UNITY IN AUTONOMY

A Federal History of the Founding of the Liberal Party

Edited By

ZACHARY GORMAN

Jeparit Press

Published in 2024 by Connor Court Publishing Pty Ltd under the Jeparit Press Imprint.

Jeparit Press is an imprint of Connor Court Publishing in conjunction with The Robert Menzies Institute.

Connor Court Publishing
PO Box 7257
Redland Bay QLD 4165
sales@connorcourt.com
www.connorcourt.com

ISBN: 9781923224414

Cover Design by Renee Gorman
Cartoon on cover by Jim Russell, used with permission of his granddaughter Ingrid Mackenzie.

Printed in Australia.

Contents

Contents

Introduction

Zachary Gorman

How do you get a group of people who place a fundamental value on freedom of thought and action to consistently unite for political purposes?

This is a dilemma that has faced the Australian liberal tradition ever since the emergence of the party system. In many respects Australian liberalism is a pre-party phenomenon, having predated the advent of colonial democracy. In the nineteenth century, liberals successfully fought for basic freedoms like trial by jury, the end of convict transportation, and the onset of responsible government, and having won them, they came to dominate colonial parliaments such that they did not feel the need for permanent extra-parliamentary organisations. There were certainly differences of opinion between liberals who leaned conservative or radical, and these could produce heated electoral battles. But it was only in the late 1880s and into the 1890s when fully-fledged political parties came into being.[1]

The dawn of party organisation was epitomised by the birth of the Australian Labor Party and its methods were an anathema to the existing liberal political culture. Labor's union dominated organisation would formulate the details of its policy, introducing an iron clad pledge to force parliamentary members to vote how they were told. MPs were thus transformed from the respected representatives of their local communities exercising 'mature judgement' and 'enlightened conscience' in the national interest,[2] into what liberals saw as mere 'ciphers' of a sectional labour movement. They were responsible primarily to their party, rather than their electorate, and this was seen as a flagrant attack on the principles of democracy.

The problem was that Labor methods proved to be quite effective both within parliament and in electioneering. Hence liberals felt the need to ratchet up their own party organisations in a manner that would encourage widespread and active participation, but crucially without shackling MPs and compromising core liberal principles. Their efforts generally proved flawed and fleeting, and were treated with suspicion by a large section of the population who came to view any party methods as inherently undemocratic. Such sentiment was particularly high in the lead up to the 1943 federal election, at a time when the One Party for Australia Movement advocated for the abolition of the party system, and they were joined by a host of independents and even a 'Women for Canberra' movement which all reflected a similar viewpoint.

As a former prime minister who had grown up around parliamentary politics and thought deeply about its workings, Robert Menzies believed that this was nonsense. A clear choice between competing approaches to governance was for him the essence of democracy; the 'very idea of… voters in a country like this being so indifferent to the political future of their country that they are content to have no Party principles or Party allegiance, but take 74 random dips in the lucky bag at each election is the height of absurdity'.[3] He felt that 'great parties' had a vital stabilising effect, and gave the elector a greater say in how their country was run because they could achieve a clear mandate, as opposed to the horse-trading that went on with a crossbench.

In these circumstances, Menzies felt compelled to justify the utility and soundness of political parties from first principles. On 15 January 1943, in the 52nd episode of his long running series of Friday night radio broadcasts made famous by 'The Forgotten People', Menzies drew on 'Edmund Burke, the greatest of practical political philosophers':

> [Burke] was himself never in a Cabinet and was never the slave of a Party. He had great detachment. He had great mental and moral powers. He was not a place-hunter. Yet, a hundred and sixty-three years ago Burke said, in language that need not be amended today:

> 'Party is a body of men united for promoting by their joint endeavours the national interest, upon some particular principle in which they are all agreed … Men thinking freely, will, in particular instances, think differently. But still as the greater part of the measures which arise in the course of public business are related to, or dependent on, some great, leading general principles in government [Menzies's underlining] a man must be peculiarly unfortunate in the choice of his political company, if he does not agree with them at least nine times in ten.'

Dismissing the idea that party politics automatically involved subordinating an individual's conscience, Menzies went on to say that:

> The notion that the discipline of Party supresses and destroys the individual conscience is purely academic. In fourteen years as a Party politician I have on three occasions voluntarily resigned from office, and, as many people could tell you, there is nothing unusual about me. But the point is that three major matters leading to resignation each left me a Party member in general agreement with my fellows and, I hope, with an unimpaired conscience. There is always room, within the structure of a general agreement in broad principle, for the most acute differences in detail or application.[4]

Burke in this instance functioned not just as an answer to critics, but as a call to action. If Australia's liberal tradition was to have a permanent political entity, it needed to be united around clear principles. The problem was that in recent decades Australian liberals had not been particularly good at formulating or expounding such principles. After coming together in the short-lived Commonwealth Liberal Party (1909-1917), liberals had found themselves in political parties based on specific circumstances rather than broad principles. Most recently, the United Australia Party had been founded to deal with the Great Depression, but had outlived the economic crisis which justified its existence – with disastrous results in terms of unity and at the ballot box.

For this reason, Menzies and numerous other liberals believed that the UAP needed to be replaced by 'a party with a philosophy' – an impetus made all the more powerful by emotionally-charged wartime contemplation of the question 'what kind of Australia are we fighting for?' Menzies answered the question through his series of 105 radio broadcasts, but as the following chapters document, this was just the most enduring and influential of many explorations of what liberalism meant which were produced in the 1940s.

Menzies's position as 'first among equals' when it came to espousing Australian liberal thought during this era is similar to his role in the founding of the Liberal Party. As Ian Hancock put it, Menzies was 'necessary for the Liberal Party's creation but not sufficient for it to happen'.[5] Debate over Menzies's centrality is an important theme explored in the existing historiography on the founding of the Liberal Party, from Gerard Henderson's *Menzies' Child*, Hancock's *National and Permanent?*, John Nethercote and Nick Cater's *Road to Freedom*, and most recently in Nicolle Flint's chapter in *The Menzies Watershed*.[6] This book finds its originality in picking up another point raised by Hancock: that the party cannot have a single founder since it scarcely exists as a single entity, and is instead made up of the state and territory divisions.[7] In doing so, it also takes inspiration from P Loveday, AW Martin and RS Parker's thoroughly federal *The Emergence of the Australian Party System*, which focused on the period circa 1890-1910.

The premise of this volume is to examine the foundation story of each Liberal Party division, in order to shine a light on figures that deserve to be better remembered, understand what is distinct about the varied political cultures that make up the Liberal Party and the Australian polity more broadly, and get a better grasp on how the party juggles the complexities produced by the fundamental liberal value of local autonomy. At a time when federal election results suggest great disparities between what voters want out of the party in places as diverse as Queensland and Victoria, and when the party system ushered in 80 years ago shows signs of fracturing, the book has a timely resonance. Yet the aim is that its original research will make an ongoing contribution to our understanding of the Australian liberal tradition which will stand the test of time.

While the book is centred around telling the story of (almost) eight divisions, it must first establish the 'leading general principles' that united Australian liberalism's disparate adherents. In chapter one, David Kemp examines what being 'a party with a philosophy' involved and why it has proven essential to the Liberal Party's success and endurance. He skilfully unpacks how politics is a battle of ideas, and that it is the depth of the wellspring of liberal ideas - which can be traced all the way back to Magna Carta – that give liberalism its great strength and cultural resonance. Yet, in the context of Australia in the 1940s, it was Menzies who distilled liberalism's essence in a manner that saw its potential to both facilitate progress and protect the political process from degenerating into a competition between special interests. Through his Forgotten People broadcasts and then the Unity Conferences, Kemp argues that Menzies created a 'narrative' that was powerful enough to carry Australia's liberal and conservative forces along the road to cohesion and victory.

Even with a clearly articulated philosophy, the problem remained that some liberal principles could prove centrifugal in rejecting all central authority or direction. Andrew Kemp's chapter explores how this and other anti-party tendencies had greatly inhibited the Liberals' predecessors, but were ultimately overcome in a delicately balanced approach to organisational federalism. Despite the continuous complaints of federal party organisers, it was a forlorn hope that state organisations would cede their autonomy to a centralised body. The task was to find a workable way of ensuring they did not need to, something which the energising effects of the bank nationalisation issue helped to provide. The chapter is particularly illuminating in its demonstration that it was not Menzies alone who was captivated by the power of ideas; there was an animating spirit of the era that inspired a whole generation of party organisers.

Anne Henderson's chapter makes it clear that this spirit captured a number of pioneering liberal women, whose role in the party's early success would prove crucial. She highlights that despite the UAP's ultimate demise, the party had been highly successful in broadening the centre-right's appeal to encompass a much larger segment of Australian society than had previously been the case. Through the remarkable figure of Enid Lyons, this broadened base would be carried over to the new Liberal Party, which was made to realise the direct imperative of having policies and positions for women. While their parliamentary representation still had (and has) significant room for improvement, the party learned that it needed women not just as voters but as energetic activists, and they in turn learned that the party could give them a greater say in public affairs than older female-exclusive organisations like the Australian Women's National League.

Having set the scene at a national scale, the stories of each division form overlapping puzzle pieces which fit together to make a more complete picture than any single narrative could achieve. We begin with the 'mother colony' of New South Wales; the epicentre of the nineteenth century's pervasive liberal culture and home to the prototypical Australian Liberal Party in Joseph Carruthers's Liberal and Reform Association. My chapter looks at how from these great heights, NSW descended to become one of the most divided states at the time of the Unity Conferences, and one where Labor achieved a reputation for being a natural party of government. I argue that the latter came about from a combination of the narrow north Sydney base that the NSW Liberals came to represent, and NSW Labor's reputation for approachable conservatism. Although one should not discount the possibility that the home of George Reid and the free trade tradition had been alienated from liberalism by the post-federation victory of tariff protectionism, and subsequent Melbourne-centric orientation of centre-right politics. It is perhaps no coincidence that the centre of political gravity has shifted northwards as Australia has come to re-embrace an older mercantile heritage.

One might assume that Victoria has taken the opposite trajectory, but Stephen Wilks's chapter reveals that the Port Phillip district still took a while to establish itself as 'the jewel in the Liberal crown'. This was in large part due to the peculiarities and strengths of the Victorian Country Party, which not only resembled Labor's 'sectional' approach to politics but was more than happy to work hand in hand with the ALP. However, it also reflected problems endemic to the various Liberal divisions, including a power struggle between the organisation and parliamentary party that in Victoria culminated in disendorsements, expulsions and flirting with the adoption of a Labor-style pledge. Wilks suggests that despite some early bloodletting, these battles hardened a robust extra-parliamentary organisation which 'proved itself to be more than a revamped UAP', and which would lay the platform for Henry Bolte's extended electoral dominance.

If Victoria was the spiritual home of the Liberal Party providing the largest section of Unity Conference delegates, Queensland was the opposite, with the Queensland People's Party declining Menzies's invitation and enduring with its own branding into the late 1940s. Lyndon Megarrity's chapter explores how of all the states, Queensland arguably had the most idiosyncratic political culture, shaped by geography, an unusually broad distribution of population, and more recently its proximity to the war. While the QPP reflected a liberal opposition to socialism, it had a significant anti-party element to its rhetoric, and its support for compulsory unionism – a principle which Menzies had spent a whole Forgotten People broadcast denouncing as an attack on freedom of association[8] – gave a policy manifestation to the QPP's temporary separation from the Liberal project. While the QPP ultimately fell into line with its interstate counterparts, its story reveals Queensland's distinctiveness as would be realised in the modern LNP – and indeed Megarrity also tracks how mergers with the generally larger Country Party have a long prehistory in the sunshine state.

South Australia also witnessed a Coalition merger in the early 1930s, but it was so successful that it might otherwise be forgotten since the Country side of the equation has since been fully absorbed into the state's Liberal division. Baden Teague's chapter charts how far ahead SA was of the other states, not just in terms of Coalition relations, but in having a unified and electorally successful extra-parliamentary organisation, the Liberal and Country League, that was able to attend the Unity Conferences as a single entity. Teague argues that because the South Australians got their house in order and fully bought into the mission, they were able to give Menzies tremendous support which facilitated the creation of the nation-wide Liberal Party. The overwhelming South Australian predominance in the National Service Group – Menzies's splinter group within the UAP that presaged his political revolution – provides clear evidence that SA may even rival Victoria in its role in the foundation story.

Western Australia's distance from the eastern states might lead to an assumption that it was far from being at the centre of events – indeed many of its leading Liberals had first become involved in politics specifically to campaign for secession during the 1930s. But as Sherry Sufi documents, WA punched above its weight in providing the party's first federal director and achieving the Liberals' first change of government at the 1947 state election. WA's isolation meant that it had a particularly strong interest in upholding the Liberal Party's principle of organisational autonomy, but Sufi maintains that its early electoral success was based on universal campaigning lessons such as good candidate selection, shrewdly targeting specific seats, and working closely with the Country Party.

While WA can boast of being the first state division to win government, Tasmania holds the unenviable distinction of being the last.[9] Like their beleaguered New South Wales counterparts, Tasmanian Liberals had to contend with a distinctively conservative Labor Party – epitomised by the fact that it was once led by future UAP Prime Minister Joseph Lyons. But unlike NSW which had geographic and demographic reasons for its Labor dominance, Stefan Petrow suggests that Tasmania should have been the state 'most politically fertile for non-Labor'. In a thoroughly detailed study of not just the birth of the Liberal division, but the history of its predecessors, his chapter reveals that great efforts being put into fostering an extra-parliamentary organisation do not automatically result in electoral dividends, particularly if there are failures in leadership and policymaking. A telling insight into the fickleness of seeking electoral success is how after deliberately moving on from older MPs in the name of placating a demand for a fresh and vigorous outlook, post-election prognostications complained of the excessive youth and inexperience of candidates. Nevertheless, Petrow concludes that in recent years Labor's university educated membership and flirtations with the Greens may have eroded its conservative reputation and therefore the electoral advantages it once enjoyed.

While the ACT Division has not gone so far as to embrace the Greens, it is unique in being the only Liberal division to have formed a formal coalition with left-of-centre MPs. Gary Humphries's chapter offers both an academic and an insider's view into how Liberals have tried to organise, survive and win government in what is effectively enemy territory. In doing so, he reveals how the ACT offers up some significant conundrums for the principles of Australian liberalism. Firstly, how do you reconcile a belief in subsidiarity and decentralisation with a city that is itself the product of centralisation? Secondly, to what extent should a 'party with a philosophy' adapt or mollify its philosophy to suit the local culture? The whole premise of *Unity in Autonomy* is that the party should reflect local conditions and local wishes, but only so far as that it never compromises the core principles which give it its raison d'etre. Those conditions and wishes appear to be uniquely resented when it comes to Canberra, partly due to their exception from mainstream Liberal opinion, and because the affluent constituency which supports them is subsidised by the national taxpayer. However, it should be pointed out that 'horizontal fiscal equalisation' means that the latter has been true of many of the states over the years.[10]

Both the ACT and Northern Territory Liberal parties got off to a belated start due to a lack of truly democratic institutions through which to contest the battle of ideas. But while the ACT Liberals eventually won independence from NSW and their own fully-fledged division, the NT Liberal Party (which was oddly tied to the Victorian Division) had only a brief existence. Its main significance, as documented by Shane Stone, is acting as the midwife for the birth of the Country Liberal Party, along with its similarly defunct Country Party counterpart. Nevertheless, NT Liberals still deserve recognition as the Territory has gone on to have a disproportionate national influence, embodied by Stone himself. The CLP is also interesting as the 'fourth member' of the federal Coalition, with a unique non-binding convention that its House of Representatives members are expected to sit with the Liberals, while its senators are expected to sit with the Nationals. This raises questions as to what truly differentiates the parties, particularly given its implication that had Jacinta Nampijinpa Price won Lingiari in 2019 she may have effectively become a Liberal – removing the impasse over portfolio allocations that occurred prior to her being appointed a shadow minister.[11]

In his memoir *Afternoon Light*, Menzies said that in 'substance' the Coalition parties had 'the same political philosophy',[12] but this does not appear to have been his view 20 years earlier. In the final chapter of the book, John Anderson and Terry Barnes explore just how close the Country Party came to joining the unity push and merging with the new Liberal Party. They note that there were numerous obstacles, including the fact that the Country Party was essentially as divided and fractious as their UAP cousins, but one of the main opponents appears to have been Menzies himself. In pushing for a party united behind 'leading general principles', he did not want those principles to be muddied by alleged sectionalism. But in a way, the Country/Nationals Party and particularly the Coalition itself, can be seen as the ultimate embodiment of *Unity in Autonomy*, as they allow for localism and difference of opinion, while maintaining a powerful common purpose and combined action. Both elements have proven essential to the successes of the previous 80 years, and maintaining both will surely prove as essential in any successes to come.

---

[1] This varied between the Australian colonies. For a detailed account see P Loveday, AW Martin and RS Parker, *The Emergence of the Australian Party System*.

[2] Edmund Burke, 'Speech to the Electors of Bristol', 3 November 1774. Menzies would refer to this in his 30 October 1943 broadcast on 'The Sickness of Democracy'.

[3] Robert Menzies, 'The Party System' Broadcast, 15 January 1943.

[4] Ibid.

[5] Ian Hancock quoted from correspondence with Georgina Downer, 1 February 2023.

[6] There are earlier works which related to the topic, such as Katherine West's *Power in the Liberal Party* or Graeme Starr's *The Liberal Party of Australia: A Documentary History*, which are cited throughout this volume. But they did not have the sense of perspective, provided by the party's endurance, to function as true foundation narratives.

[7] Hancock, *National and Permanent?*, pp. 3-4. Some states already have thoroughly researched books covering the foundation and history of their division, including Hancock's *The Liberals: The NSW Division 1945-2000*, however, they do not have the comparative element which is essential to this volume.

[8] Robert Menzies, 'Compulsory Unionism' Broadcast, 14 August 1942. Later published as chapter 24 of *The Forgotten People and other Studies in Democracy*. An attempt to abolish preference to unionists in government employment (itself a form of compulsion) had also notably been one of the issues over which Liberal Prime Minister Joseph Cook had called a double dissolution in 1914.

[9] This is complicated by the fact that the Queensland Liberals were the junior Coalition partner, but even they had a premier for a week after the Country Party's Jack Pizzey died in office in 1968.

[10] Barring mining booms and other causes of exceptional prosperity, the smaller states have been subsidised, though seldom to a level that can be described as affluence.

[11] There was commentary both before and after Price's appointment over the fact that it made the Nationals 'overrepresented' in the shadow cabinet.

[12] Menzies, *Afternoon Light*, p. 55.

1

A Party with a Philosophy

David Kemp

The formation of the Liberal Party of Australia in 1944 was an idealistic but practical project to save liberal democracy in Australia from forces threatening to undermine it. These forces were not merely fascism, communism and militarism abroad – threats which were not without domestic echoes. The immediate political issue was a governing party with a socialist objective that threatened to continue wartime economic and social controls into peacetime in pursuit of economic and social equality.

Reflecting in his memoirs on the formation of the Liberal Party at a conference in October 1944, Menzies described this event as 'the creation of a new party with a modern philosophy'.[1] The Liberal Party came into existence as a party with a philosophy. This philosophy was key not only to its successful foundation and to its survival over 80 years but to the success of its policies and to its electoral appeal. Politics is ultimately driven by ideas. This chapter examines what it means to say that a party has a philosophy; how the party obtained, and has sought to maintain, its philosophy; and the likely contribution of the philosophy to its success.

The Liberal Party has taken Menzies's description of it as a 'party with a philosophy' seriously. The legacy of the party's beginnings remains obvious. Policy positions enunciated in parliamentary debates and recommended by state councils have generally been debated over the years with a self-conscious awareness that policy should reflect values and beliefs associated with the party. Today the websites of Liberal Party divisions in the various states detail the values and beliefs for which the party is claimed to stand. Parliamentary leaders of the party since Menzies, especially at the national level, have taken opportunities from time to time to state their beliefs and the policy implications of these.

Following Menzies's retirement from parliament, and the subsequent loss of government in 1972, the federal executive established a philosophy sub-committee to review the party's positioning on the role of government, the liberal economy, Aboriginal policy, federalism, bureaucracy, justice and legal system, political parties and the 'liberal style of politics'.[2] This committee was an attempt to move beyond brief statements of 'our aims' into more detailed assessment of the implications of the party's philosophy for policy in complex new areas. Lecture series were established over the following decades by university Liberal clubs, state parties and think tanks, named after political 'heroes' of Liberal politics such as Alfred Deakin, Robert Menzies himself, Malcolm Fraser and, more recently, John Howard. These lecture series have provided attractive platforms for party leaders to publicly state their credos and political philosophies, as well as address major policy issues.[3]

After the defeat of the Fraser Government in 1983 the party's federal executive established a committee led by John Valder, president of the NSW Division, to review the performance of the party in office and assess the implications of social and economic change.[4] It analysed the party organisation and a range of policy areas, concluding that being seen by the public to stand by its philosophy, including its economic elements, remained important for the party's electoral credibility and success.

The 'party with a philosophy' has been markedly successful. For some 50 years, the party, in coalition with the Country/National Party, has formed Australia's national government. Measured by its primary support in the electorate, the Liberal Party today is the largest single political party in Australia. How far the party's philosophy has contributed to that success requires more examination than is possible here, though the case that philosophy and effective leadership go together has been made,[5] for reasons that will become apparent in this chapter. In this context it is important to observe that the party's success has varied from state to state for reasons that separately require examination. At the federal level the party's leaders most associated with a philosophical approach to government – Menzies, Howard and Fraser – have retained office longest, for over 18 years, 11 years and 7 years respectively.

A party with a philosophy is a distinctive creature. Many if not most major parties of government, in Australia and elsewhere, claim to have guiding philosophies, but few have the level of definition of the philosophy bequeathed to the Liberal Party of Australia by its founders. Denis White, in his classic book *The Philosophy of the Australian Liberal Party*, defines a political philosophy as 'a systematic set of basic ideas which make sense of the human world'. Political philosophies, he states, are concerned with 'human nature, human relationships, social and political organisation, the dynamics of change, and the kind of life which befits human beings.'[6]

Not all parties have philosophies. Some see themselves as principally serving specific interests in the electorate. Some are pragmatic, notionally responding to events as they occur. Some have ideologies: ready-made policies that the party is determined to implement, come what may, without serious consideration of practicality or consequences. The Communist Party at the time of the Liberal Party's formation was an ideological party. Menzies believed the Labor Party, or key sections of it, in the 1940s had such a character. The Greens today and the socialist left of the Labor Party can be understood primarily as promoting ideologies. Those in the grip of ideology rarely provide rational analysis and argument to justify their policies. Policies themselves become the shibboleths that dominate thinking.

The Unity Conference 1944

The Liberal Party owes its philosophy to the nature of its foundation 80 years ago. Robert Menzies, in September 1944, then national leader of the United Australia Party (UAP) and the federal Opposition, invited his senior colleagues, and the fragmented liberal and conservative parties from all states, to attend a conference in Canberra to discuss the formation of a new political party. Divisions of the Country Party, an already functioning separate organisation with which the UAP had mostly been in coalition, were not invited.[7] Achieving unity and providing the leadership to formulate and present a program of wide appeal – to claim a branding as more than a 'business' party, but rather a party looking to the future, with the interests of all at its heart – was the challenge, and Robert Menzies was determined to demonstrate that, despite doubters, he was the person to do this.

Menzies's leadership strategy, in today's parlance, was to create a 'narrative' so persuasive that it could scarcely be resisted at the conference. A narrative so compelling is a rare thing in politics, and in 1944 probably only Menzies in Australia could produce one. The power of Menzies's narrative derived not only from its intellectual strength, but its political payoff. It offered a solution to the immediate problem of disunity among liberal and conservative forces, while its electoral promise came from its appeal to widely held values in Australian culture.[8]

In presenting a philosophically based narrative, Menzies was reinforced in turn by, and drew upon, a reviving international liberalism determined to address a perceived 'crisis of democracy'. Menzies's narrative addressed current problems while having long-term policy implications and offering future electoral appeal to a new party. His 'narrative' demonstrated his skill in what he called 'the art of politics'. 'The art of politics', he wrote, 'is to convey ideas to others, if possible, to persuade a majority to agree, to create or encourage a public opinion so soundly based that it endures and is not blown aside by chance winds; *to persuade people to take long-range views*'.[9]

Those attending varied according to the degree of disunity in their home states, nor were their hopes for the future identical. The vision Menzies presented was not for a business party parallel to the trade union party that was Labor, but for a party that would safeguard Australians from the creeping totalitarianism of a densely regulated society, and enable each person to flourish in freedom and strive to realise their own dreams. Moreover, it would be a party that would be democratic in its structure and control, whose members would be individual Australians, men and women. It proved to be a compelling 'narrative', and on one weekend in October 1944 delegates to his Unity Conference agreed to build the instrument through which they would strive to achieve this vision.

Political context

Menzies was not alone in seeking a new party. Indeed, several small 'breakaway' parties had already been formed in the states. By 1944 difficult unity discussions were taking place in several of the states in efforts to re-form a successful major party out of the ruins of the United Australia Party. The disagreements were about how that new party might be formed and structured, what role it would give existing organisations and interests, and what its name, objectives and policies might be.

Menzies's proposal was that the new party would completely replace the United Australia Party, then in disarray following its defeat in the August 1943 federal election with a mere 22 per cent of the national primary vote. The Labor Party had won 49 per cent in that election. In the wake of defeat, the UAP had fragmented, giving rise to new parties and a chaotic political situation among the Opposition forces.

Menzies's invitation to existing organisations, in September 1944, to come to Canberra to attempt a nationally unified party did not therefore come out of the blue. Following his return to the leadership of the UAP after an election in which the party had been led by WM 'Billy' Hughes, he immediately took steps with others to create the new politics that he had been campaigning for over many years. Since he had first embarked on a parliamentary career in 1928 Robert Menzies had continually sought a politics of principle and purpose, rather than one focussed on the satisfaction of selfish interest claims. During his career he had resigned several times on matters of principle, in 1929,[10] 1939,[11] and again in 1941[12] and few doubted his serious intention, while wondering about his political skills. He sought a party principled in its philosophy and he had become alert to the need for it to be practical in its policies.

In 1942, in a series of radio talks on 2UE, and on associated stations in other states, he had spelled out his political philosophy in some detail and published a collected version of the talks in 1943 under the title of *The Forgotten People and other Studies in Democracy.*[12] Since the election he had seen the opportunity for a reconstruction of Australian politics through the linkage of a liberal philosophy with a new party. He had worked to bring his parliamentary colleagues behind his vision, and had met with, and persuaded, the press barons, Sir Keith Murdoch and Warwick Fairfax, to support his plans.[14] He kept himself closely informed about unity talks taking place independently in several states. Attending such talks, he had indicated his intention to provide national leadership to the process of reunification of the liberal and conservative forces.[15] When he had sent out his invitation to a conference, he hoped to use the occasion to bring to fruition at last all the elements for a new political architecture for Australia that would replace a political life he saw as dominated by selfish interests – a politics with which he was deeply dissatisfied.

Led by the Labor 'breakaway', Joseph Lyons, the UAP had come into existence as an amalgam of liberal and conservative organisations, based around a nationwide mobilisation of non-party groups dissatisfied with the major parties of the time, with weak central arrangements.[16] Its one clear goal was to beat the Depression. Across successive election victories in 1931, 1934 and 1937 the UAP had broadly achieved the economic recovery it sought. Following Lyons's death in 1939, Menzies had become prime minister and laid the essential basis for the war effort.[17] However when the finely balanced parliament after the 1940 federal election led to cabinet division he decided to resign in August 1941 – some said mistakenly and in pique[18] – to be succeeded as prime minister by the leader of the Country Party, Arthur Fadden. In October 1941 the Fadden

Government was defeated in the House of Representatives and John Curtin, leader of the Labor Party, became prime minister.

Despite his resignation, Menzies, remarkably, remained leader of the United Australia Party, the larger of the two Coalition parties, until Labor came to power. Then WM Hughes took on the UAP leadership. Fadden however remained as leader of the Opposition, a position the Country Party continued to hold through the 1943 election by agreement with the UAP. Menzies told his colleagues that this agreement had made the UAP subservient to the 'sectional' Country Party and was the UAP's 'death warrant.'[19]

Not only did Labor's wartime victory in the election of August 1943 under Curtin produce a wave of despair throughout the UAP membership and beyond. Equally, it provoked a growing level of mobilisation on the liberal/conservative side of politics as Labor's partisan approach to fighting the war – it had refused to join a wartime national government, unlike British Labour – together with its socialist objective, and attempt to gain additional powers by referendum, aroused fears of long-term damage to basic liberties and to a successful post-war recovery. Menzies regarded Curtin well as a man, but Evatt, Ward and others, strong anti-business partisans, were influential and willing to use the circumstances of the war to advance their cause.

Though some in liberal/conservative politics doubted Menzies, especially after his surprise resignation, it is a tribute to Menzies's persistence on the national platform since giving up the prime ministership that the 1943 election loss led to his immediate return to the leadership of the UAP in September 1943. He made his re-election to the position subject to two conditions. First, that the UAP leader should become the leader of the Opposition, and second that he 'should have *carte blanche* to take all necessary steps towards gathering up all existing organisations into one Australia-wide organisation, with a new name – the "United Australia" name having ceased to be up-to-date or self-explanatory – and a carefully prepared platform.'[20]

Menzies saw his liberal philosophy, already well established and articulated by him, as a key instrument to achieve the goal of unity and write the platform of the new party. He told his colleagues that he believed a new party should have a name that communicated a clear message to voters that it represented 'one of the natural classifications of political thought', as did the terms fascist, communist and socialist. Labour was a self-explanatory name. 'My own opinion', he wrote, 'is that our side of politics should stand for Liberal Democracy … I therefore believe that we should set about establishing a LIBERAL DEMOCRATIC PARTY'.[21] He called for unity discussions between the UAP or its successors and other liberal organisations in each state. He defined key features he wanted in the new party:

- It should be Australia-wide in its organisation, federally organised.
- It should have a federal executive, with a chief executive, and under it, state executives in each state.
- Membership should involve a substantial fee, giving the party a level of financial independence from business finance committees, whose role had conveyed the message to electors that the UAP was the party of 'big business'.
- The new party should have a duly elected finance committee, with people from a variety of backgrounds as its members.
- The chief executive of the party should focus on organisation, and there should be paid agents in many of the seats the party hoped to win.
- An effective public relations officer should be appointed, whose background ideally would be that of a leading journalist of 'a great daily newspaper'.
- There should be a policy committee, comprising both parliamentary and non-parliamentary representatives, 'charged with the duty of constantly revising and reflecting our political beliefs.'

- 'The search for new candidates should begin at once' and a good party journal established.[22]

Disunity in the states

The different political traditions in the states were reflected in the character of unity and disunity in 1944. In New South Wales the 1943 election outcome had shattered the UAP into two organisations: the Democratic Party (a merger of the UAP and a new ex-servicemen's party, the Commonwealth Party), and a smaller, expressly liberal, Liberal Democratic Party, led by Ernest White.[23] A coalition of the Democratic and Country parties in the May 1944 NSW state election had netted the combined force less than 30 per cent of the primary vote.

In Victoria the UAP had always functioned as an alliance between the United Australia Organisation, the Young Nationalists, and the Australian Women's National League (AWNL). A new liberal-leaning party, the Services and Citizens Party, had emerged in Victoria in 1943 led by WH Anderson, following the UAP's poor performance in the June 1943 state election, when it had obtained only 23 per cent of the primary vote.

In Queensland the liberal/conservative organisations in September 1944 were the People's Party, the Country National Organisation and the Women's Electoral League, and in Tasmania the Nationalist Party, the United Australia Party and the AWNL. South Australia had a united organisation: the Liberal and Country League (SA) led by Thomas Playford, while Western Australia had a state Nationalist Organisation, and a federal United Australia Organisation. The women's organisations in Victoria, Tasmania, and Queensland each sent delegates to the Unity Conference. Woman delegates also attended from the NSW Democratic Party and the South Australian Liberal and Country League.

One of Menzies's main concerns was to replace the business funding committees with fundraising by the party itself. He wanted the new party to break free from the characterisation of the UAP as a business party and to be recognised for progressive liberal policies. 'Big business' leaders had traditionally allied with the liberal/conservative side of politics in an organised relationship since Alfred Deakin, in the form of fundraising committees. The most influential of these committees in 1943-44 were the NSW Consultative Council and the Victorian National Union. Menzies did not see their role as benign. In his view, they exercised power without responsibility, improperly interfered in preselection of candidates and even in party leadership contests, and threatened to distort policy in pursuit of selfish interests. In 1944 business leaders were active in politics but divided about their role in helping to secure unity among the fragmented UAP and its relationship to a possible new party.

In 1942-43 new organisations in the eastern states calling themselves Institutes of Public Affairs (IPAs), comprising leaders of some of the largest manufacturing, retail and media enterprises, had come to the conclusion that business should defend its own claims to a high level of economic freedom against Labor's socialism. The IPAs came into existence to promote economic understanding in industry and public opinion in order to more effectively defend private enterprise against widespread anti-capitalist ideology and Labor's socialist big-government aspirations. These new institutes challenged the traditional role of the UAP's business funding committees, particularly the Consultative Council and National Union,[24] and took an active role in promoting party unity in 1943-4 in both New South Wales and Victoria. Noting this, Menzies invited the IPAs to the Unity Conference. The IPA in NSW, hoping to maintain the role of a funding committee with influence on the parliamentary party, chose to send delegates to the Unity Conference. The Victorian IPA, with a focus on developing a progressive policy defence of the liberal economy,[25] decided to maintain its independence from any new party that might emerge and to concentrate on policy development and public education, sending only observers to the Unity Conference.[26] It was a role Menzies appreciated and rewarded with his public support at the conference.[27]

Finally, attendees included delegates or observers from a new political organisation, the Australian Constitutional League(ACL), that had been established as the main vehicle for mounting a campaign waged by liberal/conservative forces against Labor's constitutional referendum on 19 August 1944, the so-called 'Fourteen Powers' referendum. The single question referendum sought wide powers for the federal government for five years to introduce a wide range of social and industrial policies. The ACL had developed its skills and organisation during a successful 'No' campaign. The referendum was lost 54:46 per cent. The victory greatly heartened the liberal/conservative groups, providing a supportive context for Menzies to emphasise that the new party was about important ideas. Delegates or observers from state branches of the Constitutional League came from Victoria, Tasmania, and Western Australia.

Menzies's objective was that his conference would unify 'those political groups which stand for a liberal progressive policy and are opposed to socialism with its bureaucratic administration and restriction of personal freedom'. [28]

Australian Constitutional League advertisement from *The Bulletin*, 2 August 1944.

An electoral base for a party with a philosophy

The challenge for liberal-minded and conservative politicians was to regain the trust of the voters that they had lost, and to identify and mobilise those interests in the electorate who could be persuaded to support a government promoting broad economic and social freedom. In his 1942 Forgotten People radio talks Menzies had argued that Australian politics, as then organised, failed to properly represent the middle class. The organised working class had powerful voices in the trade union movement and the Labor Party, while those 'who control great funds and enterprises … are as a rule able to protect themselves'. But 'we cannot exclude [the middle class] from the problem of social progress', he had argued.[29]

The middle class comprised 'salary earners, shopkeepers, skilled artisans, professional men and women, farmers and so on' who 'for the most part are unorganised and unself-conscious'. Menzies identified himself with them and described them as 'the backbone of the nation'.[30] They believed in the home, in a patriotic duty to defend it, in opportunities for their children, in education, in independence and assumed personal responsibility for their own future, in thrift and saving. The home often had a spiritual quality. They aspired to a better life.[31] They would be the political base of the new party. The appeal to them would be on the basis of their values and interests, and these, in Australia, were fundamentally values that would respond to liberal leadership and guide the new party's policies. It was the insight that would give the new Liberal Party an electoral base. The challenge was to provide it with the political leadership and organisation that would allow the values of this middle class to find a voice.

Menzies later recalled:

> In 1944, it was clear that my main task, as Leader of the Opposition, was to secure the organic and mental unity, of fourteen fractions. This, of course, was far more than a problem of mechanics. A unity artificially attained will

> not last long if there is no genuine community of thought, of basic principles and applied ideas. [32]

He argued that the 'community of thought' he sought could be found in Australia's liberal tradition. Without guiding ideas and principles, the party would be at the mercy of the disparate state, economic, gender, and generational political interests that, by 1944, had torn the UAP apart.

In his Forgotten People talks he had provided, what he called, 'a summarised political philosophy' that might be the basis for unity among the now divided liberal/conservative forces.[33] He was not alone in his sense that liberal democracy was facing a crisis. Internationally, voices for liberal ideas were strengthening. In the 1930s English economist John Maynard Keynes had redefined the role of government in preventing mass unemployment,[34] philosopher Karl Popper was exposing the inherent authoritarianism of Marxism,[35] the Austrian political economist Joseph Schumpeter had championed the entrepreneur as the saviour of capitalism,[36] and another Austrian political economist and philosopher, Friedrich Hayek, had stressed the importance of personal and economic freedom to sustaining democracy.[37] Hayek pointed to the danger that democratic systems, with their increasing regulation, high taxation and interest in social reconstruction, were heading in an anti-liberal, anti-capitalist, totalitarian direction.

The most obvious weakness in Labor's plans for post-war reconstruction was the absence of a wide understanding in the party of economic thought, and hence of policies best designed to produce opportunity and prosperity. The main exception was its attraction to Keynes's role for public spending to fight deflation. Warwick Fairfax had recently criticised 'the intellectual barrenness' of the labour movement.[38] Labor's policy perspectives derived largely from the interests of its trade union base, focussed on anti-competitive policies, controlling owners, managers and profits rather than on the central role economics gave to the creation of wealth, competitive enterprise and employment. Socialist intellectuals such as Sidney and Beatrice Webb[39] and Harold Laski[40] had turned against private property, the liberal market economy and its economic freedoms, neglecting the role of individual choices in ensuring outcomes that reflected, to some significant degree, the values and aspirations of most citizens.

Menzies would find at the Unity Conference that there were many who shared his concerns: his senior parliamentary colleagues, and delegates and observers such as Ernest White of the NSW Liberal Democratic Party, WH Anderson of the Services and Citizens, Elizabeth 'May' Couchman of the Australian Women's National League, and CD Kemp of the Victorian IPA, who would support him in his efforts to construct a new political force for liberalism in Australia.

Menzies's philosophy and the 'Liberal Revival'

Menzies's opening address to the Unity Conference must be judged as one of the outstanding speeches of his long career. Indeed, it is one of the very important speeches in Australia's political history. He set out to overwhelm any doubters among the delegates by building enthusiasm for his concept of a party with a philosophy. Aware of competing state and interstate factions and groups that would seek influence over any new party, he invited the delegates to unite around a common set of ideas. He later wrote in his memoir that 'I set out to inject into the meeting a sense of significance and urgency … There were one or two doubters, who were naturally attached to their own particular groups, but their doubts were soon swept away by the general enthusiasm'.[41] He was too modest to say that this enthusiasm had been largely generated by himself.

Menzies put to the delegates that there was already available to them a well-established tradition of ideas around which the purpose and direction of the new party could be built, and in a way that would appeal to the moral and aspirational middle class whose members wanted to control their own lives and to take personal responsibility for their actions. Policies based on these ideas would lead the nation back to prosperity and opportunity. This tradition was liberalism. He told delegates:

> What we must look for, and it is a matter of desperate importance to our country, is a true revival of liberal thought which will work for social justice and security, for national power and national progress, and for the full development of the individual citizen, though not through the dull and deadening process of socialisation.[42]

The 'liberal thought' to which Menzies referred was a tradition of ideas that placed the individual person at the centre of a just society. This tradition traced back in English speaking countries at least as far as Magna Carta in 1215 which established the principle of the rule of law and, through the parliamentary tradition, came to incorporate ideas of freedom of speech within parliament, and later from the eighteenth century, outside parliament.

From John Locke in the seventeenth century, and the foundation of economic thought and policy analysis in the eighteenth century by Adam Smith and Jeremy Bentham, this tradition flowered with the demonstration that widening personal freedom and enforcing justice for the individual had profound implications for social and economic life. The antislavery campaign led by the Christian evangelical, William Wilberforce, firmly entrenched concepts of the equal human dignity of all people, regardless of race, in the British political class. The colonial governors of NSW, especially Arthur Phillip, Lachlan Macquarie, Richard Bourke and George Gipps, had sought to govern according to these principles in Australia. Nineteenth century liberals such as the political economist and philosopher John Stuart Mill further supported freedom of speech, equality for women, and ready access to property in land.[43]

The policy implications of liberal thought were broad, and as a liberal Menzies had, throughout his political life, emphasised how the ideas of respect for the individual and personal freedom had guided his own thinking: in his belief in parliamentary government and the rule of law, in his dislike of censorship and the legal enforcement of morality, in his belief in freedom of conscience, thought and expression, in his opposition to propaganda stirring hatred against the Japanese, in his recognition of the need for freedom of religion, his belief in education and rational policy making, and in his support for a co-operative workplace rather than one dictated to by unions and compulsory arbitration.

All these issues arising from liberal thought were important, and from time to time central to the political agenda. Nevertheless, especially in the context of the time, liberal policy, in his view, had to focus in its practical and public expression on the economy and on the benefits to individuals and families of profitable ventures and enterprises that created both employment opportunities, wealth and rising standards of living. He would write later, in his account of the record of his government in his memoir, *The Measure of the Years*:

> [T]he basic philosophy of Australian Liberalism is that the prime duty of government is to encourage enterprise, to provide a climate favourable to its growth, to remember that it is the individual whose energies produce progress, and that all social benefits derive from his efforts.[44]

At the heart of Menzies's confidence lay his beliefs about the role of government and the inevitable trade-off between authority and freedom. Australians could choose to rebuild the country either by directing people through the authority of government, or by empowering individual choice:

> How do we propose to get these things? By looking primarily to the authoritative action of Government, or by looking primarily to the encouragement of individual skill and initiative? As to this, I believe that we can have no hesitation…We must aim at the fullest development of individual capacity.[45]

It is probably true to say that no leader in Australian federal politics before Menzies had so deeply analysed the nature of government and its limitations, and how an excessive role for government could undermine a society. The great political choice, Menzies told delegates, which went to the heart of the decision voters must make between Labor and a party based on liberal thought, was the conflict between, on the one hand, government's capacities to achieve results by the exercise of its authority and power and, on the other, by protecting and empowering individual liberty or personal freedom.

The war had reinforced in Menzies his belief that the central limitation of government arose from the fact that its main tool, authority, was only good for imposing uniform solutions. Government never knew enough to replace the knowledge of citizens themselves about their own interests or the options that freedom would make available. Each citizen knew their interests better than government knew them. To attempt to exercise government authority beyond what was necessary for society to function and for shared and humane values to be achieved, would stifle individuality, innovation, diversity and creativity, undermine leadership in other institutions, choke enterprise and prevent the creation of wealth and lasting employment opportunities. Freedom and individual initiative were necessary to achieve the diversity of options required for choice, and for the life satisfaction and meaning that choice could bring.

It was on this basis that Menzies would argue that 'any activity in which choice and personal confidence are essential is not an activity for which a socialist solution is appropriate'.[46] If a uniform outcome were optimal to achieve a public good, a government-imposed solution would be a reasonable approach. In the central areas of life, however: in thought, speech and expression, religion, housing, health, education, lifestyle, products and services; citizens wanted choice and government could protect, but never define or replicate, these choices, for each citizen wanted different things.

A prosperous, harmonious, progressive society, and indeed individual security itself, therefore depended on individual capacity and freedom:

> I see the individual and his encouragement and recognition as *the prime motive force* for the building of a better world. Socialism means high costs, inefficiency, the constant intrusion of political considerations, the damping down of enterprise, the overlordship of routine. None of these elements can produce progress, and without progress, security will turn out to be a delusion.[47]

Establishing the Liberal Party of Australia

The Liberal Party of Australia may be said to have been formally established on 16 October 1944, when the delegates of the liberal organisations, invited to Canberra by Robert Menzies, determined that they would come together into a new party and decided the name of their creation. After a weekend's debate and drafting, on Monday 16 October 1944, the delegates determined:

> That the name of the unified organisation shall be the LIBERAL PARTY OF AUSTRALIA, which name shall be adopted in the Federal sphere and by all the States except that, in view of the unity already attained in South Australia, that branch shall be permitted to retain its present name if it so desires.[48]

The decision on the name was accompanied by adoption of a detailed statement of the objectives of the new party, based largely around those Menzies had proposed in his opening address, and a decision to hold a second conference to agree to a constitution.

The Unity Conference largely endorsed the structure of the new party Menzies had foreshadowed. The party was to have a federal organisation with the states equally represented on a federal council, which included the leader of the parliamentary party in each House and a federal executive, again with equal representation from each state. There would be a joint standing committee on federal policy, consisting of an equal number of members of parliament and non-parliamentary members of the federal council, together with the federal leader of the parliamentary party who would be chairman. All states would be represented on this committee. The members of the new party would be individual citizens, none being delegates from corporate interests as in the Labor Party.

Menzies also announced to the press that a permanent secretariat would be established at Canberra, and that state branches would have 'substantial autonomy' in relation to state organisation and affairs. As he told the delegates:

> When I consider the structure of the Australian Labour Party and realise that the political warfare to which we have been committed for a long time by the choice of our own is a struggle between political armies, I am driven to wonder how we could ever imagine that a concerted force under one command and with one staff is to be defeated by divided units under separate commands, and with no general staff.[49]

Later, he would write:

> We took the name 'Liberal' because we were determined to be a progressive party, willing to make experiments; in no sense reactionary, but believing in the individual, his rights and his enterprise ...[50]

Menzies described the conference as 'remarkably successful' and predicted that 'as a result a great and powerful body of Australian public opinion which for some time has felt itself dissipated by internal differences will become vocal and effective.'[51] The IPA observers from Victoria reported back to their council:

> No single factor contributed so much to the success of the Conference as Mr. Menzies' personality. His good humour, his patience, his skilful handling of the business of the meetings, were at all times outstanding. ...[52]

The details of its organisation were defined in a constitution adopted at a second Unity Conference in Albury in December and implemented the following year. The constitution and the platform of the new party declared the principal ideas of its philosophy and policy implications. Menzies would however always emphasise in the years ahead that the essence of Liberalism lay in the spirit that lay behind it, rather than the words in which key documents defined it. As he told the Western Australian Division of the Liberal Party in 1970: 'Liberalism is an attitude of mind and of faith, aiming at the highest standards of life, both material and spiritual'.[53]

Can Robert Menzies accurately be described as 'the founder' of the modern Liberal Party? Clearly many played important roles, and the organisation of a nationwide party could not have come into existence without leadership in each of the states by significant individuals. Menzies was supported at the Unity Conference by his deputy in the House (Eric Harrison) and the Senate Opposition leader and deputy leader (George McLeay and John Leckie, his father-in-law), and eight other senators and MPs. Opposition and party leaders came from each of the states. He would later refer to the 'founding fathers (and mothers)' of the Great Australian Liberal Revival.[54] His role was nevertheless that of a unifying and persuasive leader. As he later wrote: 'the duty and the initiative fell upon me. I had to do the duty and maintain that initiative. With great help, as I proudly acknowledge, but the burdens were, in a real sense, mine'.[55]

Menzies wrote: 'I shall always remember two people who typified the prevailing spirit: Mrs. Couchman (later Dame Elizabeth) and WH (later Sir William) Anderson', who became president of the Victorian branch of the party (1945-48) and federal president (1951-56). Menzies provided the leading voice to the liberal revival that was taking place both internationally and in Australia.

For Menzies, the distinction between a philosophy and an ideology was of central importance. He saw the Labor Party's socialism, with its suspicion of 'capitalism' and markets, and exceptional faith in government, as just such an ideology. Ideologies, because of their simplifications of reality, could have great temporary power, but because they were not based on any valid understanding of human nature or society, their policy prescriptions would be flawed. The socialism he criticised saw government spending and regulation – government authority – as the answer to almost all social and economic problems, while private property, choice and economic incentives – fundamentally important to human motivation and behaviour – had little prominence. Socialism's rhetoric was divisive at best and at worst hateful, based as it was on what Menzies referred to as the 'foul doctrine' of the class war:[56] private capital was the oppressor, labour the oppressed. Despite its rhetoric, socialism did not lead to a harmonious society, but the reverse. It pictured a society engaged in a notional civil war between sectional groups – a war that could not be resolved until one group was eliminated and another centre of power erected.

Today's 'identity politics' and 'critical race theory' are socialism's successors (some would say socialism in disguise) – merely programmatic ideologies promoting expanded central control over citizens without basis in a valid understanding of the real world of humanity. Like socialism, which relied on the idea of class war to justify its social and economic controls, the neo-racism and neo-sexism of the Marxist inheritance generates social conflict between racial, gender and other identity groups rather than a harmonious society. In 1944, Menzies reflected later, 'it was our firmly held belief that the great issue to which Liberalism must direct itself was that of Socialism. It must be taken out of the academic realms of the debating society and presented as a real issue of practical politics.'[57]

The politics of philosophy[58]

Menzies believed a liberal party philosophy addressed what he saw as two great problems of democracy: that political activity tends to be largely driven by selfish interests, and that policy too often reflects the interests of the powerful. He had become all too familiar with these weaknesses as a representative of the Nationalist and United Australia parties respectively at state and federal levels. He saw the

Labor Party and the Country Party as chiefly representing powerful interests that wanted the politicians simply to do their bidding, rather than give attention to the shared interests of all.

Policies with a sound philosophical justification had the great advantage that they provided a party with arguments that could oppose selfish claims on the public platform. Menzies further believed that a party with a valid philosophy would direct citizens to the kinds of objectives that would create a better society in the longer term. A philosophy would support long-term policies:

> If we come to life only at election times and go back to indifference or grumbling criticism for the years that intervene, our political judgement, being based on no continuing principle, will be spasmodic, uncertain and inconsistent. We shall take only short views, and the candidate who plays up to them will be elected. Yet a moment's reflection should tell us that only long-range thinking and planning can save either democracy or the world.[59]

Instead of policies that suited only the powerful and loud voices – often at others' expense, a philosophy enabled members of parliament, candidates and members of the general public to be more than simply agents for special interests. It would enable politicians to become voices for the shared interests of all. A party with a philosophy would attract into politics those who wished for a politics that could achieve a better world, those Menzies regarded as 'the cream of the nation'.[60] A party with a philosophy would elevate politics and answer those who regarded politics as 'fit only for loud-mouthed careerists':[61]

> There has been no doubt that this democracy of ours has been very sick. If and when it can be cured, it has great work to do. But it will never be cured unless we see the past clearly, and recognize frankly that we cannot ignore politics and treat democracy as a mere matter of loaves and fishes and demean the politician, and at the same

> time sensibly demand that 'government of the people, by the people and for the people shall not perish from the earth'.[62]

Democratic politics, Menzies believed, was 'the noblest and highest of civil vocations'[63] and only a party with a philosophy could elevate democratic politics in the eyes of its citizens. 'I believe in democracy as the only method of government which can produce justice based upon a recognition of enduring human values.'[64]

A party with a philosophy would enable members of parliament, belonging to a disciplined party, to protect themselves against pressure by presenting a united phalanx against strong special interests. In this way a philosophy would help the party address the inequality of power and influence that always threatened to undermine democracy, based as it was on the idea of the political equality of all citizens. The political party would be the bulwark against, not the voice of, selfish power.

Efforts by citizens to control the very powerful has been a continuing theme in the history of Australian colonial and federal politics from the imposition in the early colony of constitutional constraints on the 'exclusives' (free immigrants with capital) through ever wider representation. Democracy had been successfully used by those who wanted free selection of land to prevent the growth of a local landed aristocracy. Industrial battles were waged over the scope of ownership and management authority within private enterprises by trade unions from the 1890s. Citizens disputed with the churches over the use of law to enforce morality. Industries and parties had contested over the extent of freedom of trade and industry protection in the economic framework. Two world wars had inflated the power of government, and over time the ambitions of political parties and politicians had expanded.

Further, the tendency of politicians in a democracy to promise policies simply to buy votes had inflated the power of government over the lives of citizens. 'As we know, authority tends to feed upon itself',[65] Menzies told the delegates to the Unity Conference in his opening address. Only a party committed to a liberal philosophy emphasising the central importance of personal freedom could protect individuals against the unlimited state and the concentrations of special interest power.

Menzies believed passionately that politics was a battle of ideas, and that 'unity' should mean one Australia-wide organisation with 'the guidance of well-formulated common ideas'.[66] He saw Australia as engulfed in a crisis of its political culture, producing a politics that he believed would ultimately destroy social harmony and the country's capacity to rebuild after the war. The new party he was working to bring into existence would be engaged in a political battle about the nature of Australia, about society, about human nature and about the way in which the country he loved should be governed. Today, the contest of ideas in Australian politics has many similarities to that which Menzies believed that the new Liberal Party should join.

The mere statement of beliefs and values by a party or its leaders from time to time, does not of course guarantee that these will be expressed in the policies of the party. Careerism and the pressures of selfish interests, and a policy culture distorted by the illiberal successes of selfish interests in the past, might sometimes – perhaps often – seem to bar the way to a principled approach to policy. During the Great Depression, Menzies had seen the need to cut through the confusion of interest demands to achieve a clear direction based on principle. In September 1931, as new president of the Victorian National Federation, the state party organisation of the time, he had declared the belief that inspired him through difficult times and would result in 1944 in the new Liberal Party of Australia:

> I believe that a large majority of the public today is perfectly ready to give its adherence to a party which will display political principle and political courage … We have suffered far too much from people who have no political convictions beyond a more or less genteel adherence to

> our side of politics. That kind of adherence is worthless. We must have people who believe things, and who are prepared to go out and struggle to make their beliefs universal.[67]

Appendix

To summarise Robert Menzies's political philosophy in the manner attempted below is something Menzies himself never attempted. He did regard his *The Forgotten People* book as a 'summarised philosophy' and wrote and spoke from time to time about important elements of his thinking, but he likely would have regarded an attempt to be more systematic as tempting political fate. He was always careful to emphasise liberal values in a form where their policy implications were fairly evident and preferred to be seen as a practical and effective statesman rather than as a philosopher.

When invited by the Western Australian Division of the party in 1970, after his retirement, to give a set-piece lecture, speaking on 'The Foundations of Australian Liberalism', he warned his listeners against focussing too much on the precise words of the party's federal constitution and platform. He said: 'The thing to remember constantly is that Liberalism is an attitude of mind and of faith, aiming at the highest standards of life, both material and spiritual'.[68] Nevertheless, in making his arguments he would frequently state basic values and beliefs, and the following provides a brief summary statement of some of the most important of these. Specific references are given for most of the propositions. Those not footnoted are attempts at summaries or logical conclusions of longer or dispersed statements.

Menzies's political philosophy: a summary

Foundations: Menzies believed that 'liberal thought' embodied two foundational propositions. One is that the individual person is supremely important.[69] The other is that all people have equal human dignity.[70]

These foundations imply that regardless of any differences or inequalities between people, each counts for one, and none for more than one. Democracy, a system of government in which all have equal votes, is therefore the right form of government for human societies.[71]

Public policy, social policy, and government itself, should all recognise people's equal dignity and importance. People therefore all deserve equal chances.[72]

Men and women are all citizens with a common interest and a common task.[73]

Democracy: Personal freedom should be the principal object of the democratic system. Democratic government should express a spirit of respect for all.[74]

Individuals and groups within a society have the capacity to discern vital values, to crusade against tyranny and force, and lead the way to a better world.[75] Democracy is a method of government which can produce justice based upon a recognition of enduring human values.[76]

Democratic Australia must restore the authority and prestige of parliament as the supreme organic expression of self-government.[77] To achieve this, the parliamentarian, as Edmund Burke said, must bring 'mature judgement' to decisions and not be intimidated by public pressure nor see the role as being equivalent to a paid agent of the influential.[78]

Democracy assumes national sovereignty because the nation defines the people who will govern and, through their chosen government, exercise control over policy, foreign and domestic.[79] International institutions cannot be democratic because popular election by equal individuals is not possible.

Freedom: Freedom in a democracy is freedom under law.[80] Law is necessary to protect people against oppression, to defend individual dignity, to secure the provision of essential services that can only be provided collectively, and to enable people to build the lives they seek. People are entitled to the freedom necessary to construct their own lives.[81]

People bear responsibility for their own decisions and actions.[82] Personal responsibility is the foundation of a moral order that supports civic harmony and fosters a good society. Without personal responsibility and self-discipline there cannot be freedom, and their absence leads to autocracy.

Personal freedom must include freedom of expression; freedom of thought, conscience and religion; and freedom of association.[83] These give human reality to the equal dignity of all in a democratically governed society.[84]

If truth is to emerge and ultimately triumph, the process of free debate – the untrammelled clash of opinion – must go on.[85]

Choice: Choice – real choice – is necessary for freedom to be real.[86] Government authority can be effective in imposing uniformity, but it does not have the knowledge to create the variety of goods and services that reflect people's values and that encourage creativity and innovation.

Government should therefore enact and enforce laws which provide security, opportunities, and justice. It should help people to advance their individual capacity.[87] Any activity in which choice and personal confidence are essential is not an activity for which government should attempt to determine outcomes, but where people should be free.[88]

Limited Government: Liberalism recognises the limitations of government. Liberal government should emphasise creating a framework of just laws within which personal freedom can flourish, justice to individuals and economic security be maintained, and human dignity be achieved.[89]

The source of economic and social progress within a framework of just laws is individual initiative and skill. Government should encourage the fullest development of individual capacity.[90]

Parliamentary government based on the separation of powers[91] and on free and regular elections, is essential to maintaining the rule of law, and giving the people control over the exercise of political power. A written bill of rights would give the High Court power to legislate and use political criteria. The responsibility of governments to parliament (responsible government) is the most effective way of maintaining the rights of citizens.[92]

Excessive government centralises decision-making and power. By imposing conformity and reducing freedom, it chokes progress increases unequal power, encourages corruption, and undermines democracy.[93] Federalism, by creating states that have independent authority, is an important way to devolve power.[94]

People's values should predominate in economic life – in production, distribution, and exchange. Life satisfaction, human happiness and productive motivation in economic and social life are dependent on people's values being satisfied.[95]

Government has a duty to encourage enterprise and provide a climate favourable to its growth, to remember that it is the individuals whose energies produce progress, and that all social benefits provided by government derive from individual efforts in creating wealth.[96]

The Public Interest: Given the equal rights, responsibilities and dignity of all, liberalism's aim includes promoting the shared interests of all citizens: the national interest and the public interest. Liberalism abhors prioritising sectional demands that are the selfish interests of a powerful few.[97]

The shared interests of all include national security, a framework of law, equal opportunities to gain education, a culture of non-discrimination, a decent standard of economic security and material well-being, the encouragement of enterprise, resourcefulness and efficiency, co-operation between employers and employees in the workplace, the conservation of natural resources fundamental to life and future prosperity. Government must avoid policies that confer privileges – social or economic – on a select few that are not in the shared interests of all.

Community: A liberal culture that recognises the equal dignity, rights and responsibilities of all provides the only secure basis for community life. Community depends on strong individuals with a sense of responsibility,[98] not bureaucratically managed government programs imposing solutions and diminishing freedom of choice.

Government policies should not discriminate between individuals on the basis of gender, race, colour, religion or associational membership, as such policies directly contravene the equal dignity of all.

Politics: Democratic politics is the noblest and highest of civil vocations[99] and only a party with a philosophy can elevate democratic politics in the eyes of its citizens.

The art of politics is to convey ideas to others, as far as possible, to persuade a majority to agree to those ideas; to create or encourage a public opinion so soundly based that it endures without being blown aside by chance winds; *to persuade people to take long-range views.*[100]

Essentially, a worthwhile political program needs to address two matters: first, what do we want to achieve for the Australian people? Second, how do we propose to go about it? There is no useful place in Australia for a party of reaction or negation.[101]

The Liberal Party: The Liberal Party must be a progressive party, willing to make experiments; in no sense reactionary, but believing in the individual's rights and enterprise …[102]

---

1 Menzies, *Afternoon Light*, p. 281

2 The philosophy sub-committee was chaired by party President Sir Robert Southey. Its main product was Puplick & Southey, *Liberal Thinking*.

3 See Gregory (ed), *The Menzies Lectures*. In 1970 Menzies himself delivered the Inaugural Sir Robert Menzies lecture to the Western Australian State Division on the topic 'Foundations of Australian Liberalism.'

4 John Valder (Chairman), *Report of the Liberal Party Committee of Review*, 'Facing the Facts', Canberra, September 1983.

5 Kemp, 'A Leader and a Philosophy'. A more thorough examination of links between philosophy and performance is provided in Kemp, *A Liberal State* and, for the period 1966-2022, in Kemp, *Consent of the People*.

[6] White, *The Philosophy of the Liberal Party of Australia*, p. 11.

[7] The texts of Menzies's invitation and other key documents associated with the formation of the Liberal Party are to be found in Starr, *The Liberal Party of Australia*, Ch.2.

[8] The development of an inherent liberalism in Australian culture is examined historically in Kemp, *The Land of Dreams.*

[9] Menzies, *The Measure of the Years*, p. 8.

[10] From the Victorian Nationalist Party ministry over a deal with the Country Progressive Party.

[11] From the UAP/Country party cabinet over its decision to renege on National Insurance undertakings.

[12] As prime minister, over divisions within the cabinet – in order, he said, to secure national unity.

[13] Menzies, *The Forgotten People and Other Studies in Democracy.*

[14] Kemp, *A Liberal State*, details the views of Fairfax and Murdoch, pp. 279-80; 289-90; also Bramston, *Robert Menzies*, p. 109.

[15] One such meeting is documented in Kemp, *A Liberal State*, pp. 288-9. Fairfax's views can be found in *Men, Parties and Politics*, pp. 5, 67-9.

[16] See Kemp, *A Liberal State*, Chs. 5-7; also Henderson, *Joseph Lyons.*

[17] Martin, *Robert Menzies,* Vol. I, p. 386 cites the comment of FG Shedden, the public service head of the Department of Defence, and the man largely responsible under Menzies for Australia's war organisation, who wrote to Menzies in December 1942: 'Tribute has yet to be paid to the great foundations laid by you at a time when you lacked the advantage of the effect on national psychology and morale of a war in the Pacific'. See discussion of Menzies's wartime resignation in Kemp, *A Liberal State* pp. 239-44.

[18] This was the view of Calwell in *Be Just and Fear Not*, p. 71.

[19] Menzies, 'Some Lessons of the Election', reproduced in Bramston, *Robert Menzies*, pp. 322-4, 323.

[20] Menzies, *Afternoon Light,* p. 283.

[21] Menzies, 'Some Lessons of the Election'.

[22] Ibid.

[23] Hancock, *The Liberals*, pp. 47-52.

[24] Kemp, *A Liberal State*, pp. 287-8.

[25] Head & Walter (eds), *Intellectual Movements and Australian Society*, pp. 257-61

[26] The role of the IPA in NSW, which initially replaced the Consultative Council as a funding and controlling organisation, is described by Hancock, *The Liberals*, pp. 48-53. The role of the Victorian IPA is described in Kemp, *A Liberal State*, Ch. 12.

[27] Opening Speech, p. 12. Menzies quoted the Victorian IPA publication *Looking Forward*, p. 29

[28] *Forming the Liberal Party of Australia*, p. 3.

[29] Menzies, *Forgotten People*, pp. 1-2.

[30] Ibid., pp. 1-2.

[31] Ibid., pp. 3-9.

[32] Menzies, *Afternoon Light*, p. 287

[33] These were Menzies's words in his Foreword to *The Forgotten People.*

[34] Keynes, *The General Theory of Employment, Interest and Money.*

[35] Popper, *The Open Society and Its Enemies.*

[36] Schumpeter, *Capitalism, Socialism and Democracy.*

[37] Hayek, *The Road to Serfdom.*

[38] Fairfax, *Men, Parties and Politics*, p. 4.

[39] Webb, *Soviet Communism.*

[40] See e.g. Laski, *Democracy in Crisis.*

[41] Menzies, *Afternoon Light*, p. 285.

[42] Ibid, p. 2. This statement was extracted from his opening address and included at the front of the record of the conference, emphasising its importance. See also David Kemp, 'The Political Philosophy of Robert Menzies'. A summary of major aspects of Menzies's political philosophy can be found in the Appendix to this chapter.

[43] Kemp, *The Land of Dreams* provides a detailed account of the arrival and development of the liberal tradition in Australia.

[44] Menzies, *The Measure of the Years*, p. 55.

[45] *Forming the Liberal Party*, p. 10.

[46] Menzies, *The Measure of the Years*, pp. 121-2.

[47] Menzies, *Forming the Liberal Party of Australia*, p. 11.

[48] Ibid. The Melbourne *Argus* later reported that, as Menzies announced the formation of the Liberal Party to the press, the heavens opened and the drought which had affected the Canberra area of NSW was broken, *The Argus*, 21 October 1944, p. 11.

[49] Menzies, *Afternoon Light*, p. 284.

[50] Ibid., p. 286.

[51] Ibid. p. 16; see Appendix to this chapter for a summary of Menzies's political philosophy.

[52] Institute of Public Affairs, Papers, Report on Canberra Conference.

[53] Menzies, Foundations of Australian Liberalism, p. 1.

[54] Menzies, *Afternoon Light*, pp. 289-90

[55] Ibid., p. 296.

[56] Menzies, *Policy Speech* 1946.

[57] Menzies, *Afternoon Light*, pp. 294-5.

[58] See White, *Philosophy of the Liberal Party*, Ch III lists reasons why a party benefits from having a philosophy.

[59] Ibid., p. 176.

[60] Ibid., p. 174.

[61] Ibid., p. 175.

[62] Ibid., pp. 178-9.

[63] Ibid., p. 175.

[64] Ibid., p. 184.

[65] *Forming the Liberal Party of Australia*, pp. 10-11.

[66] Ibid. 285.

[67] Martin, *Menzies*, Vol. I, p. 99.

[68] Menzies, 'The Foundations of Australian Liberalism', p. 1.

[69] Menzies, p. 211.

[70] Menzies, *Forgotten People*, p.183; in his 1970 speech, *Foundations* p.2, he condemned socialism as a 'reactionary doctrine' that 'does scant justice to the dignity of man'.

[71] Ibid., pp. 176-7.

[72] Ibid., pp. 8, 43.

[73] Menzies, *Policy Speech*, 1946.

[74] Menzies, *Forgotten People*, p. 178.

[75] Ibid., p. 173.

[76] Ibid., p. 184.

[77] Ibid., p. 185.

[78] Ibid., p. 178.

[79] Martin, *Menzies,* Vol. II, p. 428.

[80] Menzies, *Opening Address to Unity Conference*, p. 9.

[81] Ibid., p. 9.

[82] Menzies, *Forgotten People*, p. 35.

[83] Menzies, *Opening Address*, p. 9.

[84] Ibid., p. 9; Menzies, Policy Speech, 1949.

[85] Menzies, *Forgotten People*, p. 13.

[86] Menzies, *Opening Address*, p. 9.

[87] Ibid., p. 9.

[88] Menzies, *The Measure of the Years*, pp. 121-2.

[89] Menzies, *Forgotten People,* Ch. XXXII.

[90] Menzies, *Opening Address*, p. 10.

[91] The two key powers of government that should remain independent are the legislative and the executive, and the executive and the judicial.

[92] Menzies, *Foundations*, pp. 11-2.

[93] Menzies, *Forgotten People*, p. 178.

[94] Menzies, *Foundations*, p. 8.

[95] Ibid., p. 55.

[96] Menzies, *The Measure of the Years*, p. 55.

[97] Menzies, *Forgotten People*, p. 17

[98] Ibid., p. 10.

[99] Ibid., p. 175.

[100] Menzies, *The Measure of the Years*, p. 8.

[101] Menzies, Opening Address, p. 8.

[102] Menzies, *Afternoon Light* p. 286.

2

Organisational Federalism

Andrew Kemp

In October 1945 – before the Liberal Party's federal secretariat even had an office – the party's publicity officer, Eric White, privately remarked to Donald Cleland, the straight-laced and ambitious inaugural federal director, that their appointments had garnered little enthusiasm at a recent party conference.[1] White put it down to their 'lack of political experience'; indeed, only days later, Sydney's *Daily Telegraph* called out Cleland as a 'political cleanskin'.[2]

Cleland was affected enough by the comment to mention it in his diary. The next day he dined for the first time with the federal parliamentarians of the new Liberal Party and sensed the scepticism that White may have been referring to. Some members, he thought, saw little reason for the new body to exist at all beyond organising publicity. Others wondered why the new body was taking so long to get going.[3] Cleland was, moreover, already aware of friction between Menzies and the organisation's president, the self-made businessman Thomas Malcolm Ritchie. Despite this, he was confident enough to feel the experiment would work, even if 'there is a long trial and a hard one ahead'.[4]

The diary of Donald Cleland, written across 1945 and early 1946, is a fascinating document of a moment when the Liberal Party of Australia barely existed beyond a name and a promise. It had a constitution and the bare bones of a federal organisation, neither of which had been tested at a general election. Menzies remained politically vulnerable, respected by many but actively disliked by some. Cleland saw first-hand the federal leader's brilliance (his intelligence) and his vulnerabilities (arrogance). The only electoral test federally was the Fremantle by-election, held in July 1945 following the death of John Curtin. None other than Cleland himself was the Liberal candidate. But the result did not bode well for the future; Cleland was trounced by the 27-year-old Kim Beazley Snr, with barely a swing in his favour. Without a secretariat behind him, he relied on Menzies's own press secretary to organise the campaign, which included rudimentary speaker's notes compiled by Menzies's office.[5] These were the earliest of days.

There are clues in Cleland's diary as to what the party would become; what hopes and ideals were behind it; and who was behind it. Cleland is introspective, idealistic, and not a little judgmental. Few impress him, and yet he is crying out to be impressed. Like Menzies, he wanted a political organisation worthy of the philosophical ideals he believed in. This was a generational ambition not limited to the parliamentary leader alone. As early as 1941, Cleland wrote to his wife of plans to revitalise liberal politics in Western Australia, his home state.[6] In the late 1930s, he delivered radio lectures on 'Ideals in politics', 'Democracy – our heritage', 'The challenge to democracy', and 'Liberalism'.[7]

The early years of the Liberal Party's founding, before the federal victory of 1949, were the most idealistic years of the party's history. By the late 1950s, party members would wistfully refer to the 'Spirit of '49'. Every state division had its Donald Clelands, each demanding a decisive break from the past. 'We beg that the Liberal Party shall not be regarded as a compound of old material and old ideas', declared the *Free Beacon*, the official journal of the Tasmanian Division, in May 1945.[8] A year later, Victorian State President WH Anderson, fumed at sitting members 'putting over to the people dead and gone stuff which is best buried. At times it is painful sitting on platforms listening to the deeds of 1066, all of which have the effect of undermining our publicity to the effect that this is, in fact, a <u>new</u> Party' [his emphasis].[9] The turbulent beginnings of the NSW Division came about in large part because one faction sought to prevent 'a camouflaged replica of the old sections of the old United Australia-Democratic Party machine, the puppet of big business, without genuine liberalism'.[10]

This idealism tested the boundaries of what a truly Australia-wide organisation could look like. In October 1945, Cleland and White visited every state division and reported the next month that 'the Party consists in reality of six separate entities, each with its own special problems'.[11] Uniformity was their recommendation, in candidate selection, record keeping, and state constitutions. This was an impossible task. In reality, six divisions meant at least six different conceptions of the ideal, each built upon a liberal tradition that had organically developed – and regressed – over many years.

State identity remained paramount. Cleland felt more moved by the inaugural state council of the WA Division ('a very good meeting and so different to old National Party') than with the first federal council ('solid but not inspiring').[12] There was an artifice to the federal organisation that had to be overcome. This was the challenge laid down by the party president, Tom Ritchie, who told the delegates to the inaugural council that they 'did not represent any State', but had been sent 'to act as an individual on an Australian Council, and the most urgent work in front of this Council would be to develop the Australian conception of the Party'.[13]

This was easier said than done. The more common sentiment was expressed by Jim Paton, president of the WA Division, who warned of the 'tendency to concentrate power in one centre; a corresponding tendency to override the states; a most dangerous cult of uniformity particularly in legislative proposals; and a tendency for full-time officials to be clothed with directive powers'.[14] This was the challenge laid down by the state divisions, who protected their autonomy with righteous conviction.

To a degree, the zeitgeist was on Ritchie's side. The war had expanded the size and ambitions of the federal government, and with it, the public's expectation of what it can and should do. Australians had been mobilised, regulated and regimented. Australian government spending and taxation levels had never been higher. Innovative minds turned to 'post-war reconstruction'. While not against appropriate state intervention, liberals were increasingly suspicious of anything that smacked of 'planning', if such a thing meant more regimentation, rationing and regulation. The rhetoric and ruminations of the mid-40s are therefore uniquely philosophical. 'Policy matters, I think, are minor compared with the statement of great principles', Alex Mair, the NSW deputy leader of the Opposition, wrote to Menzies in 1944.[15] The effect was to encourage liberals across the country to think nationally, and turn their own minds to great principles. This was the undercurrent of the centrifugal forces unifying the liberal and conservative groups.

The mirage of an Australian-wide party, pre-1944

By the early 1940s, liberal politics had regressed not just philosophically but organisationally. Election defeats around most of the country were only half the story. What Joseph Lyons had called the United Australia Movement, on 28 March 1931, had become a gaggle of separate interests that could not even share a common name across Australia, let alone a common purpose. The UAP was not a federation in the same way that its Nationalist predecessor was. It had no federal constitution, no federal platform, no federal council, executive, or secretary. Its lifeblood was in the leadership of the federal parliamentarians, namely Lyons, and in the New South Wales and Victorian organisations, which were themselves decaying by the 1940s.[16]

An informal assessment of the political situation in Victoria and New South Wales, written by the NSW branch of the Institute of Public Affairs in 1943, revealed the extent of the decay. 'Actually functioning branches appear to be few in the whole of Victoria', the note read. 'There appears also to be a complete absence of electorate conferences, a central council and a central executive'. The situation was better in NSW. There were active branches in competitive electorates; the central executive continued to meet regularly; there were headquarters with a (small) secretariat; but numbers had dwindled, and a shortage of funds meant the party could not afford paid organisers. The assessment did not even need to mention the divided state of the organisations opposing Labor: at the Canberra Unity Conference of October 1944, representatives of no less than thirteen political parties were present.[17]

How did it come to this? The reality was that the United Australia Party was built on unstable foundations. Joseph Lyons was the face of it, but he saw it and regarded it as the parliamentary manifestation of a popular movement, which, at its peak, reached hundreds of thousands of members spread across popular citizens' movements. These organisations had emerged during the worst depths of the Great Depression and prided themselves on their rejection of party politics. This was a problem when the time arrived to establish the UAP. Many of the members and movement leaders discouraged the formation of proper party machinery on the grounds that it might further corrupt true parliamentary democracy.[18] When the populist wave receded, little was left organisationally.

The secretive financial sponsors, however, remained – the National Union in Victoria, and the Consultative Council in New South Wales. These committees existed independently of the parliamentary parties and were composed of well-connected businessmen who could deliver funds at election time. The mysterious nature of these committees, which kept their business behind firmly closed doors, took on a degree of notoriety that badly damaged the UAP brand. At all levels – parliamentary, grassroots, and business – the time was ripe for a new party to emerge.

Deciding on an Australian-wide party: the lead up to the Canberra Unity Conference, October 1944

For almost a year, from late 1943, Menzies had watched the unity developments in Victoria and New South Wales with a mixture of interest and apprehension. Neither showed signs of a breakthrough. The Victorian unity committee was amicable but slow. Menzies was kept informed of its progress, but expressed his frustration that the politicians, himself included, were not more involved in its workings.[19] In NSW, rumours that a new state party might form the basis for a new federal organisation were particularly disconcerting. Writing to Alex Mair, then UAP leader, Menzies urged restraint in adopting any kind of federal policy until all the states could be brought together for an Australia-wide party.[20] In the end it did not matter. Within two weeks, discussions broke down, and a hastily re-named 'Democratic Party' was badly defeated in May 1944.

There was no consensus as to what an Australia-wide organisation would look like, how it would be formed, or even who would lead it. Although Keith Murdoch could observe, in late 1943, that Menzies 'regarded himself as the Commander-in-Chief of the anti-socialist forces, and his office in Canberra as the headquarters of these forces', this viewpoint had to be impressed on the states.[21] In this respect, the failure of the unity discussions at a state level was of great assistance to the federal leader. Menzies's proposed Unity Conference offered something of a lifeline to others.

Diversity of opinion was evident across all Australian liberal groupings. This was obvious in the written responses to the Unity Conference invitations. Everyone agreed on the necessity for an Australia-wide organisation. The Western Australian Nationalists saw broad continuity with the status-quo, with minimal amendment to their own constitution other than linking up with a federal organisation – 'State organisations should remain separate and autonomous on the basis of existing State organisational bodies'.[22] The elderly James Shaw, secretary of the Country-National Organisation of Queensland, recommended an Australia-wide party with 'unity of name and unity of organisation', with a strong federal executive that could determine federal policy.[23] Mair in NSW was less confident of a unified federal organisation ('a central organisation with affiliated state parties would be better than nothing'), but his rival Ernest White, leader of the Liberal Democratic Party, was more ambitious, suggesting an 'Australia-wide Party speaking with one voice and answering to one control', with mass membership and a clear break from the opaque arrangements with financial donors.[24] He suggested the new party be called the 'Australian Liberal Party'.

The federal ambitions of the Canberra conference were put into effect with a federal method of achieving them: two committees, each comprised of two representatives from every state, were appointed to decide on the name of the party and its objectives, as well as the organisational structure. The latter committee recommended a federal structure with state branches, governed by a federal council comprising seven delegates from each state. A federal executive, made up of an equal number of state representatives, would be answerable to the council. The committee further recommended a joint federal standing committee on federal policy, again with equal state representation; a permanent secretariat in Canberra; and 'substantial autonomy on the part of State branches in relation to State organisation and affairs'.[25]

The Albury conference of December 1944 solidified these federal principles. It established a provisional constitution and a provisional executive. It made it clear that the party 'would raise and control its own funds … [and] would be free of any possibility of control from outside itself and would determine its own destiny'.[26] State councils, comprised of representatives to be annually elected in a manner left to each state, would govern the state branches. Party members were therefore members of their respective state divisions, not of a central or national organisation. Policy was to remain the purview of the parliamentarians – befitting the Burkean tradition of the politician as trustee, not delegate – but the joint standing committee on federal policy would link the organisation with the parliamentary party – a feature entirely absent from the UAP. The policy committee was to 'advise the Parliamentary Party upon matters of Federal policy'.[27]

A declaration of 'substantial autonomy' for the state branches (later to be called state divisions), eased the concerns of state party officials, but ruffled the feathers of those seeking a new start and more radical change driven from the centre. Donald Cleland was intensely disappointed to find the draft constitution of the Western Australian Division almost identical to the old Nationalist constitution. He offered up his services to the drafting committee.[28] A similar situation was occurring around the states, with divisional constitutions drafted to reflect long-standing arrangements and local circumstances. Victoria provided for equal representation of men and women across multiple levels of the organisation, reflecting the influential position held by the Australian Women's National League in that state. New South Wales had no such arrangements but produced a more convoluted set of rules to accommodate existing diversity, even disunity, among the old UAP group and rival liberal groupings.[29] The relatively youthful Queensland People's Party, a liberal and urban organisation that had absorbed the state's UAP, simply refused to join, suspicious of Menzies and what it perceived to be the south-eastern conservative elites. South Australia chose to retain its branding and structure as the Liberal and Country League.

Building a nationwide party: 1945

Despite this diversity, Menzies was delighted by the membership drives occurring across the country in early 1945. This was perhaps the greatest accomplishment of the party in its first calendar year. Surviving correspondence gives a sense of the atmosphere. 'We are receiving letters and enquiries from all over the island asking for more information about the Liberal Party, and from canvassers wanting to know the answers to questions hurled at them', one Tasmanian official wrote. In South Australia, 'branches which have been dead for many years have sprung to life'. A young Victorian party member and future senator, Alan Missen, compared the opening of one branch to a revival meeting of the kind led by Billy Graham.[30]

By March 1945, around 42,000 members were enrolled – excluding Queensland. By April, 61,000. When the inaugural federal council met in August, the party's federal executive could boast around 100,000 members spread across almost 800 branches. At the state level, these numbers told interesting stories. In the first few months of recruitment, South Australia had more branch members than either New South Wales or Victoria, at 22,000 (see Table 1). The SA Liberal and Country League had largely ignored the Nationalist and UAP rebranding of the previous decades but had amalgamated with the Country Party – the primary source of its added numerical strength. This was a tantalising prospect for the federal organisation, which held out early hopes for a Liberal-Country amalgamation.

Table 1: Total members per state division and as a percentage of enrolled voters, April 1945

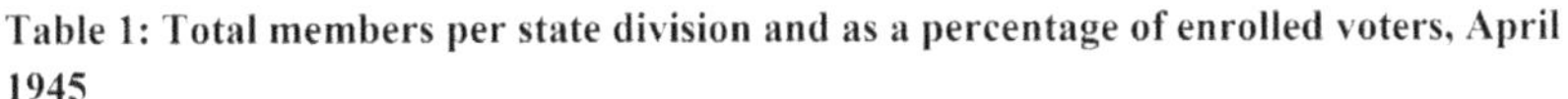
Table 1: Total members per state division and as a percentage of enrolled voters, April 1945

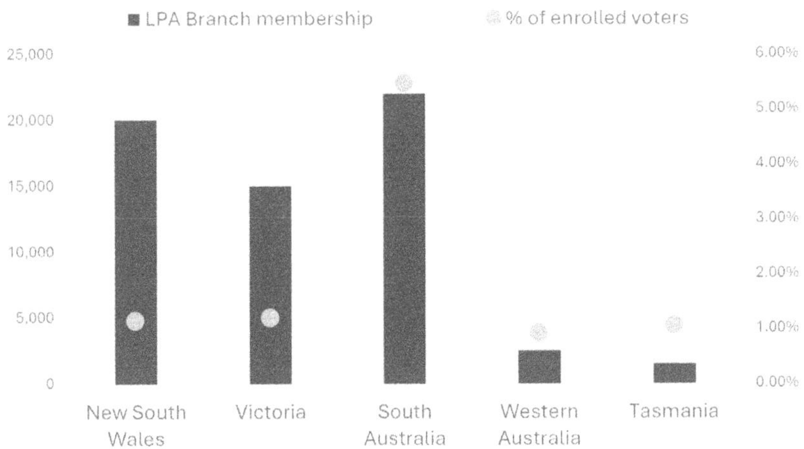

Source: member figures from Hancock, *National and Permanent?* p. 39. Enrolled voters are based upon enrolment numbers for the 1944 '14 powers' referendum, held on 19 August 1944, Handbook of the 44th Parliament (2014), Part 5 – Referendums and Plebiscites – Referendum Results, *Parliamentary Library of Australia.*

Those with long enough memories had, of course, seen such bursts of enthusiasm and recruitment before. The citizens movements in the early 1930s were larger and more intense. But the new party was determined to provide a structure that could retain membership. 'All States are meeting with success in the formation of branches', Jim Paton, the WA Division president, wrote to Menzies in March, 'but unless these branches are guided in their work, the initial enthusiasm is bound to wane'.[31] He wanted the federal executive 'to be a truly co-ordinating body', providing party news, research and information to all state divisions.

The new federal president, the 'square-jawed, beetle-browed' businessman, Thomas Malcolm Ritchie, had grand plans for an influential and well-funded central organisation to do just that.[32] Envisioning a party of one million members, operating on £2-3 million per annum, Ritchie desired a federal secretariat budget of £1 million – each state contributing on a proportionate basis relative to their membership. He wanted the secretariat to provide economic and political research to the parliamentary wing and state divisions; to assist in co-ordinating the functions of the state divisions; and to provide improved publicity.[33] Most of this required, in differing degrees, a transferral of responsibility from the states to the federal organisation. But the first federal executive report, written by Cleland and Eric White in November 1945, made clear that such ambitions would be difficult to achieve.

Cleland and White's report did not make for comfortable reading. The party organisation was found to be 'weak and spasmodic as compared to the over-all organisation of the anti-Liberal forces'.[34] The state divisions varied 'in efficiency and in extent'. With one exception, no state division had a publicity or research team. Record keeping of membership files was all over the place. Processes to select parliamentary candidates differed across every division.

Ritchie saw himself, along with '[m]ost of the men and women with whom I have come in contact in the Party', as a newcomer to politics.[35] He shared an idealistic optimism with Cleland, and indeed with other new officers to the party. This was perhaps the most important distinction from the old UAP. Ritchie urged party members to consider themselves as 'Liberals', not 'Conservatives', and to regard the party as standing 'for something new and progressive'.[36] He wasn't afraid of making pronouncements on Liberal policy, sometimes to the raised eyebrows of party members. But after making public his million-dollar fundraising plan, Menzies scolded him in private for the insensitivity towards voters 'who are not at heart socialists, but who have considerable apprehension about the power of money'.[37] Menzies respected Ritchie but found his perceived political naivete and managerialism galling. Cleland noted Menzies's 'casualness and lack of appropriate attention to the office of the President', which may have explained the irregular contact between the two in 1945 – a point raised by Ritchie in one angry letter written in August.[38]

Both men approached organisational questions from a different basis. Menzies saw a parliamentary party in need of an organisation subordinate to it; Ritchie regarded the organisation as the arteries of the party, which if left in a sclerotic state could bring the whole project to its knees. Labor, with its affiliated unions, resolved this tension by imbuing the membership with a sovereignty of its own. Party conferences were themselves 'little parliaments', in Arthur Calwell's words, where the federal conference, dominated by unions, held supreme authority over the parliamentary wing.[39] Liberals could not accept such an arrangement that breached the sacrosanct principle of the politician as trustee of the public good, not a delegate to a sectional interest. The parliamentarians were therefore accorded a high degree of autonomy and policy making power by the party's constitution, paralleling all previous liberal party arrangements.

This presented in-built challenges to the federal aims of the party's structure. Menzies could be frank to the point of insulting in federal executive meetings over the efficacy of the secretariat's work – usually over matters of publicity – while Cleland was being pulled in another direction by the representatives of the state divisions – forever unhappy over the financial burden of a central body less attuned to local conditions than themselves. By mid-1947, Cleland was writing nervously to Menzies about the prospect of the secretariat being confined 'to a restricted role of minor importance', should the states cease to fund it adequately; 'then its real usefulness and purpose in the Federal build up will be destroyed'.[40]

Building a nation-wide party: Finance

A federal secretariat was hardly a new idea, but funding it had proved elusive for the United Australia Party. As early as 1932, Lyons was urged to establish a research and publicity bureau to undertake the kind of work later envisaged by Ritchie in 1945.[41] The prime minister approached both the National Union and the Consultative Council more than once to discuss such an organisation, but nothing eventuated.[42] This was but one of many deficiencies of the financial arrangements prior to 1944, and it was hoped that with greater party control of funds, the more opportunities there would be for long-range strategic work.

Convincing the traditional donor bodies to cease their role as money collectors was a difficult process made easier by the new faces of the party. Men like Ritchie and Bill Spooner (state president) in NSW, or the Victorian State President WH Anderson, harboured no loyalty to the old way of business and actively sought to do away with it. In this they were successful. By January 1946, Spooner could publicly declare that the party would simply not accept donations from associations or groups of donors. Victorian Division Treasurer William Kirkhope had the unenviable task of writing to confused business donors that the National Union had no association with the Liberal Party, while Anderson, after learning the National Union intended to remain a conservative fundraising body, suggested in one frustrated memorandum that 'possibly some straight talk will need to be indulged in, and so that interested people may be well aware of the hollowness of the Union'.[43]

The state fundraising silos of the old UAP did at least have one unintentional benefit, which was that donors knew exactly where to send their money. In mid-1945, after Ritchie addressed a business luncheon in Melbourne, the natural question from contributors was whether to write a cheque to the new federal organisation or the state divisions. After successfully raising £50,000 from larger donors, Ritchie was inclined to carve out a section of Australia-wide businesses exclusively for federal purposes.[44] This was an obvious red flag to Anderson, who conferred with the Victorian state finance committee and strongly recommended that there be 'only one collecting agency in this State'.[45] Irritated, Ritchie could not help but respond that 'the "six Liberal Parties" development has not left Victoria unscathed'.[46]

This was an argument that Ritchie could not win. Anderson was probably right to remark, as he did in his characteristically frank way, that 'Mr. Ritchie unduly emphasises the importance of the Federal activities and does not realise that at least 80 per cent of the work must be performed and 80 per cent of expenditure incurred by the State Division'.[47] The states had the field workers and the organisers; they found and trained the candidates; they knew the local conditions well enough to tailor more suitable publicity than what the federal organisation could provide. And so they largely kept their fundraising autonomy, but at a cost – especially in the early years – of a federal secretariat operating effectively on probation. It would have to prove its worth, or risk the states withdrawing what little they provided.

Building a nation-wide party: Publicity

The big test of the federal organisation was in organising publicity for the federal parliamentary party. A lot of thinking had gone into what it could do; what the state divisions were good at and not so good at, and what a truly national campaign would look like. In January 1946, the federal executive defined the publicity functions of the federal body as confined to a national radio campaign, while providing state divisions with advertising and broadcast materials as desired.

Despite uncertainties over responsibilities, national campaigns, it was believed, were becoming not only more effective, but more necessary. The expansion of Commonwealth power inevitably drew state politics further into national debates. Even local events took on national meaning in a political environment still standing in the shadows of a hot war and entering the realm of a cold war. Industrial strikes affected everyday life for most Australians, who were also calibrating the real and perceived threats of radical ideologies like communism. 'WA Labor lost the elections on the waterfront of NSW' one Labor-leaning individual remarked to Ross McDonald, a former WA Liberal leader, reflecting on the 1947 state election.[48]

The 1946 federal election campaign was a premature test of the federal secretariat's capabilities. After devoting most of their efforts in 1945 to setting up the body, campaign preparation was a rushed and rather unsatisfactory affair. A typical criticism was of the low quality of the material produced, a complaint that extended over into later referendum campaigns.[49] Divisions were used to a two-tiered structure with state headquarters (and assistance from the federal leader's office) owning the national messaging while local electorate committees undertook the real work of boots-on-the-ground campaigning. But the grey area of what was expected of federal and state headquarters necessitated a re-think after the disappointing 1946 result.

Advertisement authorised by the federal secretariat, emphasising Chifley's failure to facilitate homeownership. From *The Bulletin*, 8 May 1946.

State election campaigns were entirely the purview of the divisions, though the federal organisation could and did provide resources to the smaller states. A publicity officer from the federal secretariat was sent to Tasmania to assist with the 1946 state campaign; 'gestures as these show the solidity of our Australian wide structure', the state president wrote to Cleland, but in New South Wales, Menzies was effectively asked not to participate at all in the 1947 state campaign.[50] 'What the N.S.W. people decide politically is their own affair entirely, but it would be ludicrous for me to keep right away from New South Wales as if I were under a quarantine order!' Menzies wrote to Cleland.[51]

Even the federal director himself, initially operating out of the NSW Division headquarters, was cautious not to appear too often at NSW executive meetings.[52]

To better co-ordinate state activity, and to appreciate state sensitivity to federal activity, state secretaries, publicity officers, and the federal secretariat began to meet regularly. What began as a series of 'staff conferences' evolved into the public relations planning committee, later simply called the staff planning committee (SPC). This was the forum for the states and the federal secretariat to say their piece, 'to share experiences, report on the current political situation, exchange advice, prepare and endorse memoranda on matters such as publicity, postal voting and electoral redistributions, and construct the "political appreciation" which formed the starting point of any federal or state election strategy'.[53]

Over the years, the personalities of the SPC were as significant as the committee's purpose. John Verran McConnell, the Victorian general secretary, was a trusted confidant of the prime minister and held his position right up until his death in 1971. John Carrick in New South Wales dominated his state's organisation with a political shrewdness and an unusually philosophical approach to party politics; he served as the NSW general secretary from 1948-71. Bob Willoughby, Menzies's former personal assistant, succeeded Cleland as federal director in 1951 and retired in 1969. McConnell and Carrick were returned serviceman; Willoughby had witnessed the evolution of liberal politics from his teenage days working as a clerk for the South Australian Liberal Federation in the 1920s, through to the UAP and then the Liberal Party. These men 'got' the Liberal Party, to the extent that they were involved in its formative years, understood why it formed, and took its core philosophy seriously. Their retirement ushered in a more professionalised era of politics, but one less anchored to the mid-century liberalism that formed the basis of the party's existence.

Building a nation-wide party: Candidates

At the Albury conference, Menzies asked the party to focus its efforts on the selection of quality candidates. As 'one of the great problems' facing the old organisations, he wanted the new party to throw its weight behind 'real candidates', 'people who through their intellectual and moral force, their experience and skill, were fit to sit in Cabinet. ...[54] Few could disagree with the sentiment, but almost immediately the issue became the first battleground for determining just how centralised or federalised the organisation was to be. The Albury conference agreed to a uniform method of candidate selection for federal electorates, with WA and SA exempted after internal protest.[55] This was a short-lived experiment. Nine months later, the party constitution was amended to give all divisions freedom to adopt whatever method they saw fit.

Cleland observed at the first annual WA council the intensity to which candidate selection could be debated by party members. His subsequent tour of the state divisions revealed a variety of methods along a democratic spectrum. They ranged from the most democratic – South Australia provided for a plebiscite under which any party member within the relevant electorate could vote – to a more centralised hybrid, where state executive delegates and a small number of elected branch delegates participated in the selection process (e.g. Western Australia).[56]

In the minds of the federal secretariat, the 1946 federal election confirmed the deficiency of state autonomy for such a responsibility. In an angry post-election report, Ritchie attacked the quality of the candidates and the lack of a uniform method of selection.[57] The absence of any federal control was obvious by the failure to secure Richard Casey, a former treasurer under Joseph Lyons, a Lower House seat. Although the federal executive expressed its 'unanimous wish' that Casey find his way back to parliament, and identified a range of potential electorates, local branches had no intention of abandoning their say in the matter.[58] Press reports of the party 'cold shouldering' Casey, a potential leader of the party, were embarrassing but wrong.[59] This was the federal structure of the party at work. Nonetheless, it gave some party officials pause to consider whether 'the ultra-democratic provisions of the [party's] constitution' were a problem.[60]

Building a nation-wide party: Policy

From its inception, every rank-and-file member had a say on Liberal Party policy; the bigger question was who, if anybody, would listen. A policy idea might emanate from a local branch and be submitted as a motion to be considered at state council. If carried, the motion may be forwarded to the federal council, should it pertain to federal policy. The federal council could pass, reject, or amend the motion. Whatever the outcome, it was not binding on the parliamentary party. To the extent that parliamentarians listened, it was the informal ties that mattered: personalities, organisational-parliamentary relationships, the political climate, the urgency or importance of the matter being debated. These informal factors could breathe a dynamism into party activity, or suffocate it with a deadening hand.

The joint standing committee on federal policy (JSCFP) was built to listen. It arrived with high ambition, began promisingly, then muddled through and disappeared – dormant for almost eight years before its revival in 1957. It played a central role in drafting the first federal platform, Menzies's 1946 election speech, and the policies adopted for the 1946 election. Submissions made to JSCFP by the state divisions were backed with impressive research and equipped the federal Opposition – then without the benefit of a bureaucracy – with the information to advocate a fighting policy.

Yet there were problems from the beginning. Cleland found the JCSFP 'not really effective because of its make-up and the difficulty of frequent meetings etc …'[61] At first its functions were not clearly defined. A gap emerged between what the federal president desired of it, and what the federal parliamentary leader expected it to do. Neither did policy development lend itself neatly to committee work, certainly not a committee with representatives scattered across Australia. On urgent matters requiring fast turnaround, it could do little. Various iterations and sub-committees could make improvements at the margins, but there was a larger barrier in the supremacy of the parliamentary leader, whose co-operation such a committee relied on.

The question of uniform taxation was one instance in which the party's policy development apparatus was tested. As a wartime measure, the Commonwealth had taken over the administration and levying of income tax, replacing the dual system that had been in place since World War I. States were compensated by federal grants, but the subsequent loss of fiscal autonomy inevitably meant the policy settings would be revisited after the war. The federal council resolved in 1946 to appoint a special committee to examine the issue, consisting of a representative from each state, which would submit a recommendation at a future council. Its work was delayed by a federal election in late 1946 and then by subsequent state elections, so it did not meet until mid-1947 – one of many instances in which the federal committees struggled to co-ordinate all the state delegates into a single place at a single time.[62]

There was never much of a likelihood that a single committee could distil a satisfactory solution from so divisive a problem. Victoria had long been in the vanguard of opposition to uniform taxation, having been a net loser from its fiscal arrangements. The smaller states were more comfortable with the status quo, and NSW State President Bill Spooner was openly supportive of it.[63] Nonetheless, the special committee found a middle ground: a continuation of uniform tax collection, with the condition that states could apply their own rates.[64] But what was obvious to the committee was decidedly less obvious to many rank and file members. The matter was debated again at the federal council in 1948, which resolved only to review the matter when in government.[65] Keenly aware of the policy's complexity, Menzies simply chose to stay silent on the issue in the 1949 campaign. Once in office, it was a working party of Commonwealth and state treasury bureaucrats that were tasked with finding a solution – not the party organisation.[66]

Such was the fate of the JSCFP, which could not compete with a well-resourced public service at the hands of Liberal ministers, to the extent that it did not meet at all from the 1949 victory until 1957. An internal organisational review was blunt: 'To put it boldly, the Government has rarely accepted the advice of the organisation on Policy matters, and rarely carried out recommendations and suggestions'.[67]

This was a low point in the organisation-parliamentary relationship, but state interests had their own way of being heard – aside from informal talks with party members – either through the federal cabinet, the backbench, conferences with the state Liberal leaders, or the annual premiers' conference and loan council meetings. As Menzies consolidated his own hold over the Liberal leadership, the most productive (if tense) flow of federal-state policy communication was between himself and the Liberal state leaders.

Australia's federal system, aided by the personalities of influential state premiers, did much of the work in transmitting state interests to federal policy. Thomas Playford, the 'Holy Terror' as Menzies called him, was regularly on the phone to South Australian MPs and senators whenever there was a state interest to pursue. Playford mastered the loan council meetings probably better than any other premier. Henry Bolte was another professional haggler over Commonwealth tax reimbursements to the states, with political capital in Menzies's hometown. 'Henry Bolte … is prepared to throw himself into whatever the campaign needs are', John Buchan, Victorian state president, wrote to the federal president in 1961 during a low point in the federal government's popularity, 'but he emphasises that the Commonwealth must do certain things which will greatly assist in appealing to Victorian electors … '. Here was an opinion that Menzies could not afford to ignore.[68]

The Spirit of '49

The first five years of the Liberal Party can be divided into two distinct phases: before and after Ben Chifley's announcement, on 16 August 1947, of his government's intention to nationalise Australia's banks. The effect was to turbo charge the membership, organisational activity, finances, and electoral success of the Liberal Party – both its federal and state parliamentary wings – and to consolidate its political and philosophical purpose, providing the state divisions with a common language and set of principles to pursue state interests. In this respect, Ben Chifley can be credited – in the most ironic sense – as an unofficial shaper of the modern Liberal Party.

Consider the *cri de coeur* of William Kirkhope a year earlier, that 'our bank balance [of the Victorian Division] was sufficient for a month's expenditure'. Organising another drive for funds was 'the last thing I wished to do. I decided, however, to give it a go and see if the public really wish the party to survive, or will it cease through lack of funds?'[69] By 1949, the money was flowing in; according to one source, £150,000 was raised in two years.[70] In 1943, field organisers were almost entirely absent from the United Australia Organisation in Victoria; there were forty-eight employed by 1949, a number considerably higher than the fourteen employed in 1967.[71] Membership peaked in 1950 – above 45,000 in Victoria, and almost 200,000 across Australia.[72] In 1947, the minority state Labor government was forced to resign after the Legislative Council blocked supply, largely in opposition to Chifley's bank policy.

Yet neither bank nationalisation nor the coal strike of 1949 were circuit breakers for resolving organisational federal-state tensions. Campaign control remained a point of contention. The South Australian Division – numerically the most impressive, considering its relatively smaller population – simply did not want federal advertising material. When asked how many federal pamphlets it would like in the lead up to the federal election, its Chief Secretary AS Dunk replied 'None'; 'They intended to run a campaign based on the personality of the candidates and the Liberal philosophy'.[73] Note the language here – *they* owned the campaign.

More importantly, however, for the party's fortunes was the growing convergence in purpose between the divisions. '[M]ore and more people were rallying to Liberalism', retiring Queensland People's Party State President AL Hume reported at the 1949 annual convention.[74] The next day, the QPP changed its name to the Liberal Party. At a meeting of the state general secretaries in March 1949, a NSW divisional organiser, reflecting on a successful state by-election held earlier that month, reported that the result 'satisfied him that we had got to convince the people that Liberalism has replaced Labour'.[75] This was the core message of Robert Menzies's weekly broadcasts that began in July 1949: the Liberal way or the Socialist way. Not only was the message resonating, but Menzies himself was beginning to win over doubters. 'We believed we could perceive nearly twelve months ago a growing warmth towards yourself, and following your tour here this has enormously increased', Charles Porter, the Queensland Liberal president, told the federal leader in September.[76] The NSW Division, having tried to keep Menzies away in 1947, took great pains to secure his presence as much as possible.[77]

The success of 1949 was a mixed blessing for the federal organisation. On the one hand the contrast with 1943 could not have been greater. It validated every argument for a professional extra-parliamentary organisation. It could receive the wave of membership from 1947-50 with a political infrastructure that embedded a degree of continuous activity in a way that the UAP could not. But it also proved that electoral success could be achieved without the kind of centralised structure envisaged by Ritchie and Cleland. More members and more resources simply emboldened the state divisions. Even after six years, Federal President WH Anderson would ruminate on the 'very nearly autonomous' state divisions which, among other challenges, were threatening the party's job 'to establish a permanent liberal tradition'.[78]

The counterpoint to Anderson's argument was that a number of factors were drawing the divisions closer together, if not organisationally then in other informal ways: political attitudes, philosophy, and a new nomenclature of anti-socialist politics. Cold war politics was the external factor that sharpened the liberal ethos, but Menzies was the great articulator of a revived liberalism that gave a foundational coherence to the Liberal Party. State autonomy was the buy-in for this project to succeed; there was no chance that such a diverse range of state interests would cede organisational control to an untested central body. But as history proved, they did not need to.

---

[1] Sir Donald Cleland Diary, 1 October 1945, Papers of Donald Cleland, NLA, MS 9600/6/10.

[2] *Daily Telegraph,* 7 October 1945, p. 7.

[3] Cleland Diary, 2 October 1945.

[4] Ibid., 3 October 1945.

[5] Martin, *Robert Menzies,* Vol. II, p. 31; Menzies to Jim Paton, 19 July 1945, Papers of Sir Robert Menzies, NLA, MS 4936/14/417.

[6] Donald Cleland to Rachel Cleland, 7 October 1941, quoted in Lutton, *My Dearest Brown Eyes,* pp. 146-153.

[7] Ibid., p. xx.

[8] *Free Beacon,* May 1945, Papers of Sir Robert Menzies, NLA, MS 4936/14/417.

[9] WH Anderson to Robert Menzies, 6 September 1946, Papers of Sir Robert Menzies, NLA, MS 4936/14/417.

[10] Statement from Ernest K White and supporters, 30 April 1945, Papers of Ernest K White, NLA, MS 6455/1/3.

[11] Donald Cleland & Eric White, *Report and Recommendations to the Federal Executive,* Liberal Party of Australia, 26 November 1945, Records of the Liberal Party of Australia, NLA MS 5000/7/170.

[12] Cleland Diary, 30 May 1945, 28-30 August 1945.

[13] Record of Proceedings including Minutes of Meeting of the Inaugural Federal Council Meeting, 28-31 August 1945, Papers of Sir Robert Menzies, NLA MS 4936/14/415

[14] Quoted in Starr, 'The Liberal Party of Australia', p. 35.

[15] Alex Mair to Robert Menzies, 17 September 1944, MS 4936, Consignment 1993, File 11, Box 573.

[16] Lloyd, 'The Formation and Development of the United Australia Party, 1929-1937', pp. 220-1.

[17] The note is titled 'Comparison of political organisations, Victoria and New South Wales', author not specified. Institute of Public Affairs (Victoria) papers, 1943. Privately held.

[18] See for instance Cunningham, *Mobilising the Masses,* Chapter 5.

[19] Notes of Unity Meeting held on 5 September 1944, Institute of Public Affairs (Victoria), privately held.

[20] Robert Menzies to Alex Mair, 5 November 1943, Papers of Sir Robert Menzies, NLA MS 4926 14/410.

[21] Quoted in Kemp, *A Liberal State.*

[22] Ross McDonald to Robert Menzies, 3 October 1944, Papers of Sir Robert Menzies, NLA MS 4936, 1993 Consignment, File 11, Box 573.

[23] Ibid., James Shaw to Robert Menzies, 2 October 1944.

[24] Ibid., Alex Mair to Robert Menzies, 27 September 1944; Ernest White to Robert Menzies, 3 October 1944

[25] *Forming the Liberal Party of Australia.*

[26] Quoted in Starr, *The Liberal Party of Australia,* p. 81.

[27] Ibid., p. 116.

[28] Donald Cleland to Rachel Cleland, 7 October 1941, quoted in Lutton, *My Dearest Brown Eyes,* pp. 146-153

[29] Starr, 'The Liberal Party of Australia', p. 34.

[30] Hancock, *National and Permanent?*, p. 39.

[31] Jim Paton to Robert Menzies, 19 March 1945, Papers of Sir Robert Menzies, NLA, MS 4936/14/417

[32] *Daily Telegraph,* 14 October 1945, p.22.

[33] Proposals for Federal Organisation, Liberal Party of Australia, submitted by the Chairman, 6 June 1945, NLA MS 5000/7/204

[34] Cleland & White, *Report and Recommendations to the Federal Executive.*

[35] Quoted in Martin, *Robert Menzies,* Vol. II, p. 33.

[36] *The Daily Telegraph,* 14 October 1945, p. 22.

[37] Robert Menzies to Thomas Malcolm Ritchie, 6 August 1945, Papers of Sir Robert Menzies, NLA MS 4936/14/410.

[38] Sir Donald Cleland Diary, 2 October 1945, in Papers of Donald Cleland, NLA, MS 9600/6/10; Thomas Malcolm Ritchie to Robert Menzies, 8 August 1945, Papers of Sir Robert Menzies, NLA MS 4936/14/410.

[39] Quoted in Maddox, 'The Australian Labor Party', pp. 205-6.

[40] Donald Cleland to Robert Menzies, 16 June 1947, Papers of Sir Robert Menzies, NLA MS 4936/14/410.

[41] Lloyd, 'The Formation and Development of the United Australia Party, 1929-1937', pp. 221-2

[42] Ibid., 222

[43] University of Melbourne Archives, Records of the Liberal Party of Australia (Victorian Division), 19850148, Executive Files: Correspondence, WH Anderson, Memorandum, 21 February 1946.

[44] Ibid., Thomas Malcolm Ritchie to WH Anderson, 30 July 1945.

[45] Ibid., WH Anderson to Thomas Malcolm Ritchie, 3 August 1945.

[46] Ibid., Thomas Malcolm Ritchie to WH Anderson, 7 August 1945.

[47] Ibid., WH Anderson, Memorandum, 8 August 1945.

[48] Ross McDonald to Robert Menzies, 21 March 1949.

[49] Hancock, *National and Permanent?*, p. 74; see also University of Melbourne Archives, Records of the Liberal Party of Australia (Victorian Division), 19850148, Executive Files, Victorian Division Executive Committee Meeting No. 29, 8 April 1948.

[50] JM Fotheringham to Donald Cleland, 10 December 1946, Papers of Sir Robert Menzies, NLA, MS 4936/14/417.

[51] Robert Menzies to Donald Cleland, 20 March 1947.

[52] Cleland Diary, 4 March 1946.

[53] Hancock, 'The Liberal Party Organisation, 1944-1966', pp. 82-83

[54] Quoted in Starr, *The Liberal Party of Australia,* p.83.

[55] Cleland & White, *Report and Recommendations to the Federal Executive*, p. 5.

[56] Ibid., Appendix A.

[57] Hancock, *National and Permanent?*, p. 71.

[58] Minutes of the Federal Executive, 2-3 July 1946, Robert Menzies Papers, NLA MS 4936/14/415.

[59] *The Argus,* 15 July 1946, p. 3.

[60] Quoted in Hancock, *National and Permanent?*, p. 74.

[61] Donald Cleland to Robert Menzies, 8 July 1949, Papers of Sir Robert Menzies NLA MS 4936/14/410

[62] Federal Director memorandum to State Secretaries, 26 June 1947, S14/47, Papers of Sir Robert Menzies NLA MS 4936/14/415

[63] Hancock, *National and Permanent?*, pp. 95-6.

[64] *The Herald,* 1 September 1947, p. 8.

[65] *The Advertiser,* 29 September 1949, p. 3.

[66] Saunders, 'The Uniform Income Tax Cases', p. 69.

[67] Quoted in Hancock, *National and Permanent?*, p. 160.

[68] University of Melbourne Archives, Records of the Liberal Party of Australia (Victorian Division), 19850148, Executive Files: Correspondence, John Buchan to Phil McBride, 15 December 1961.

[69] University of Melbourne Archives, Records of the Liberal Party of Australia (Victorian Division), 19850148, Executive Files: Correspondence, William Kirkhope to Alec Fitzgerald, 17 July 1946.

[70] Aimer, 'Liberal Organisation in Victoria 1945–68', p. 124.

[71] Ibid.

[72] Hancock, *National and Permanent?*, p. 121.

[73] Minutes of the Staff Conference Held in Sydney, 17 March 1949, Records of the Liberal Party of Australia, NLA MS 5000/1/15

[74] *Courier Mail,* 8 July 1949, p. 3.

[75] Minutes of the Staff Conference Held in Sydney, 17 March 1949, Records of the Liberal Party of Australia, NLA MS 5000/1/15

[76] Charles Porter to Robert Menzies, 6 September 1949.

[77] Hancock, *National and Permanent?*, p. 112.

[78] Ibid., p. 159.

3

Founding The Liberal Party of Australia – How Women Made A Difference

Anne Henderson

It was eloquent, richly written, and delivered in a long practised and well-trained lilting voice which surprised listeners in Australia's House of Representatives on the evening of 29 September 1943. It came from a backbench of the chamber and was the voice of the first woman elected to that Lower House of parliament, a mother of 12 and widow of one of Australia's longest serving prime ministers. It was the voice of Dame Enid Lyons (1897-1981) making her maiden speech.[1]

In her own words, Enid Lyons caught the historical significance of the moment as she began:

> It would be strange indeed were I not tonight deeply conscious of the fact, and not a little awed by the knowledge, that on my shoulders rests a great weight of responsibility; because this is the first occasion a woman has addressed this House. For this reason, it is an occasion which, for every woman in the Commonwealth, marks in some degree a turning point in history.[2]

The times were indeed against this small woman in her dark outfit standing amongst a chamber packed with men of distinction. She would write much later of how she had not eaten before her delivery and was extremely nervous, saying 'my lips were stiff when I started but all the men were wishing me well'.[3]

Enid Lyons was in parliament as the new representative for the federal seat of Darwin in north-west Tasmania. She was a member of the federal Opposition and the United Australia Party, a political party depleted by its own internal wrangling and diminished by a bad loss at the 1943 election, at which Enid Lyons had, unexpectedly, won a seat. The news of the day was likewise bleak as the war in Europe, North Africa and the Pacific raged on, enhancing masculinity as the quality for leadership. It was no surprise, then, that former Labor and Nationalist Prime Minister Billy Hughes – who would become a Dame Enid ally in parliament house – referred to her arrival as like 'a bird of paradise among the carrion crows'.[4]

Labor Prime Minister John Curtin was quick to acknowledge the significance of Dame Enid's achievement and responded warmly as she resumed her seat. He spoke of the fight for female franchise and said that Dame Enid was a member of the parliament not because she was a woman but because she had been elected by the people of Australia. He added:

> That this great event in the development of Australian citizenship should occur during the greatest war that our country has ever waged is, I think, not a mere accident; it occurs because women, as women, and men, as men, have come to look at problems as problems. I have no doubt whatever that the electors of Darwin elected their representative because they believed that of the candidates offering she would make the best member … We do not any longer sit here as men, nor does the honourable member for Darwin attempt to suggest that she sits here as a woman: we all sit here as persons upon whom our fellow citizens have imposed a duty by preferring us to others who offered at the polls.[5]

Enid Lyons's presence in the federal parliament had been a long while coming. Her background in politics was, by 1943, well known. As the wife of Labor's Joe Lyons – a Tasmanian state MP from 1909 till 1929, and minister, Opposition leader and premier in that state – Enid Lyons had enjoyed a heady ride into federal politics when, after the 1929 election, Joe was elected member for the federal seat of Wilmot (in north and central Tasmania) and became post-master general and then acting treasurer. This was followed by the tumultuous political year of 1931 when Joe Lyons left Labor and was elected leader of the newly established United Australia Party (UAP), going on to win one of the biggest landslides in federal election history in December.[6]

Enid and Joe Lyons would establish themselves, over three successive election wins, as the steady couple that led Australians through the Great Depression, uniting middle Australia from opposing sides. The Lyons' of Labor background had joined forces with Opposition Nationalists in a move that would broaden the voting base of what, in time, would become the Liberal Party of Australia. In Robert Menzies's Forgotten People radio broadcasts of 1942 – now famous for articulating a broad underpinning of ideas for the party that would be established under Menzies's leadership just two years later – there can be seen a softening and broadening of what had been the Nationalist outlook prior to the 1930s.

The Lyons experiment in 1931 had brought such a diversity of citizens together under the UAP banner – which in time affected Menzies's appreciation of mainstream voters and their aspirations. As one reporter put it at the time of the UAP's emergence at the head of citizens' groups, the popular front that took the UAP to resounding victory reflected the 'camps and enlistment depots of 1914 and 1915; clerks, bank managers, labourers, small shopkeepers, accountants, barristers, a mixed audience but all inspired by a wave of patriotic ardour.'[7] These were the exact same people to which Menzies's seminal broadcasts would appeal.

In addition, Catholic Joe Lyons as leader of the UAP drew many to vote for the first time for what, until then, had been seen as a Protestant establishment party. Historian Michael Hogan has recorded that, in the Labor loss of votes from 49 per cent of first preferences in 1929 to just 27 per cent in December 1931, many Catholic voters had for the first time switched their allegiance to non-Labor. The ALP could no longer rely on this vital safety net of voters.[8]

The divide between the newcomers from Labor and the select social rank of some of the Nationalist heavyweights is best described in Enid Lyons's interview with Mel Pratt for the National Library. There she discussed the early impressions Labor traditionalists such as Jim Fenton – who had joined Joe Lyons in crossing to the UAP – had on confronting the conservative ladies of the Australian Women's National League (AWNL).[9]

As Enid Lyons described them to Pratt, the AWNL were the 'last word in conservatism' and the butt of cartoonists. They regarded anything Labor as anathema. With the formation of the UAP, the AWNL was shocked that suddenly the party they supported was to be led by a Labor figure and include a handful of former Labor MPs. They were loathe to join as members of the UAP when the new party was formed. They also respected their independence – something that would be overcome in the formation of the Liberal Party over a decade later. Recalling an occasion soon after the formation of the UAP, Enid Lyons described how 'poor Jim Fenton nearly died at facing the prospect of these ladies of social standing'. But, somehow, he came through. Enid, on the other hand, with her poise and grace, was warmly received by many an AWNL meeting. One of her first engagements after winning her seat of Darwin was to speak at a Melbourne meeting of the AWNL on her way to Canberra.[10]

Perhaps it was a case of going with the strength, but in the years Joe and Enid Lyons remained in the Lodge, and until the formation of the Liberal Party, the AWNL became a consistent supporter of the UAP, working electorates at elections and welcoming UAP speakers at their meetings.

Challenging a woman's place

The public world that Enid Lyons – alongside her Senate Labor colleague Dorothy Tangney – entered in September 1943 as the first women to sit in Australia's federal parliament is hard for voters of the twenty-first century to imagine. Women, literally, were accepted as the engineers of the nation's private space with men the operators of all public space. Here and there, a woman had emerged to challenge that notion – Edith Cowan into the Western Australian parliament in 1921; Millicent Preston Stanley in Sydney for the NSW Legislative Assembly in 1925; Irene Longman winning Queensland's third largest seat in 1929; Millie Peacock entering the Victorian Legislative Assembly in 1933. All four were conservatives involved with non-Labor/Nationalist politics but none of them survived more than one term in parliament.[11] For all that, such was the expectation that women had no chance of success in public arenas that Irene Longman's opponent in 1929, the English born Mr AH Wright, opined: 'Well, you know, I am only being opposed by a woman.' At the election, 13,000 voters in Bulimba thought otherwise.[12]

The women's suffrage movement had a profound effect on representative politics from the late nineteenth century. In this, Australia was well ahead of other nations – with the exception of New Zealand where women gained the vote in 1893. Women gained the vote in South Australia and Western Australia in 1894 and 1899 respectively. In 1902, all Australian women over the age of 21 gained the right to vote in federal elections. By 1908, all states in Australia had granted women the right to vote. Such was the success of women's suffrage in Australia, local suffragists like Vida Goldstein linked with international activists like Dora Montefiore and the Pankhursts to show leadership in the fight for suffrage more widely.[13]

Yet, for all the progressive steps towards suffrage for women, the movement was not easily embraced by women of a conservative inclination. As Diane Sydenham has argued in relation to conservative women in Victoria, 'Opposition to female suffrage was still grounded in concerns over women's role and the degrading effects political participation would have on womanhood … Woman suffrage was now portrayed as offering support to the socialist cause.' In other words, working or Labor women would use their right to vote and thus female suffrage was a plus for Labor.[14]

The strongest voice for conservative women that emerged in the first half of the twentieth century was undoubtedly the Australian

Women's National League begun in 1904 in the opulent splendour of Lady Janet Clarke's Melbourne townhouse *Cliveden*. The Clarke status and wealth undoubtedly gave the league significant uplift and it grew quickly with some 10,000 members in Victoria alone by 1908. Its highest membership was achieved in the years of World War I when, in 1916, it registered 54,000 members and 500 branches.[15] In the years that followed, the Country Women's Association sapped AWNL numbers but in 1945 it could still boast some 12,000 members and a powerful political network for non-Labor at election times. All of which was the reason Robert Menzies was so keen to have the AWNL fold into the new Liberal Party of Australia in 1944.

In its first two decades, the AWNL strongly endorsed women making a difference in public affairs but drew back when it came to taking public roles. Its defining ethos as the league developed could be summed up as follows:

> The League was initially very much committed to the belief that men and women had different 'natural' spheres of interest and activity. Although working to provide a voice for women's specific concerns and offering some political influence for women, the League did not support the idea of women taking on political leadership.[16]

This approach to politics for women could not last, even in conservative circles. By 1922, at the AWNL's annual conference, Elizabeth 'May' Couchman argued that the words 'we do not wish to send women to Parliament' should be deleted from the AWNL preamble. Her interest was in allowing women who 'put public good before personal ambition' to have a public role.[17] Couchman's motion was defeated but, by 1924, the AWNL no longer opposed women being elected to parliament – in fact the organisation now strongly encouraged women to stand, albeit with little success. In 1927, Couchman was elected president of the AWNL and her leadership, while failing to gain preselection herself for a winnable seat, would be a strong influence on conservative women's burgeoning place in the political process.

Couchman (née Ramsay) would bring a smooth pragmatism to the AWNL. She was a graduate of the University of Western Australia where she had gone from her home in Geelong to take advantage of free tertiary education. At first, she taught at the Methodist Ladies College in Melbourne and in the music faculty of Melbourne University before marrying Colonel Claude Couchman – a marriage that advanced her connections in upper middle class Melbourne. In her familiarity with various women's organisations, she was a master at conducting meetings and participating in round table discussions. Claude Couchman's death in June 1931 left Elizabeth a widow, but her strong links to the Melbourne establishment were undiminished.[18]

Couchman had forthright views but was no radical. She pushed the education of women, emphasising their supportive strengths. While empowering, this ignored vast areas of social policy taken up by women of the left and even Enid Lyons with her more homespun (Labor) background. But Couchman's pragmatism was well ahead of her feminist sisters by some decades and her mastery at playing a vital role in the formation of the Liberal Party would, in time, reveal how her contemporaries in Labor ranks were struggling to find a workable political niche.[19]

Leadership for conservative women in the public sphere

Enid Lyons first stood for election to parliament in the Tasmanian winter of 1925 – she was thrown into Labor's election campaign as a candidate for the Tasmanian multi-member electorate of Denison (Hobart). Joe Lyons was then Labor premier of Tasmania, which had passed legislation allowing women to stand for parliament.[20] In order to draw off votes from an independent woman who had chosen to stand in Denison, Enid agreed to put her name forward. In spite of family sickness and seven children (one of whom was a baby of six months), Enid went to nightly meetings and almost won a seat. In the party, she was regarded as a mere distraction with no chance of winning. For all that, her public persona made a difference.

The idea that women could be successful at the polls had a long way to run in the 1920s and 1930s. But leadership can take many forms and the presence of women at podiums or in positions of influence grew steadily. Enid Lyons may not have won a seat in 1925, but she was seen increasingly as a public voice in support of her husband on many occasions. This continued with the Lyons leadership of the UAP. As prime minister, Joe Lyons openly encouraged Enid to make speeches knowing it would help capture the female vote. An appreciation and acceptance of the woman's point of view was growing.

Personalities like Enid Lyons caught the public's attention, but likewise women's organisations had started to attract interest with their growing lists of members and the willingness of their leaders to make statements in the public interest. An open meeting under the auspices of the All For Australia League, in Melbourne in March 1931, advertised speeches to be given by National Council of Women President Mrs Moss, Dr Georgina Sweet, Mrs Herbert Brookes, Mrs FW Head and Mrs A Rapke – otherwise known as Julia Rapke a secretary of the Victorian Women's Citizens Movement.[21]

International gatherings and associations also brought women to the fore as representatives for women on global platforms. Couchman, arriving back in Australia in December 1934 after months abroad attending conferences at the League of Nations in Geneva and the International Council of Women in Paris, spoke of ten days of 'solid discussion on questions of great importance and interest to women'.[22] What trade union organisations did for (mostly) male workers, women's associations from temperance unions to women's electoral leagues were doing for women.

In November 1934, Melbourne hosted the Women's International Congress in its exhibition buildings. Women from across the globe made speeches, emphasising the need for women to play a role in public life. They stressed the qualities of good citizenship and the way women could improve both the atmospherics of civic life and its realities. Women were seen as making a wholesome contribution to harmonious democratic politics, with a stress on women being trained in civic virtues and public policy. It took an Australian, however, to strike a keynote. Irene Longman, the former Queensland MP for just one term, called out the 'disabilities' under which women laboured in spite of so-called equality with men. These disabilities, she added, were largely due to economic dependence and the fact that 'women had no voice or influence in the halls of legislature'.[23]

As a significant group of influence in the public sphere, meetings of the AWNL were addressed by leading figures of the UAP and often reported on in daily newspapers. Couchman's election as president of the AWNL was acknowledged in *The Argus* on 2 March 1927, describing her as having made 'a special study of sociology, constitutional history and economics' to which it added that her 'theoretical knowledge of social reform will be of great value to her new office'.[24] Four months later, reporting on a protest gathering of women's organisations opposing beauty pageants, *The Argus* noted Couchman, representing the AWNL, as among the prominent speakers.[25]

Couchman was a good friend of businessman Herbert Brookes and his wife Ivy, a daughter of Alfred Deakin. Their impeccable political connections in Melbourne and across non-Labor circles gave Couchman invaluable support and guidance. As the non-Labor elements around the Nationalists stirred in early 1931, uniting with spontaneous groups bursting onto the political scene such as the All For Australia League, Elizabeth May Couchman announced she would submit her name for election to the Senate as a Victorian candidate, adding that 'there were 30,000 more women in Victoria than men, and it seemed that the time had arrived when women should take part in the government of the country. The principles of household budgeting were, or should be, those employed for running the affairs of the country'.[26]

Couchman was now firmly supporting the need for women to stand for parliament. However, as the United Australia Party took shape with the AWNL refusing to become part of the party itself,

Couchman was not chosen as a Senate candidate for Victoria at the 1931 federal election but was made an emergency candidate instead. She would fail again to be nominated for the Senate ticket in Victoria at the 1940 federal election.

And then there was Enid Lyons

If any female figure stood out for taking the lead to demonstrate women could be successful at politics and public life it was Enid Lyons. Australian politics had seen nothing like her. Tasmanians had accepted the very young wife of the Labor leader taking to the podium here and there and generally working electorates at election times. But, in the federal sphere, as wife of the hugely popular Prime Minister Joe Lyons, Enid was a stand out.

Married at 17 to a man 18 years her senior who was already a leading figure in the Tasmanian government, Enid took some years to become prominent at the podium. But Joe Lyons, unlike many men of his day, was never threatened by his wife's personality and presence in public life. He encouraged her to speak at the podium as they made appearances across the state or joined in at Labor conferences where they would often take different sides in debates. Joe Lyons was Enid's tutor over years in both political strategy and presentation. And Enid, regardless of the immense load of her domestic charges, loved the limelight and the freedom it gave her from home duties.

This was not a wife who was only seen accepting bouquets of flowers (which she did often) and sitting quietly while listening to her husband at the podium (which she also did many times over the years). This was a political figure who also faced wild hecklers while at the podium in 1931, supporting the re-election of Jim Fenton and helping him defend his seat after leaving Labor.[27] This was a wife who joined her husband as prime minister in rowdy meetings in Perth in late March 1933, arguing against secession by West Australians. At one meeting of women, with Joe and Senator Tom Brennan, the audience refused to listen to the men and called for 'Mrs Lyons'. The chairwoman, activist Bessie Rischbieth, suggested calling a policeman as the women heckled. The resourceful Enid refused the offer and chose instead to talk directly to the audience rather than make a speech. Getting her audience to listen, she managed to encourage something of a back and forth, question and answer format. Enid had abandoned her fine speech notes in favour of tackling the issues as they were fielded to her.[28]

Writing to his wife in 1935 just before their overseas trip to Europe, the UK, the US and Canada, Joe Lyons told Enid of his pride in her abilities:

> I am thrilled to death with the reports of your speech – you're a marvel! What with the packing, travelling, children, dress worries and all the rest there isn't anyone in the world who could do as you did. It was just wonderful and it's just impossible for me to describe my pride and admiration for you. I'm almost reconciled to the London trip when I think of the way you'll put it over the natives there.[29]

With Joe Lyons's sudden death in April 1939, Enid Lyons became the tragic widow and in time no longer part of the political scene, retiring to the family home in Devonport with her daughter Enid whose husband was on active duty. After a year or so of healing and home, it was Enid jnr. who realised her mother needed to get back into public life and urged her to put her name forward for the seat of Darwin on the retirement of Sir George Bell in 1943. As Enid Lyons describes her reaction, her thirst for politics shines through:

> It was a chance to earn my own living, as I had always wanted to do … It was work I felt myself quite capable of doing after my years in the political field with Joe, and it had advantage over most other forms of employment: I could arrange its duties so that I could be home with the children during the school holidays. Finally … I believed with all my heart in the right of women to a place

> in government. All my active public work in more than twenty years had been aimed at rousing women to a sense of their powers and responsibilities.[30]

The story of Enid Lyons's success in Darwin stands tall as a lesson for all women taking up the challenge of preselection and a chance at a seat in parliament. It would also become a lesson to the future Liberal Party not to underestimate the appeal of women in politics. In time, Labor would come to allocate seats more out of factional deals but for the most part, whatever party, taking up the challenge is the first step. The UAP could hardly refuse the nomination of Dame Enid Lyons. Therein lay a first lesson: make the most of all advantages you have. Enid did just that in spite of there being already two men nominated to contest the UAP's seat of Darwin. In a state used to selecting multiple candidates for state seats under the Hare-Clark system, this was not unusual. But, of course, no one at party headquarters expected a woman to beat either of the other male candidates. At best, Enid was seen as something of an extra who might draw votes away from moderate Labor candidates in a preferential system.

The team that stood by Enid Lyons and organised her campaign were people she had known from campaigns for Joe. It was very much a personal effort. Enid travelled the electorate even going into the heart of Labor territory in a freezing west coast visit to mining towns Queenstown and Zeehan. She used radio endlessly with the newspapers advertising her times in paid advertisements and her schedule was listed along with other candidates. In her lively account much later, she described the comical moments of the west coast visit and the cracking pace of her campaigning. 'It was the period of the radio "bed-time story" and whenever I was in range of a broadcasting station, I made a feature of five minute broadcasts at 10 pm for which the complexities of rationing provided wonderful material,' she recalled.[31] On one occasion, she simply read out new, verbose and complicated coupon regulations for drapers issued by the government – as she put it, 'Read aloud exactly as it was written, without pause or inflexion of voice, it created an impression of near lunacy on the part of the framer and, by implication of the government responsible.'[32]

After many days and eight counts of preferences, Enid Lyons was declared the winner of the seat of Darwin with 51.49 per cent of the preferred vote. She had not only won but had beaten a strong Labor rival in Eric Reece, a future premier of Tasmania. It was a win very much against the odds, with the Curtin Labor Government recording one of Australian political history's largest landslides. Robert Menzies said it was like being run over by a steam roller, while Billy Hughes telegraphed Enid that 'Your victory compensates for many defeats'.[33]

Enid Lyons's arrival in the parliament was greeted warmly. More than that, she would be the first woman not only to take a seat in the House of Representatives but also the first of those who had won seats in the various houses of parliament across the nation to keep her seat over forthcoming elections until she chose to retire at the 1951 election. Furthermore, after meetings in 1944 led by Robert Menzies, Enid Lyons would be one of the team that became the Liberal Party of Australia – her presence forever confirming that women could make a difference however hard the road to success.

Women must be in the team

In the year leading up to the August 1943 federal election, the Curtin minority government had been under such pressure from its parliamentary Opposition that it was reported Curtin was not enjoying minority government, even that he had considered resigning the prime ministership.[34] All that would be forgotten with the stunning victory for Labor at the 1943 federal election. Which left the Coalition in tatters.

In truth, while scoring hits on Labor's leadership in 1942-43, the UAP was falling apart, its leader Billy Hughes, born in 1862, clearly was no longer up to the task. As the election year took shape, the UAP had divided with a National Service Group, of which Menzies

Liberal election advertisement centred on Enid Lyons and her commitment to child endowment. From *The Mercury* (Hobart), 24 September 1946.

was a key member, forming within its ranks and declaring it would remain as part of the UAP but not attend its meetings.[35] Writing to his brother Ken on 2 September 1943, Menzies opened up on his thoughts re the state of the UAP and what might lie ahead. He opined that the election result could well be 'in a personal sense favourable to me' and added he hoped the UAP would reconstruct itself and 'get a better name'. He further mused that he would only accept leadership of any future UAP if it became the dominant party of the Coalition – he would 'not serve as deputy to Fadden'. He concluded, 'Who-ever becomes leader must promptly set about the task of creating a fighting spirit and building a real organisation all over Australia.'[36]

After strategically outplaying Hughes and his supporters at the UAP party meeting on 22 September 1943, Menzies was re-elected leader of the UAP and agreement was reached that it would be the dominant partner in the non-Labor Coalition. It was an equivocal start as leader, however, with Menzies allowing his name to go forward for the position of chief justice of Victoria in January 1944. Even so, not being in good favour with Country Party Victorian Premier Albert Dunstan, Menzies was not chosen.[37] Fate once more saw Menzies direct his vision to a fresh start in politics. He now determined on working to establish a new party from the dispirited and divided non-Labor operatives.

The organisation for a rethink and total reconstruction of the non-Labor Opposition took many months and involved many individuals. It is certainly clear that without Menzies's leadership the coalescing of the many disparate groups would never have been successful.[38] Yet it is also obvious that within the forces coming together there were many significant individuals who played important parts.[39] Of particular significance was the AWNL and Elizabeth 'May' Couchman.

The formation of the Liberal Party of Australia was, in essence, decided at the Albury and Canberra Unity Conferences. The non-party organisations in attendance included the Australian Women's National League of Victoria and Tasmania and the Queensland Women's Electoral League, while women delegates were also sent by the NSW Democratic Party, and the South Australian Liberal and Country League. Twelve federal parliamentarians attended, including the leaders and deputy leaders in the House of Representatives and Senate, and five state non-Labor parliamentary leaders, in addition to deputy UAP leaders from Victoria and NSW. Dame Enid Lyons was not among them. Her vote for Billy Hughes, a personal friend, in the party room leadership challenge and a simmering distance after Menzies's resignation as minister in the last weeks of her husband's prime ministership also did not endear her, at this point, to Menzies.

Unlike Enid Lyons, Couchman was a good friend of Robert Menzies. They had friends in common and were both Victorians where the AWNL had a long history of campaigning for the UAP at elections. Menzies knew the AWNL was a force in the wider community and their members' hard work and electoral reach was invaluable in non-Labor circles. 50 years later, his successor as member for Kooyong Andrew Peacock was loud in his praise of the work of the AWNL: 'By God it was good. They were off to the hospitals and nursing homes without being told. They just got going. They were on the committees of various community groups. Couchman was the tower of it all.'[40] Both Peacock's mother and grandmother were AWNL members. This was something Couchman often described in her speeches – the work and wisdom of women, their practical experience and their pragmatic approach to policy, getting things done for the best outcomes; believing that these came from implementing liberalism rather than the state control of Labor.[41]

Sir John Muir Anderson served as president of the Victorian Liberal Party from 1952-56. Reflecting on Couchman he said that she was a master of information. She would ring him sometimes at 2 am: '"JM," she'd say, "Do you know such and such?" I'd say no. And she'd give me the details. She talked to a lot of people. Women were afraid of her, but they were a great source of information. She wasn't one of the blue rinse set. … And she knew how to handle men.'[42]

The outcome of the three-day conference in Canberra was a milestone in non-Labor politics, albeit learning from Labor of the importance of structure and organisation at the federal and state level. As Gerard Henderson has argued: 'At Canberra the agreement went beyond name and objectives. There was also a consensus on organisational structure. Not surprisingly it was consistent with that proposed by Menzies in his opening address.'[43]

There was still a long way to go even if there had been little disagreement at the Canberra meetings. On 7 November, Menzies addressed a special meeting of the Australian Women's National League in Melbourne. Crucial to community support, Menzies had been working to have the AWNL move on from its rejection of party membership at the time of the formation of the UAP. This was a big ask even if Couchman could see the advantages it offered. The women delegates of the AWNL at the Canberra conference had warmed to the idea that the AWNL disband and fold into the new party. They knew the best years of the AWNL were behind them. Here was a new way of being involved in politics for women. This, however, was something meetings of the AWNL needed to affirm and, as always, there were members who once again did not trust the move to surrender their organisational independence and merge with a new party.

It was not until meetings of the AWNL in January and February 1945 that the debate over the AWNL delegates' acquiescence to become part of the Liberal Party came to a head. Couchman stood her ground arguing that the women would miss an important opportunity to influence preselections and have an improved part in public life. She was strongly supported by Ivy Brookes. They were opposed by an AWNL old guard led by Mrs Berry who formed a 'defence committee' which went public arguing the Liberal Party was illegitimately taking over AWNL assets.[44] For all that, Couchman prevailed. At a meeting of 600 members in Melbourne, on Tuesday 24 July 1945, the AWNL agreed to alter its constitution 'so that the council could wind up the League and merge the organisation with the Liberal Party'.[45]

In closing the Albury conference in December 1944, Robert Menzies had especially devoted part of his remarks to the place of women in politics and the Liberal Party. His words echoed those of Couchman that it was time to look forward to where women were headed. Women, in fact, like Enid Lyons. As he described the nature of the Liberal Party of Australia, Menzies voiced a new look for any contemporary political organisation:

> … men and women will side by side be members of this organisation. … [he hoped] on behalf of the men represented here that as a result of this joint and equal membership of this great movement we will find on councils and executives an adequate representation of women.
>
> Women are unquestionably destined to exercise more and more influence upon practical politics in Australia … In the educating of the electorate in liberal ideas they have for many years been an effective force.[46]

The deal Robert Menzies had pulled off with the strong support of Couchman and the female delegates of the AWNL such as Ivy Wedgwood and Edith Haynes at the party conferences, and other AWNL members like Ivy Brookes was historic. When the Victorian Division of the Liberal Party emerged, Couchman worked to achieve equal representation of men and women on all significant committees. And she got it.

Aftermath

The Liberal Party of Australia's inaugural federal council meeting was held in Sydney on 25 August 1945 followed by a rally in Assembly Hall three days later. There was still much to do to bring the disparate groups in Sydney to a real unity. The Liberals' loss at the 1946 election would challenge the party administration in New South Wales to overcome tribal party divides, which General Secretary John Carrick would achieve by the 1949 poll.[47] The loss in 1946 also brought its own tensions and Menzies was forced to resign at a party meeting on 1 September 1947 so that he could be re-elected unopposed. And then the battle for the banks happened.

The protest over the Chifley Government's attempt to nationalise Australia's banks would be the rallying cry and spearhead that swept the newly formed Liberal Party of Australia into government on 10 December 1949. In the rallies of thousands across Australia against the legislation, women came forward from among the Liberal Party's ranks to lead their own demonstrations. On Wednesday,

22 October 1947, hundreds of women converged on Canberra in a massive rally against the legislation. Among the women leading the protest were those who had become well known for their public leadership, women such as the first female Liberal senator – Annabelle Rankin from Queensland, and Ivy Brookes from Victoria, among others. Enid Lyons MP not only spoke but had organised a deputation to the prime minister. Groups were drawn up to lobby their respective state and Senate representatives.[48] And the protest would widen and continue.

Thus, with the birth of the Liberal Party of Australia, and as the protest movement over bank nationalisation would show, decades of women's groups working on women's issues in public life could now merge with a real political operation. There was some way to go before any substantial representation of women in parliamentary seats, even as Victoria's Ivy Wedgwood and WA's Agnes Roberts would join Rankin by being elected to the Senate at the 1949 election (six of the first seven female senators would be Liberals). Nevertheless, by merging with a real party of government, women were having their voices heard as never before.

---

[1] Dame Enid Lyons, 'Maiden Speech', 29 September 1943. Recording available from the National Film and Sound Archives.

[2] CPD, House of Representatives, 29 September 1943.

[3] Lyons, *Among The Carrion Crows*, pp. 35-36.

[4] Ibid., p. 7.

[5] CPD, House of Representatives, 29 September 1943.

[6] Henderson, *Joseph Lyons*, p. 283.

[7] Macintyre, *The Oxford History of Australia Vol 4*, p. 268.

[8] Hogan, *The Sectarian Strand*, p. 214.

[9] Lyons interview with Pratt.

[10] *Burnie Advocate*, 18 September 1943, p. 5.

[11] Fitzherbert, *Liberal Women*, pp. 147-163.

[12] Ibid., p. 161.

[13] Wright, *You Daughters of Freedom*, p. 268.

[14] Sydenham, *Women of Influence*, p. 14.

[15] Fitzherbert, *Liberal Women*, p. 46.

[16] Australian Women's National Register, https://www.womenaustralia.info/entries/australian-womens-national-league/

[17] Smart, 'Couchman'.

[18] *Sun News Pictorial*, Monday, 15 June 1931, p. 5.

[19] *The Weekend Australian*, 8-9 October 1994; supplement celebrating the 50th anniversary of the Liberal Party of Australia.

[20] Henderson, *Enid Lyons*, p. 112.

[21] *The Argus*, 27 March 1931, p. 10 .

[22] *Sydney Morning Herald*, 12 December 1934, p. 7.

[23] *The Argus*, 22 November 1934, p. 12.

[24] *The Argus*, 2 March 1927, p. 10.

[25] *The Argus*, 9 July 1927, p. 33.

[26] *The Argus*, 30 March 1931, p. 9.

[27] Lyons, *So We Take Comfort*, p. 185.

[28] Ibid., pp. 212-214; *Advertiser (Adelaide)*, 30 March 1933, p. 9; *Sydney Morning Herald*, 28 March 1933, p. 9.

[29] Henderson, *Enid Lyons*, pp. 197-8.

[30] Lyons, *Among The Carrion Crows*, p. 9.

[31] Ibid., p. 14.

[32] Ibid.

[33] Henderson, *Enid Lyons*, p. 277.

[34] *Sydney Morning Herald*, 19 August 1942, p. 7.

[35] Fitzhardinge, *The Little Digger*, p. 661.

[36] Letter, Robert Menzies to Ken Menzies, 2 September 1943, Menzies family collection. Letters kindly supplied by Heather Henderson.

[37] Henderson, *Menzies at War*, p. 183.

[38] Henderson, *Menzies' Child*, p. 87.

[39] Hancock, 'Liberal Party of Australia', p. 390.

[40] *The Weekend Australian*, 8-9 October 1994; supplement celebrating the 50th anniversary of the Liberal Party of Australia.

[41] *The Argus*, 22 February 1945, p. 4.

[42] John Anderson, interview with Anne Henderson, 1994.

[43] Henderson, *Menzies' Child*, p. 83.

[44] Fitzherbert, *Liberal Women*, pp. 214-9.

[45] *The Argus*, Wednesday, 25 July 1945, p. 3.

[46] Starr, *The Liberal Party of Australia*, p. 82.

[47] Henderson, *Menzies at War*, p. 186.

[48] *Sydney Morning Herald*, 22 October 1947, p. 1.

4

'Bold We Brag' – The New South Wales Division

Zachary Gorman

'When first Australia's statesmen rose
They took the task in hand
To gain the boon of liberty
In this our Fatherland.
Of Henry Parkes and Dunmore Lang
And Wentworth bold we brag
They raised the flag we fly today
The good old Liberal Flag ...'[1]

Penned by Banjo Paterson for the 1907 New South Wales election, 'The Good Old Liberal Flag' is a campaign song which speaks to a Liberal Party which is confident that it is embedded in the state's political culture and taking ownership of its proud history. To the author and the audience he was writing for, the 'mother colony' – self-consciously Australia's oldest and largest polity – was a pervasively Liberal state. Its story read as a triumphalist narrative of Liberal victories: winning trial by jury, equal rights for ex-convicts, the ending of transportation, self-government, universal manhood suffrage, public education, widespread property ownership via the Land Acts, female suffrage and much more. Many of these earlier gifts it had also won for its sister states, fuelling New South Wales's own sense of superiority.

Yet, by the latter half of the twentieth century people were describing New South Wales as a natural Labor state.[2] To understand the NSW Division of the Liberal Party of Australia, one must explain how liberalism went from a pervasive political culture in which virtually every politician described themselves as a liberal, to being represented by a party that in its modern iteration has generally found itself in Opposition. Far from being the dominant force it once had been, in the mid-twentieth century the Liberal movement struggled to even attract full time politicians, as the talented felt it was a waste of their energy to fully commit to a lost cause. It is only in recent years, with the pre-MAGA demand to 'Make New South Wales Number One Again' that the NSW Liberals have recaptured something of their old bravado, but the scars of past failings – and their inherent causes – have never fully disappeared.

The Liberal and Reform Association

The story of the founding of the NSW Division must begin with the original NSW Liberal Party, the Liberal and Reform Association formed by then Opposition Leader Joseph Carruthers on 19 December 1902. The post-federation foundation date speaks to the fact that in the nineteenth century, NSW did not really have political parties in the modern sense. It was ruled by the faction system, in which charismatic leaders like Henry Parkes and John Roberston held office by maintaining personal followings, forging temporary alliances, and buying off 'roads and bridges' members with public works.[3] From 1887 more recognisable parties emerged with the advent of the 'fiscal issue' which split politicians into Free Traders and Protectionists, but the extra-parliamentary organisations which backed both sides were rudimentary and quickly proved fleeting.

Moreover, the tariff debate – while it had important connotations for the role of the state – was rather narrow and did not suggest a clear philosophy of approaching governance which could form the basis for a permanent political party. There were certain things which nineteenth century liberals already believed, which would ultimately form the basis for a Liberal Party: that members should be free to vote according to their conscience, that parliament should govern for all and not give representation to sectional interests, that taxation and spending should be kept low to give people the freedom to flourish, and that individual initiative was the real driving force behind national progress – but at the time they were largely taken for granted.

It was only when these common assumptions started to be questioned by the advent of the Labor Party in 1891, that liberalism was given the impetus to take a true party form. Labor thought that members should be firmly bound to the dictates of caucus, explicitly represented the sectional interests of the union movement, and increasingly believed that large-scale state intervention was the way to drive positive change. Using a balance of power position between the fiscal parties, they were able to exercise influence beyond their electoral strength.

It was Carruthers who first identified that not only did a Westminster system need a two-party divide to function healthily, but also that it would be liberalism and Labor which would form the natural 'lines of cleavage' for Australian politics.[4] Born in Jamberoo in 1856 as the son of an undisclosed convict, Carruthers had been thoroughly inculcated in NSW's liberal political culture. His father had worked on William Wentworth's grand mansion in Vaucluse and taken Joseph to Henry Parkes's political rallies as a small boy, while like many others in his era Carruthers also grew up to revere British Liberal icon William Gladstone.[5] In his father, his own career and those of his peers, Carruthers saw tangible proof that NSW was a land of tremendous opportunity and social mobility where 'in our system of education, and under our form of government and social life, no great barriers were offered to any lad, no matter how humble, from going step by step from the lowest to the highest place in the community.'[6]

Carruthers self-consciously created his Liberal and Reform Association to sit on the centre-right of politics, because he believed that while liberalism must continue to pursue its own understanding of progress, it also needed to defend what was good and successful about Australia's existing liberal order. His political program focused on twin goals: reducing spending and taxation at a time when both had been vastly increased by the onset of federation, and continuing the long liberal tradition of reform. Most notably in introducing a comprehensive system of local government – which embodied the thoroughly liberal principle that decisions are best made at the most grassroots level, and where possible by the individual themselves.

Crucially, as a former minister in both the Parkes and Reid Governments, Carruthers was also a highly experienced political organiser, who had directed several election campaigns for the old Free Trade Party (which had restyled itself as the Liberal Party when the fiscal issue moved to the federal sphere). He had been actively involved in several short lived attempts by liberals to form extra-parliamentary organisations, including the Free Trade Association (est. 1885), the Liberal Political Association (est. 1889), the Free Trade and Federation Committee (est. 1891), the Free Trade and Land Reform Committee (est. 1893), the Free Trade Council (est. 1894), and the Australian Free Trade and Liberal Association (est. 1900). One of the reasons why these organisations failed was because they were often separate from and in conflict with the parliamentary leader, presaging later clashes experienced between the modern NSW Division's organisation and parliamentary leadership.

Part of the secret to Carruthers's success was the fact that he fully bridged this divide. He used his first-hand knowledge to create an innovative and successful extra-parliamentary organisation featuring:

- A large network of local branches which would be able to control local preselections via plebiscite (subject to final endorsement by the central organisation) and elect delegates who would have a say in shaping the party platform.
- Low membership fees that would encourage people to sign up, and which were intended to create a consistent 'fighting fund' through sheer numbers rather than relying on a smaller number of powerful donors.[7]

- Very large and active women's participation in the form of the Women's Liberal League headed by prominent Swedish-born suffragette Molyneux Parkes.
- A central council made up of an equal number of MPs and LRA members, soon joined by equal numbers from the Women's Liberal League.[8]
- Organising, literary and finance committees, each specialised to focus on a key aspect of the electioneering process.
- A permanent general organiser; the talented and long-serving Archdale Parkhill. Parkhill would become Carruthers's organisational protégé, taking every electioneering lesson learned from the 1880s onwards and carrying them forward into first the Nationalists and then the UAP.

By the time of the 1904 state election, the LRA claimed to have 70,000 members. At the poll Carruthers would lead the Liberals to a landmark victory, smashing the Protectionists (who had been renamed the Progressives) and precipitating the clear Liberal-Labor divide that we have since been familiar with. The LRA's electoral success crossed all areas of the state, monopolising the suburbs, but also making significant inroads in the country and inner city.[9] They were also said to have captured the women's vote with the help of the temperance issue, even if this is much harder to verify.[10] Carruthers would go on to win the 1907 election before suffering a heart attack and being forced to retire, though he would eventually recover and go on to have a long career as a legislative councillor (playing a central role in saving the Council from Labor's abolition attempts).

The eclipse of liberalism

Historians are in accord that the foundation of the LRA is in essence, the foundation of the enduring NSW Division. Loveday, Martin and Weller maintain that 'by 1907 the basic forms and ideologies of the Liberal Party, and its successors to the present day, had been laid down in New South Wales'.[11] Ian Hancock writes that the LRA created a 'structure which would survive the changing brand names and remain in place, albeit in a more complicated form, at the end of the twentieth century'.[12] Meanwhile my own biography of Carruthers goes beyond this, arguing that Carruthers and the success of the LRA would influence the evolution of Liberal politics at the federal level – where he enjoyed strong friendships with NSW Liberal prime ministers George Reid and Joseph Cook, and a functional relationship with Victorian Alfred Deakin.

But despite this continuity in organisation and outlook, NSW liberalism would have to go through great travails before it settled into the modern 'NSW Division'. This story begins with Carruthers's successor as premier, former England rugby player Charles Wade. Wade was able to carry through Carruthers's promise to abolish state income tax for those earning under £1000 (the vast majority of people) and to abolish most forms of stamp duty. But Wade's unpopular handling of a strike would contribute to the Liberals losing office at the 1910 election.

Led by boilermaker James McGowen, NSW's first Labor government already displayed characteristics which would play an important role in its future electoral dominance: an ability to attract the Catholic vote, a knack for showing just enough conservative instincts to reassure the electorate, and product differentiation from federal Labor. Indeed, McGowen refused to back federal Labor's 1911 referendum to greatly expand the Commonwealth's powers and would be brought down by a caucus revolt over his decision to empower non-union labour to break a strike in the vital gas industry.[13]

More 'conservatism' was displayed by McGowen's successor William Holman, who agreed not to pursue divisive legislation to keep the state united during World War I, and sided with Billy Hughes during Labor's split over conscription. The result was NSW mirroring federal politics, as Holman and his following merged with Wade and the Liberals to form the NSW Nationalists, with Holman staying on as premier. Officially, the LRA itself merged into a new Nationalist Association of NSW, but in practice the latter adopted the former's constitution with some minor amendments[14] and crucially Parkhill carried on as general secretary.

However, one ominous change was that by 1919 the organisation began relying on a new Consultative Council for fundraising, a body made up of wealthy donors who demanded special access to government leaders.[15] This would allow opponents to paint the party as a vehicle for the vested interests of big business, in a direct violation of the Liberal commitment to govern for all. This commitment had deep roots in NSW history with liberals having made great capital out of opposing Squatter interests in the unelected Legislative Council. Moreover, the Consultative Council was a slap in the face for the grassroots membership. Not only was the Council being granted special access, but this influence directly contradicted the liberal concept of freedom of conscience which had manifested itself in the LRA platform never actually binding the parliamentary party.

If the Nationalists had abandoned liberal principles in funding their extra-parliamentary organisation, under Holman, they also lost the clear liberal philosophical underpinning to their policy-making. As with Hughes at the federal level, Holman's 'residual radicalism' helped to hasten the emergence of the Country Party,[16] which acted as an outlet for a conservative protest vote. Coming out of the Farmers and Settlers' Association, the Country Party once again violated the liberal view that you should not have sectional interests represented in parliament. This exacerbated the damage of the Consultative Council, because it was harder to claim that you were not representing big business when the rest of the political system was set up to represent specific interests.

The election of George Fuller as premier in 1922 augured a potential return to the liberal fold, as he was an old Free Trader who had been a backbencher behind Parkes and Reid, and he even appointed Carruthers to his ministry from the Upper House. The Fuller Government achieved some clear liberal goals: reducing taxation, producing a budget surplus, and abolishing several state-run businesses including a trawling company, timber yard, bakery, sawmill and power station – an extensive list which indicates that Labor and Holman had been actively carrying out the 'socialist objective' of 'extending the industrial and economic functions of the state'.[17] Less philosophically informed but nevertheless notable was the passage of the Sydney Harbour Bridge Bill; an icon which is unfairly associated in the popular memory with Labor's Jack Lang due to the famous incident with the ribbon cutting.

But the Fuller Government also went further than any of its twentieth century predecessors in alienating NSW's Catholic population. A sectarian undercurrent to the political divide had existed since at least Henry Parkes's infamous 'Kiama Ghost' speech responding to the attempted assassination of Prince Alfred in Sydney in 1868. The Liberals as the successors to the Free Trade Party carried this association with them. Carruthers had been able to garner support from the pervasively Protestant temperance movement, although his local option proposals ultimately left it unsatisfied.[18]

It was Fuller's Minister for Justice Thomas Ley, a man of such outstanding repute that he was later convicted for contracting a murder,[19] who brought this undercurrent to the surface. He introduced legislation to counter a papal decree known as *Ne Temere*, which innocuously outlined rules for how the faithful should be married to have their union recognised by the Church. Ley led a fanatical campaign against *Ne Temere*, arguing that it would be taken to invalidate existing marriages, allowing husbands to leave their wives and children to be treated as if they were illegitimate – a scare campaign made all the more farcical by the fact that the decree had been in effect since 1907.

Ley's Bill proposed to make it illegal to suggest that lawfully married people were not truly and sufficiently so. Many believed that the Nationalists were cynically trying to exploit the fears and prejudices of NSW's then 70 per cent Protestant majority for political advantage at the 1925 election.[20] But if that was the arithmetic they had been calculating, it did not come off, and instead the Nationalists lost office.

The birth and death of the UAP

The 1925 poll saw the election of NSW's first female MP, in former Women's Liberal League organiser and member of the Nationalists' state council Millicent Preston Stanley. Despite only lasting one term as the member for East Sydney, Stanley (later Vaughan) would spend decades as a leading voice for women's issues and liberalism more broadly; fighting a successful campaign to give women equal custody after divorce, editing a popular women's section for the *Daily Telegraph*, and spearheading the large-scale Australian Women's Movement Against Socialisation in the 1940s.[21] The latter would attract the services of famous aviatrix Nancy Bird Walton, trying to protect her industry from Labor's nationalisation plans.

More ominously, the election brought to power Jack Lang. A radical populist, he came to embody and deliberately exacerbate the social unrest associated with the Great Depression – most famously in his call for something amounting to debt repudiation.[22] In these circumstances, the Nationalists and then the United Australia Party emulated Carruthers in trying to preserve what was left of the old liberal order.

Events reached a crescendo on 13 May 1932, when the Governor Sir Philip Game dismissed Lang for ordering public servants to directly disobey federal law. Lang's actions were so extreme that he managed to split the Labor Party, and the UAP's Bertram Stevens subsequently won the 1932 election in a landslide, assisted by a 'Federal Labor Party' garnering 4.24 per cent of the vote.[23]

This would have long term repercussions for both major parties. NSW Labor would spend the rest of the decade embroiled in its own internal squabbles, but in doing so it inoculated itself against the equally devastating split of the 1950s. Moreover, unlike the federal and Victorian Liberal parties of that later decade who were able to use the split to entrench themselves as 'parties of government', the fortuitous circumstances of the mid to late 1930s were 'wasted' on the UAP.

This is not to slight the Stevens Government, which did much to heal the divisions Lang left and get the state through the economic calamity it faced.[24] But they were 'wasted' in the sense that the UAP had a couple of inherent flaws that meant it never stood much chance of a permanent existence. Firstly, the party emerged to deal with the specific and temporary circumstances of the Depression, attracting some Labor supporters and having little of the philosophic coherence of Carruthers's LRA. Secondly, the UAP emerged out of the All For Australia Leagues – a movement which openly denounced 'party machines' as inhibitors of democracy.[25]

Such anti-party sentiment was nothing new. The LRA had had to compete with a rival People's Reform League, which had a quixotic approach in which it would endorse candidates for election but then require them to resign from the organisation because it did not welcome politicians.[26] But while the PRL ultimately fizzled out, elements of the All for Australia Leagues were absorbed into the UAP creating a headache for its extra-parliamentary organisation and leading to numerous debates over how to democratise its constitution. The spectre of Lang created an initial wave of enthusiasm within the organisation nevertheless. Five full party conventions were held in a period of 12 months between 1933-34, and its National Club supporters even acquired a permanent building at Ash Street to house the party's employees and offer leisure space for its wealthy backers.[27] The UAP also boasted very active youth and women's organisations, as well as debating clubs designed to train the oratorical skills of ordinary members.

By the late 1930s Stevens faced sustained criticism from supporters for not doing enough to balance the budget, reduce taxation, and end excessive interventions in the rental market.[28] In early August 1939 he was brought down by Secretary for Public Works

Eric Spooner who resigned from cabinet and moved a censure motion which attracted the support of nine UAP members. The liberal tradition of freedom of conscience survived in the UAP such that the backbenchers who crossed the floor felt entirely free to do so. They 'did not see themselves as an undisciplined rabble; they were proud of their independent ways'.[29]

When it was still united behind its anti-Lang pro-economic recovery agenda, the UAP had been the most successful political party NSW had yet seen, winning three consecutive elections. But by the end of its life, party room clashes revealed that there was little consensus as to what the UAP stood for. This lack of discipline and purpose carried over into electioneering, and by the late 1930s the presence of independent UAP candidates standing against endorsed members became endemic, even succeeding in bringing down the revered Parkhill (minister for defence and Menzies's rival for the UAP deputy leadership in the 1935 party room vote) in his federal seat of Warringah. The exasperated party eventually gave up on this point, allowing multiple endorsements for 'safe' seats at both the 1938 state election and 1940 federal election – an experiment which produced less than satisfactory results.[30]

With these circumstances contrasting sharply with those of the newly united Labor Party led by the meticulously safe and moderate William McKell (the self-styled anti-Lang), Stevens's successor Alexander Mair was sure to be handed a poisoned chalice. His tenure fell almost entirely within the war, and particularly during the early frustrating stages of the conflict before the nation was galvanised by the threat of Japan. Hindered by Menzies's federal government which was viciously attacked in the Sydney press and likewise starting to disintegrate, in 1941 Mair led the Coalition to an almighty defeat in which the UAP lost 23 seats and the Country Party another 10.

The IPA and the LDP

The period of the early McKell Government was notable for its emphasis on wartime consensus, accepting many Opposition and Upper House amendments to legislation.[31] McKell also shrewdly targeted rural voters, setting up a scheme for the mechanisation of the dairy industry, creating a division for agricultural economics within the Department of Agriculture, and increasing funding for soil conservation.

However, despite a carefully cultivated image of moderation and incrementalism, it was still a Labor government that sort to expand the role of the state through a new housing commission, state-owned dockyards at Newcastle, and government insurance office to deliberately compete with private enterprise. This old-style Labor socialism mixed with a newer technocratic fad for 'planning' and the inevitably pervasive role of government during wartime, to create a potent statist cocktail which prompted the birth of new organisations set up to defend the liberal tradition from some of the most significant threats it had yet faced.

The first was the NSW Institute of Public Affairs. The concept of such an institute had existed since at least 1927 when an IPA was formed at the University of Virginia 'to advance the popular understanding of current public questions … particularly the domestic problems of the United States and to have them discussed in a broad and competent fashion by men charged with the task of public administration and by those who are actively engaged in public affairs.'[32] The concept also spread to England, where so distinguished a figure as Bank of England Director Josiah Stamp became IPA president. In 1938 he visited Australia for the sesquicentenary of the First Fleet and gave a speech to a 'NSW regional group' of the IPA, which was extensively reported in the local labour press for allegedly giving endorsement to some forms of socialism in specific areas of the economy.[33]

Whatever existed of that first NSW IPA seems to have petered out, but it was re-formed in February 1943 by a group of businessmen headed by Charles Lloyd Jones (of David Jones fame) and Cecil Hoskins (the industrialist responsible for building the Port Kembla

Steelworks) – who were certainly not as amenable to socialism as Stamp. Their stated aim was to create an informed public opinion along sound lines when it came to matters of economics and the political and social welfare of Australia, insisting that:

> the necessities of war-time control and regulation should not be allowed to harden into a settled body of rules directed towards the socialisation of Industry and interference with the liberty and freedom of the individual, and that some steps should be taken to keep such regulations within proper bounds.[34]

The NSW IPA was partly inspired by its more famous and enduring Victorian counterpart, but there would be two crucial differences between them. One was that the NSW version was more classically liberal, upholding the proud NSW tradition over its social liberal/Deakinite mutation (which had been given expression in NSW by Bernhard Wise, who notably ended up in the Progressive Party facing off against Carruthers's Liberals). The other was that the NSW IPA did not intend to confine itself to research, educating the public and engaging in debates, but also proposed to fund political parties which pursued its philosophical objectives, in a manner that amounted to a more above-board version of the approach of the Consultative Council.[35]

One party it would not end up funding, despite some overlap in viewpoint, was the Liberal Democratic Party. This was formed in April 1943 under the 'sponsorship' of former Sydney Lord Mayor Stanley Crick and Captain Ernest White, president of the Australian American Cooperation Movement. Created with an intent to contest the upcoming federal election, its draft platform included full employment, the progressive reduction of taxation, equal access to education, equal pay for women, the cancellation of national security regulations which were not necessary to the winning of the war, and the abolition of protective tariffs except those necessary to establish an essential industry.[36]

The LDP thus sought to revive NSW's old Free Trade tradition, but for an admirer of the US like White this had a modern impetus in the Atlantic Charter's demand to lower discriminatory tariff barriers. Other attempts to 'move with the times' included accepting elements of state planning and centralisation such that the LDP even endorsed the eventual abolition of the states – in direct violation of the liberal principles of federalism and subsidiarity.

The LDP also picked up anti-party sentiment, railing against 'extreme party government' and the 'intensifying [of] class differences'. In line with this, both Crick and White insisted that they had no personal political aspirations. While the decorated World War I captain might not have been seeking a seat, contemporary John Cramer described White as having 'dreams of being a political messiah'.[37] There was certainly a religious undertone to his political crusade, as the LDP's statement of 'political philosophy' began with 'faith in God' and portrayed free trade as a method through which to maintain world peace through cooperation.[38] Democracy was likewise upheld as a universal good which should be promulgated throughout the globe. Indeed, it was the vehicle through which the Christian ideal would be accomplished on earth:

> GOD IS LOVE
>
> AND THUS IT IS A MISSION
>
> THE MISSION TO LOVE YOUR NEIGHBOUR
>
> GOD WILL NOT DO IT FOR YOU. YOU WILL HAVE TO FIND THE WILL TO LOVE YOUR NEIGHBOUR
>
> PRACTICALLY, YOU WILL HAVE TO FIND YOUR WAY WITH THE MEANS AVAILABLE UNDER EVERYDAY LIFE
>
> TRUE DEMOCRACY PROVIDES THE MEANS TO THAT END ...[39]

Suffice it to say White had an air of fanaticism about him, and something bordering on delusions of grandeur. The fact that he thought a political party formed only in NSW, and not even contesting half the state's seats, could have a large impact on a federal poll are clear evidence of overconfidence. However, receiving 42,000 first preference votes at the party's first electoral outing was not an embarrassment, and was enough to encourage White to continue with the endeavour.[40]

If White over-estimated the ability for NSW to reshape national politics of its own volition, he was not alone, as the same 'parochial' view was taken by the founders of the smaller but as newly formed Commonwealth Party, made up largely of current and former servicemen.[41] Despite this splintering, divisions within the parliamentary party, and having already lost three federal seats in 1940, the NSW UAP was said to be in *comparatively* decent shape when it came to extra-parliamentary organisation.[42] Nevertheless, the disastrous result of the 1943 federal election, where it received a 16.6 per cent primary vote, was enough to convince the party that it too needed to press forward with a reformation ahead of its interstate counterparts. Much to the chagrin of newly elected federal Opposition Leader Robert Menzies.

It was the IPA which called together fusion negotiations between the three parties, and White's ego was given significant vindication when they agreed to appropriate both the LDP name and its philosophy (with minor but necessary amendments). It would have been further bolstered by the *Sydney Morning Herald*'s reporting that:

> [T]here is the belated recognition of the fact that the U.A.P. possesses neither the political philosophy, the organisation, the virile personnel necessary to provide an alternative, nor has it even within itself the seeds from which these might be successfully germinated without assistance … The Liberal Democratic Party, small in numbers and in financial strength and without Parliamentary representation, is not in a position to build itself up rapidly enough for any prospect of immediate electoral suc-

> cess. It has, however, something equally necessary which the U.A.P. has lost and is desperately anxious to retrieve or to share in – that is, a certain measure of public goodwill and prestige which comes from the display of a little youthful virility and progressiveness, and from the leavening of the dough of political expediency with a little genuine idealism.

But as would prove the case several times, White was a difficult man to work with, and he ultimately broke off negotiations believing that too many of the moribund UAP's personnel were being retained in the prospective new entity. This was not his sentiment alone, for White was under tremendous pressure from many within the LDP who had become involved in politics specifically because they disliked the UAP.[43] In the end the UAP 'merged' with or simply absorbed the tiny Commonwealth Party, and kept the 'burgled' LDP philosophy, becoming the Democratic Party. Among White's redeeming qualities was his acerbic skill with insults, for he responded by saying:

> The ne'er-do-well cannot live on past glories of his forebears. The old National Party got a strong blood infusion from the A.F.A., and became the U.A.P.; but in process of time this has dried up, and, with failure staring them in the face, a further infusion was sought, but in this case Dracula was brought to earth.[44]

New Leader of the Democratic Party Reginald Weaver admittedly did bear some physical resemblance to Dracula, and he brought to the role enough political baggage to weigh down a party such that it would sink into a Transylvanian swamp. As spokesman for the Protestant Defence Association Weaver had openly attacked Catholics and called for restrictions on their migration to Australia, as minister for mines he had overseen the Rothbury riot in which one man was killed and another 45 injured, and he had clashed with the Graziers' Association so the Country Party did not like him.[45]

Weaver's policy speech for the 1944 state election was notable in putting homeownership front and centre,[46] however the poll was another bloodbath, with the Coalition left with only 22 seats in an Assembly of 90. But it was not like the LDP was beating down the door either. It only mildly improved its showing from the federal election, going up to 49,325 votes, and only really contesting blue ribbon seats rather than taking the fight to Labor. For comparison, also contesting its first state election was Lang's breakaway 'Lang Labor' Party which received 118,174 votes, only 13,776 short of the Country Party.[47]

Some further fusion negotiations between Weaver and White followed, but there was never much chance of an enduring compromise without the intervention of an outside force. As John Williams put it in a 1967 article:

> On the one hand there were the amateurs of the Liberal Democratic Party who evidently conceived of a party as an entity concerned with policy formation, had no appreciation for the need to compromise, and possessed little knowledge of organization or practical politics. On the other were the professionals of the United Australia Party staff and the members of the state parliamentary party aware of the problems of organization and reluctant to disband party headquarters and dismantle the machinery of the state organization which had been created over many years. In addition, without the unifying presence of an experienced national leader, differences of policy and personalities loomed large especially among the Liberal Democrats who conceived of their leader as ruling by divine fiat and knew little of the political qualities required by a successful leader.[48]

NSW liberalism desperately needed a clear and articulated vision, which is what the LDP was imperfectly trying to provide. But what they also needed was experience. Not just parliamentary, organisational, and electoral experience; but the experience to know that they were not starting from scratch with a new political religion. They were trying to re-erect and then carry forward the 'Good Old Liberal Flag', which had resonated precisely because it was so deeply baked into NSW's culture and values. Carruthers had a profound and whiggish sense of history, and was humbled and inspired by his place in a long tradition of progress. This was a quality that White – caught up exclusively in the present moment – lacked. But it was something that Robert Menzies possessed as he called for 'A Liberal *Revival*'.

Founders of the NSW Division

Charles Hallett cartoon suggesting that NSW Opposition Leader Reginald Weaver was not the most attractive recruit for Menzies's liberal revival. From *Smith's Weekly*, 7 October 1944, p. 12.

The DP, LDP and NSW IPA all received personal invitations from Menzies to attend the Canberra Unity Conference in October 1944. The conference came on the back of the successful 'No' campaign which had defeated the powers referendum and reinvigorated the divided forces of Australian liberalism. But it is an indication of White's flawed political judgement that he came late to that party. He had initially endorsed the referendum, believing that 'If Australia is to advance to full and dignified nationhood we have got to cease being a collection of squabbling parochial states',[49] and even attacking the Democratic Party for its opposition given that it had endorsed his policy proposals in regard to federal expansion. But then when he saw which way the wind was blowing, White came to the argument that even though he believed in centralisation, the current Labor government could not be trusted with it, and the LDP thus belatedly joined the 'No' camp.

In addition to the delegates from these three organisations and the state parliamentary party, there were only two federal parliamentarians from NSW to attend the Canberra conference. Eric Harrison,[50] the UAP deputy leader and former minister for trade and customs, and Frederick Stewart, the member for Parramatta who would retire at the next election, and therefore never even face the polls as a Liberal. Harrison was exceptional in being a New South Welshman who had strongly supported Menzies in the party room – the 1940 result having suggested he was an electoral liability in NSW. Most of the others were in the Billy Hughes camp, not that there were many left given that there were no NSW UAP senators, and only four UAP MPs. These all represented blue ribbon seats, but those seats were essentially wasted on the exiting Stewart, the elderly Hughes, and the effectively independent Percy Spender. Spender had not only rolled Parkhill, but had his own radio program trying to rival the Forgotten People (Spender had dubbed the middle class the 'lost legion', but it hadn't caught on),[51] and he had defied Menzies by sitting in the Advisory War Council even after the Opposition boycotted it over Labor pursuing a partisan agenda.[52] Needless to say, new blood was desperately needed, but it would not come in any quantity until 1949.

Proceedings in Canberra and subsequently Albury went exceedingly well, and the NSW delegates left in good spirits, convinced that this time they would finally be able to resolve their differences. Early the next year the DP and the LDP met to form a provisional executive, and while major disputes inevitably ensued, they were counterbalanced by a series of accomplishments.

The first was the wise choice of Bill Spooner as chairman. The brother of Eric, Bill was another decorated World War I veteran who had survived being wounded at the battle of Ypres to become a chartered accountant – thus mixing leadership skills with an eye for detail. He also possessed 'determination, political perspicacity and [a] professional grasp on financial affairs and fund-raising'.[53] Although an independent figure not officially tied to the DP or LDP, it was White who nominated Spooner for the chairmanship.

White can likewise take some credit for the fact that another key member of the provisional executive, Eileen Furley, came to the party from the LDP. Formerly the officer-in-charge of sugar rationing during the war, she would become the division's leading female organiser in its early years. Believing that 'the women's vote can make or break any government', she would argue that the 'only way in which the Liberal or any party, can hope to succeed, is to have sufficient women on all its councils, the executive and representing it in Parliament'.[54] Correlation is not causation, but Furley appears to have been proven right. The division would be notoriously slow in pre-selecting women for winnable seats, and notoriously slow to win state government. But after Furley filled a casual vacancy for the NSW Legislative Council in November 1962, the Liberals won the next four elections.

One more skilled extra-parliamentary organiser worth noting is Thomas Malcolm Ritchie. A self-made industrialist whose life story made manifest the liberal ideal of social and economic mobility, he firmly believed that 'a measure of freedom to enjoy his life in his own way is the priceless heritage of the Australian'.[55] However, as the first federal president, Ritchie's services would naturally be concentrated on federal rather than state matters – an early example of the talent drain that would become all too common for the state party.

The NSW provisional executive had to hit the ground running, for on 3 February the Liberals contested a by-election for the state seat of Ryde, the first victory for the modern Liberal Party anywhere in the country. There followed the nation's first Liberal Party branch, formed at Mosman nine days later with Menzies in attendance. By mid-year the state boasted over 200.

Approved by state council on 30 August, the party's constitution had little to differentiate it from its UAP predecessor. In theory, a new joint standing committee on state policy gave the organisation a greater say in policy formation, but this was to have little impact.[56] Branches would be combined into electorate conferences, which would play the central role in preselecting candidates, electing delegates to state council, and raising money for campaigns. As with the LRA, the Liberals wanted ordinary aspirational voters to sign up as members, but there was greater acknowledgement that membership fees nevertheless had to be substantial enough for the party to function. Arguably the most important structural change was that despite the limitations of relying on fees, Spooner was able to win a long and protracted fight to ensure that the NSW Division would not be financially bound to the IPA – thus freeing it from the spectre of another Consultative Council.

Spooner's self-confident view that he could get on without the IPA was based in part on his accountancy skills, and in this he would be vindicated as his careful financial management and independent fundraising not only ensured that the party stayed (somewhat narrowly) in the black, but also that it was able to take on a growing organisational staff. One vital recruit was a 27-year-old survivor of Changi and the Thailand-Burma railway named John Carrick.[57] Although his life was a bit directionless when he took the 'temporary' job as a research officer in January 1946, Carrick would prove to be an expert and thoughtful proponent of Australian liberalism, even authoring a short book of political philosophy, *The Liberal Way of Progress*, in 1949.[58]

The publication reflected the wave of youthful enthusiasm which invigorated the new party in the early post-war period. Rejecting 'stagnant and reactionary collectivism', it aimed at establishing a society 'in which the individual can develop his personality in his own way'. Idealistic, but still more grounded than White's efforts, *The Liberal Way* defended freedom of enterprise, contract, speech, association, and religion, while championing decentralisation, higher education, the family and self-reliance. On the latter point, Carrick emphasised that while Liberals accepted an ameliorative role for the state, they contrasted with Labor in 'not regard[ing] social services as ends in themselves but rather as a minimum below which none may fall and upon which all may build'. Picking up another cornerstone of Australian liberalism, the book also boasted that 'The Liberal Party is the only truly non-sectional party'.

Carrick's biographer Graeme Starr describes how his subject was just one of numerous ex-servicemen drawn to the Liberals, who were:

> ambitious, independent, unselfconsciously idealistic, and convinced that individuals could make a difference and change things for the better. They were suspicious of ideology, collectivist ideas and bureaucratic ways.[59]

Having risked their lives to defend the free world, they were now determined to make that world better and more free. Moreover, they brought with them a degree of optimism and sense of human agency that had pervaded Carruthers's view of NSW as a land of opportunity, but which had since been dulled by the grim realities of the Great War and the Great Depression.

As well as enthusiastic party organisers and members, many would serve as youthful and attractive electoral candidates. Though more frequently for federal seats: partly because of their greater lure, and also because the 1949 expansion of federal parliament meant they didn't need to topple a sitting member. The Liberal desire for fresh blood was so strong that party secretary HA Warby even put out a *Bulletin* ad openly canvassing for nominations to be sent to Ash Street ahead of the 1946 federal election.[60] Likewise, Spooner and Carrick would drive to regional towns and scout local opinion for who they should press into running.[61]

The two men quickly developed a close working relationship, and such were Carrick's talents that in February 1948 Spooner would promote him to become the party's general secretary, a position from which he would outdo 'even the achievements of Archdale Parkhill'.[62] A trait they had in common was longevity and consequent fostering of institutional memory (much of which had luckily been saved from White's compulsion to burn everything to the ground and start from scratch).

Carrick would hold his post for over two decades before entering the Senate in 1971. Over this time, he would gain numerous insights into electoral politics, many of which found memorable expression as catchphrases. The two most famous were 'you can't fatten a pig on market day' – meaning that campaigning had to be perpetual, and could not wait until election time – and 'Vive la difference' – the idea that Liberals needed to emphasise their philosophical difference from their Labor opponents and offer the voters a real alternative.

An extended adolescence

Another Parkhill similarity was that Carrick was generally acknowledged to be perhaps the best party organiser in the whole country. Hancock, for example, describes the organisation of the 1949 federal election campaign in NSW (Carrick's first time in charge) as 'the best electoral planning ever undertaken by the principal non-Labor party'.[63] Yet despite this reputation, Carrick's resume is stained by the fact that for years he failed to resurrect the electoral fortunes of NSW liberalism at the level of state politics.

Part of the problem was said to be that the organisation was too focused on federal matters – they even shared a building with the federal secretariat. But conversely Menzies was initially very unpopular in NSW. So much so that after a disappointing federal election result in 1946 (there were now five NSW Liberal MPs, the most notable addition being future minister and ambassador to the United States Howard Beale, still no senators), the NSW campaign committee vetoed a candidate from inviting Menzies to address one of their meetings ahead of the 1947 state election.[64] Menzies himself is said to have returned the favour by developing 'an intense distaste for New South Wales'.[65]

Nevertheless, the division took heart from state Liberal victories in Western and South Australia early in the year. Party CEO Brigadier Frank Burton (whom Carrick would succeed in a renamed role) even commissioned full-page advertisements boasting of the 'swing to liberalism' across the country:

THE SWING TO
LIBERALISM

because:-

THE PEOPLE HAVE HAD ENOUGH of a Government which has failed to remedy industrial unrest.

THE PEOPLE HAVE HAD ENOUGH of bureaucratic controls and restrictions, of housing shortages and a chaotic transport system.

THE PEOPLE HAVE LOST FAITH in government by a Party which reserves important diplomatic and administrative appointments for defeated or retiring politicians, and conveniently forgets preference to servicemen.

In Western Australia and South Australia this year, the electors have chosen a Liberal Government. In New South Wales, too, the swing to-day is to the *Liberal Party*, and a return to good Government for our State.

A CAPABLE LEADER

The Hon. Vernon Treatt, M.M., K.C., M.L.A.
Leader of the N.S.W. Liberal Party

The Liberal Party has the leaders, the candidates and the policy to bring sane, progressive government to New South Wales

The Liberal Party stands for industrial peace and full production, and the immediate development of our State's resources to overcome shortages in the least possible time. The Liberal policy is sound and progressive, and the Party has the Leader and the team with the vigour, enterprise and ability to put this policy into effect.

CHANGE THE GOVERNMENT—*VOTE*
LIBERAL

The Bulletin, 23 April 1947, p. 6.

Despite these raised expectations, the division had to dig itself out of a very large hole in the poll held on 3 May. Hence the fact that the Coalition gained 12 seats even with White (who had resigned from the NSW executive as early as April 1945, and by now was not even an ordinary member) sniping from the sidelines,[66] is not a result worthy of condemnation.[67] It was the failure to then take the next step which was to doom the NSW party for years to come.

David Clune has argued that the real missed opportunity was in 1950.[68] This was when the backlash against Labor's post-war socialist objectives was still at its height. State Liberal Leader Vernon Treatt would have hoped and expected to capitalise on Menzies's watershed victory the preceding December. This had seen the Coalition pick up 16 additional NSW seats in a newly expanded federal parliament, a great triumph that was essential to taking and holding office, and which would produce long serving Liberal ministers like Allen Fairhall, Bill Spooner, John Cramer (also a former member of the NSW provisional executive) and William McMahon (who would become the first NSW Liberal PM since Joseph Cook – whose campaigns had featured Banjo's song). However, a combination of flawed leadership, delayed policy announcements and tensions with the Country Party saw the Coalition's state election totals fall agonisingly short.

The latter issue had been simmering away for some time. Spooner had initially advocated contesting all Country Party seats in the name of being a party of universal values. But when that was essentially vetoed by the federal executive,[69] he changed tactics and instead lobbied for a merged Liberal-Country Party, even commissioning polling which showed overwhelming support for the proposal amongst the supporters of both parties.[70] Spooner also prepared detailed amalgamation plans, which promised that the leadership and deputy leadership could never both be held by members holding metropolitan seats (vice versa for rural seats), and presaged the Queensland LNP in offering elected candidates a choice of which party to caucus with in federal parliament.

Notably the NSW Protectionists/Progressives had been something of a proto-Country Party in having a strong rural basis – even to the extent that the early NSW Country Party re-used the Progressive name. So Carruthers had essentially achieved such a merger in 1907 when he induced their leader, Thomas Waddell, to join his cabinet (the arrangement was so one-sided it was more of an absorption). But the party system had hardened in the meantime, so Spooner's efforts would come to nought. Leading to perpetual wrangling over joint policy statements and three-cornered contests.

The 1950 election result – a hung parliament in which Labor narrowly clung to office – had a fundamental snowballing effect. By the time of the next state election in 1953, the federal Coalition was highly unpopular on the back of an inflationary crisis and Arthur Fadden's corresponding 'horror budget' (Menzies was lucky enough to have an extra 15 months of economic recovery before he faced the polls). Because Labor won that election and were still in power in the mid-1950s, that access to power gave members added incentive to avoid letting the Labor Party split spread to the state. With the persuasive help of Cardinal Gilroy, conservative Catholics not only stayed within the NSW Labor tent, but under his friend Joe Cahill they practically became the face of the NSW Labor Party.[71] Indeed, at a certain point, NSW Labor began to openly court right-leaning voters by arguing it needed to be re-elected as a counterweight to the leftist Evatt within the ALP.[72]

Meanwhile, as the Liberals gained a well-earned reputation as a party of permanent Opposition, the business community found it was pointless donating to their campaigns as resources were better spent courting the entrenched Labor government. Likewise, anyone with talent was dissuaded from standing as a state Liberal candidate, and those that were elected began treating politics as a part-time occupation.[73] This was further reinforced by the fact that there was no regular Coalition shadow cabinet until 1977.[74] On top of all of this, the Coalition had to deal with a minor gerrymander, that while nothing compared to what Playford was doing in South Australia, meant that they would need 51.7 per cent tpp to win a one seat majority;[75] as well as the suspension of postal votes which tended to favour them.

Because of its reputation for relative conservatism or at least pragmatism, it can be said that Labor's electoral appeal in NSW was far broader than elsewhere – an advantage reinforced by favourable electoral geography. While we are now used to seeing electoral maps dominated by vast dark-green coloured Nationals seats, in the 1950s state Labor frequently won regional seats, as well as dominating the mining/industrial districts of Newcastle and the Illawarra. In contrast, indeed partly as a consequence, the Liberals became comparatively narrow, with support overly concentrated in the northern suburbs of Sydney.[76] The party was not only 'especially' Protestant[77] and bad at promoting women, but was said to be under the control of a Vaucluse or Mosman 'aristocracy' that had little hope of appealing to the Forgotten People.[78]

As one of six children born to a simple clerk who would lose his job during the Depression, Carrick to his credit fought tirelessly against this narrowness. Like Carruthers and Menzies, he thought that liberalism's greatest appeal was to the aspirational voter who did not already have abundant wealth but had to strive for what they could achieve. This was an appeal that had a strong resonance with recent migrants, as it had since the liberal heyday of the nineteenth century. Thanks to a post-war boom, these migrants were once again becoming an ever-larger section of the electorate, but Liberals were not capturing their votes in the way they once had. The creation of a migrant advisory council within the party apparatus hoped to rectify the situation, but achieved limited success in the short term.

Carrick also campaigned ceaselessly for the Liberals to adopt 'state aid' for independent schools, a policy which not only reflected the core liberal value of choice (*la difference*) but would function as a key olive branch to the Catholic community. This included the descendants of Irish Catholics who had long been alienated from Australian liberalism and aggrieved at paying taxes for exclusively secular schools they felt they could not use, but also a growing number of Italians and other migrant groups. Carrick was even subject to an anonymous letter circulated to Liberal branches, attacking the 'Ash Street Kingmaker' for his 'obsession over state aid'.[79]

Despite this display of vision, Carrick has been accused of scapegoating the parliamentary party for the division's numerous state election losses, rather than shouldering enough of the blame himself.[80] Success would finally come when the party found a leader who broke free of its aristocratic mould, though like his predecessors, Robert Askin was not always on the best terms with the extra-parliamentary organisation.

Askin was a man who could boast working class roots. He played reserve grade rugby league for Glebe's Dirty Reds and in times of financial distress had spent evenings sleeping in Wentworth Park. Like so many others, he was a veteran of World War II, and he also had some insight into country concerns from two stints working for the rural bank. Notoriously, Askin was also a bookmaker, but considering the Liberals' association with an uptight form of Protestantism, this was not entirely a negative – even Askin was a freemason, an affiliation which likely helped him secure preselection for the not-so working class seat of Manly.

Despite holding an electorate in northern Sydney, Askin was determined to make a sharp break from the narrow appeal and history of failure that had preceded him. On being elected party leader in 1959 he sold his interest in the printery that produced the *Manly-Warringah News* to demonstrate that he was going to be a fulltime professional politician.[81] He took the time to develop a clear policy platform well ahead of elections, rather than leaving things to the last minute as had often proven the case before. Projecting himself as more Dirty Red than Sea Eagle, Askin tried to leave behind the Liberals' 'silvertail' reputation by making his electoral pitch to the ordinary salary earner.[82] There were also major improvements in PR, with the breakthrough 1965 NSW election featuring Donald Horne's iconic advertising slogan 'with Askin, you'll get action!'.

After reneging on the idea in 1962, Askin also acquiesced to Carrick's lobbying on the state aid issue. In a state in which the Labor split had essentially not occurred, this was a landmark event.

The 'Kiama Ghost' had finally been exorcised, as respected journalist Brian Johns reported that state aid and transport were the most important issues in determining the 1965 election result, having been shown as such by Labor's private marginal seat polling in the lead up to the defeat.[83] Perhaps the most remarkable display of the Liberals' broadened appeal was picking up the seat of Wollongong-Kembla where Labor had won 58.45 per cent of the primary vote in 1962,[84] while they also made inroads in Carruthers's old stomping ground of St George by taking Hurstville.

Conclusion

For all that changed for the division in 1965, some scars remained. Despite Carrick's post-election boast that NSW was a 'Liberal state', they had a long way to go before they were a natural party of government. They had finally been elected, but narrowly, and in part just to clean house after Labor's long incumbency had seen them become complacent and corrupted by the 'Tammany Hall' nature of how they ruled.

Askin's success was not fleeting – he won four consecutive elections, a record for an individual leader. However after he left office, Askin would be the subject of major corruption scandals which stained his party's reputation in an enduring and psychologically damaging fashion. In both of the Coalition's subsequent returns to office they won as self-styled corruption-busters, but ultimately found themselves caught up in controversies stemming from the all-powerful anti-corruption body (the Independent Commission Against Corruption) which they created and to which they gave extraordinary reach that goes beyond all the normal safeguards and limitations of law enforcement.

In the more recent instance, this ate away at significant gains the Liberals had achieved in Western Sydney, where Barry O'Farrell 'not only breached the defences in Labor's heartland but occupied much of the citadel'.[85] The breadth of Labor's appeal has been weakened as it struggles to balance the interests and views of an increasingly affluent and educated constituency with those of its traditional base. Whether the NSW Liberals can seize upon this vacuum to recapture the self-confidence and cultural dominance with which they once raised the 'Good Old Liberal Flag' is still to be seen. A Liberal record run of 12 years in office was certainly a positive step, but the 2023 NSW electoral map shows how rapidly things can backslide. The LRA won the 1904 election by dominating the aspirational suburbs; 120 years later its successor's path to victory still lies in those same outer suburban seats.

---

1 … '*Chorus:*
The good old Liberal Flag my boys,
The good old Liberal Flag.
And Joe Carruthers he's marching on
With the good old Liberal Flag.
Verse 2:
From deaf old England's distant shores
The immigrants may come.
From Scottish hills and Irish dales
To make this land their home.
The absentees who hold our lands,
From off their perch we'll drag;
We'll find a home for every man
Beneath the Liberal Flag
Verse 3:
As long as freedom holds her sway
So long that flag shall fly.
Our watchword is the people's will
And down with tyranny.
The country's laws must be obeyed,
And though Bill Lyne may brag,
Unfair taxation we resist
Beneath the Liberal Flag.
Verse 4:
So Liberals all in strength arise
United we must be;

Tomorrow's fight must show your might -

March on to victory.

And when the fight is fought and won,

No more the foe will brag;

You'll see it floating up aloft

The good old Liberal Flag'

AB Paterson, 'The Good Old Liberal Flag', 1907, quoted in Earnshaw, *One Flag, One Hope, One Destiny,* p.134. Notably the song was also adapted for use in Joseph Cook's federal election campaigns.

[2] Turner, 'A Labor State?'.

[3] See Loveday & Martin, *Parliament, Factions and Parties.*

[4] Gorman, *Sir Joseph Carruthers.*

[5] For Gladstone's importance to Australia's liberal political culture see Gorman, 'A Flawed Saint'.

[6] 'Lecture by Mr. Carruthers', *Sydney Morning Herald*, 22 April 1890, p. 8.

[7] In the end the money earned from basic memberships would have to be supplemented by more expensive 'Central Body' fees, and even then the LRA was never flush with cash. Hancock, *The Liberals,* p. 21.

[8] Loveday, Martin & Weller, 'New South Wales', p. 227.

[9] Michael Hogan, '1904', p. 53.

[10] Evatt, *Australian Labour Leader*, p. 166.

[11] Loveday, Martin & Weller, 'New South Wales', p. 248.

[12] Hancock, *The Liberals,* p. 10.

[13] 'Deep Disappointment', *Sydney Morning Herald*, 16 January 1911, p. 10. & Nairn, 'McGowen'.

[14] Hancock, *The Liberals*, p. 23.

[15] Berzins, 'The Nationalist Party'.

[16] Nairn, 'Holman'.

[17] This objective had initially been adopted into the Labor platform as early as 1905. McMullin, *The Light On The Hill,* p. 56.

[18] See Bollen, *Protestantism and Social Reform in New South Wales.*

[19] Berzins, 'Ley'.

[20] Moore, 'Sectarianism in NSW: the Ne Temere legislation 1924-1925', pp. 7-8.

[21] Radi, 'Preston Stanley'.

[22] See Clune, *Jack Lang*. On the Afternoon Light Podcast Clune directly compared Lang to Donald Trump.

[23] Green, *New South Wales Election Results.*

[24] See McCarthy, 'Bertram (later Sir Bertram) Sydney Barnsdale Stevens'.

[25] 'All for Australia League', *Sydney Morning Herald*, 20 May 1931, p. 12.

[26] 'State Politics', *Sydney Morning Herald*, Monday, 10 August 1903, p. 5.

[27] Hancock, *The Liberals*, pp. 32-4.

[28] Ward, 'Stevens'.

[29] van der Jadt, 'Mair, Alexander', p. 239.

[30] Hancock, *The Liberals*, p. 37.

[31] See Clune, 'Labor government in New South Wales'.

[32] 'Guide to the Papers of the Institute of Public Affairs 1927-1953', University of Virginia Special Collections, 2011.

[33] 'Towards Socialism', *Worker* (Brisbane), 8 February 1938, p.2. & 'Trend to Socialism', *Westralian Worker*, 25 February 1938, p. 3.

[34] 'Fight against bureaucracy', *Sydney Morning Herald*, 8 May 1943, p. 11.

[35] Cunneen, '1944', p. 213.

[36] 'New Party Formed', *Sydney Morning Herald*, 17 April 1943, p. 11.

[37] Cramer, *Pioneers, Politics and People.*

[38] 'Democracy as Faith', *Sydney Morning Herald*, 4 November 1943, p. 7.

[39] 'The Philosophy of the Liberal Democrats', a political pamphlet which survives in White's papers at the NLA.

[40] Cunneen, '1944', p. 213.

[41] Williams, 'The Emergence of the Liberal Party of Australia', pp. 10-12.

[42] 'Comparison of political organisations, Victoria and New South Wales', author not specified. Institute of Public Affairs (Victoria) papers, 1943.

[43] 'Letters to the Editor', *Sydney Morning Herald*, 13 November 1943, p. 6.

[44] 'UAP and LDP', *Sydney Morning Herald*, 29 November 1943, p. 3.

[45] Bourke, 'Weaver', & Clune, 'Labor government in New South Wales', p. 215.

[46] 'Democratic Party's Policy, *Sydney Morning Herald*, 4 May 1944, p. 3.

[47] Green, *New South Wales Election Results*

[48] Williams, 'The Emergence of the Liberal Party of Australia', p. 13.

[49] 'Liberal Democrat's View', *Sydney Morning Herald*, 23 February 1944, p. 9.

[50] Harrison's role in keeping the Liberal flag aloft in NSW in very difficult circumstances, and then laying the platform for the party's federal success from 1949, deserves to be better remembered. Born into modest circumstances, Harrison had gone straight from public school into a job in the textiles industry at the age of 13. By the age of 21 he had become the manager of a whole factory, and his belief in the Liberal ethos was thus imbued with this personal experience of hard work reaping dividends. He served as the only federal parliamentarian on the NSW Liberals' provisional executive, and frequently travelled interstate to assist with campaigning. By the time he retired to become High Commissioner in London in 1956, he had set a record as the

longest serving Liberal deputy leader that would last almost 50 years until it was finally eclipsed by Peter Costello. His daughter Shirley Walters would follow in his footsteps by becoming Tasmania's first female senator and an outspoken proponent of the pro-life movement.

[51] 'The Middle Class has its say', *The Herald* (Melbourne), 6 April 1943, p. 5.

[52] 'UAP expels Mr Spender', *Sydney Morning Herald*, 24 February 1944, p. 4.

[53] Boxall, 'Spooner'.

[54] 'Women's Vote Vital', *The Sun*, 1 June 1945, p.6.

[55] T Malcolm Ritchie, 'Why I believe in Liberalism', *Pix.*, 25 May 1946, pp. 16-17.

[56] Hancock, *The Liberals,* pp. 60-61.

[57] See Starr, *Carrick.*

[58] Carrick, *The Liberal Way of Progress.*

[59] Starr, *Carrick,* p. 124.

[60] *The Bulletin*, 2 January 1946, p. 17.

[61] Starr, *Carrick,* p. 146.

[62] Hancock, *The Liberals,* p. 66.

[63] Ibid., p. 76.

[64] *Sydney Morning Herald*, 18 March 1947, p. 2.

[65] West, *Power in the Liberal Party*, p. 231.

[66] White was not a member of the Liberal Party by 1947, as he told the *Daily Telegraph*, 18 June 1947, p. 9. But he appears to have later rejoined, for he would be expelled from the party in 1954 for standing against an endorsed Liberal candidate in the seat of Warringah – abandoning his old pretension of not directly seeking office. See Cuneen, 'Sir Ernest Keith White (1892-1983)'.

[67] See Clune, '1947'.

[68] Clune, '1950'

[69] Hancock, *The Liberals*, p. 61.

[70] Report of the NSW State Executive to State Council, 27 August 1948.

[71] Golding, 'They called him Old Smoothie'.

[72] Clune, 'Labor government in New South Wales', p. 111.

[73] West, *Power in the Liberal Party*, p. 152.

[74] Smith, 'The Opposition in New South Wales', pp. 202-3.

[75] Clune, '1950', p. 292.

[76] Smith, 'The Opposition in New South Wales', p. 199.

[77] Starr, *Carrick,* p. 169.

[78] Loughnan, 'A History of the Askin Government', pp. 44-5.

[79] NSW Liberal Party Records, Mitchell Library MSS 2385, K53626,3.

80 Loughnan, 'A History of the Askin Government', p. 27.

81 Goot, 'Askin'.

82 Loughnan, 'A History of the Askin Government, p. 72.

83 Brian Johns, 'The Liberals' Saturday Night', *The Bulletin*, 8 May 1965, p. 15.

84 Green, *New South Wales Election Results*.

85 Clune, 'Why Labor Lost'.

5
The Origins and Early Years of the Victorian Liberals

Stephen Wilks

The origin story of the Victorian Division of the Liberal Party has not left a slew of revered sites around Melbourne. Rare is the political history enthusiast who seeks out Scots Church Hall or former party offices in Queen Street. But what is remembered widely is that Victoria was once 'the jewel in the Liberal crown', a proud sobriquet attributed to the state's most famed Liberal leader, Henry Edward Bolte, premier 1955-72. Peter Blazey, writing at the very end of Bolte's long career, concluded that by then the premier's 'power over his parliamentary party was more complete than that of any other modern Liberal leader.'[1]

Debatable as this claim is, it is certainly the case that the long Bolte era has come to overshadow the Victorian Division's extended adolescence – several years of shifting parliamentary alliances, clashes between the parliamentary party and party managers, and even the occasional accusation of treachery. Yet sitting beneath all this like the foundations of a Collins Street edifice, albeit with discernible cracks, was the development of a party organisational apparatus hitherto unknown outside the Labor Party, animated by an invigorating spurt of philosophical ardour. The division sought to signal its difference from its United Australia Party predecessor by casting itself as an entity that was professionally led while also being democratic, purposeful, and socially inclusive, particularly in its formal provision for female representation.

Replacing the UAP

The UAP in Victoria and elsewhere was, wrote Robert Gordon Menzies, 'a whole series of unrelated organisations, without cohesion or common purpose'.[2] Its extra-parliamentary wing, the United Australia Organisation (UAO), was by 1944 accordingly widely held in contempt. The National Union, a party fundraising committee of up to six business leaders and graziers, was viewed with suspicion, not least as its membership was secret. *The Age* described it as 'repugnant to all democratic concepts', while the UAP's own Victorian parliamentary leader, Thomas Tuke Hollway, condemned it as a 'small financial coterie which seeks to control a great party representing all sections of the community'.[3]

The UAP did have two lively satellites, both Victorian-based. The Young Nationalist Organisation (YNO) was founded in 1929 by Menzies and others. It grew increasingly distant from the UAP, culminating in re-dubbing itself the Nationalist Party in September 1944. The Australian Women's National League (AWNL) was formed in Victoria in 1904 to promote women's awareness of politics and oppose socialism, but did not at first endorse women running for parliament. Although formally autonomous, it was partly financed by the UAP, and assisted it during election campaigns. But from the late 1930s it was closer to the YNO than the UAP, and under the presidency of Elizabeth 'May' Couchman was to play a major role in creating the Liberal Party.

The first and last UAP-led Victorian government was that of Stanley Argyle, which took office in 1932 in coalition with the Country Party. It was replaced in 1935 by a minority Country Party government led by Albert Dunstan, a figure known more for party partisanship and fiscal frugality than any evident qualities of statesmanship, yet who was 'pivotal to the chances and changes of Victorian politics over thirty years'.[4] At the June 1943 state election the UAP lost ground by winning just 13 out of 65 Legislative Assembly seats. It did slightly better in Victoria at the national election two months later: the UAP held all of its Victorian House of Representatives seats when the party lost 10 nationally.

Menzies began distancing himself from the UAP apparatus well before its replacement by the Liberal Party of Australia. As early as November 1941 he had proposed a radical reform of the UAP by emulating the ALP's strong organisational structure, with a financial base free from external direction. He proposed to a Melbourne meeting of UAP parliamentarians a national conference to work out what he and Hollway foresaw as 'a vigorous reconstruction of the party organisation', with 'a revision and restatement of policy'.[5]

UAP decline also spawned in Victoria a mixed array of new political entities. These were loosely allied mainly through their rejection of established party politics, and fear that the Curtin and Chifley Governments intended to re-engineer Australia into something very different from the pre-war nation. Labor's efforts to consolidate and build on wartime controls and planning raised the spectre of a seemingly socialist Australia, that the UAP was too weak to resist. Unwittingly, these new entities provided a basis for amalgamation into a new major party.

The Services and Citizens Party, formed in February 1943 originally as the United Ex-service Men's and Women's Political Association, made abundantly clear its fear of 'the mounting growth of bureaucratic government and the onward march of Socialism'.[6] It contested five seats at the 1943 federal election, without success. More significantly, some of its leaders later featured prominently in the Liberal Party, notably William Hewson Anderson, an outwardly austere corporate accountant with the Shell Company of Australia Ltd. who wanted 'to implant the service spirit in citizen life, to remove the sordid and selfish from our politics'.[7]

Different in function but sharing similar objectives was the Institute of Public Affairs (Victoria). The IPA was founded in 1943 by the Victorian Chamber of Manufacturers with finance from business interests to challenge the left intellectually by educating government and the public on the merits of free enterprise, something the UAP had manifestly failed to do. Although never institutionally part of any political party, it played a significant role in crystallising ideas that animated the early Liberals. It was not organisationally tied to its more overtly politically partisan New South Wales counterpart. The IPA and the Services and Citizens Party formed the Australian Constitutional League during 1944 to aid the fight against the Curtin Government's referendum on Commonwealth powers needed to implement its postwar reconstruction plans. A yet more minor body, the Kooyong Citizens' Association, was established in June 1943 mainly as a campaign committee in Menzies's seat.

Efforts in Victoria to draw new entities together into a united party to oppose Labor predate the Canberra conference of October 1944. The 1943 national election defeat saw increasingly open discussion of major party reform. In late November, for example, Harold Holt told the AWNL's South Yarra branch that the UAP needed to 'match the highly efficient political machine of the ALP with its hundreds of branches and tightly-knit Federal organisation'.[8]

In early October 1943 the formally apolitical IPA entered into talks with the National Union on replacing the withering UAP. But these 'most nebulous'[9] discussions, as *The Age* described them, were soon overshadowed by an interstate initiative in the form of talks held in Melbourne on 11-12 October between the Victorian and New South Wales IPAs. Menzies attended these briefly, but they still floundered over Victorian reluctance to adopt the UAP's personnel and apparatus, and New South Wales insistence on a controlling role over the putative new party. The Victorian IPA made its own more discreet efforts to unite the various anti-socialist bodies by sponsoring four secret conferences over June-September 1944 with the UAO, Services and Citizens, the YNO, and (initially) the AWNL. These were chaired by Herbert Taylor, another corporate accountant later prominent in the Liberal Party.

A separate 'preliminary unity conference' of senior UAP figures held in Melbourne on 16 June 1944 had eight Victorians amongst 23 attendees. This was mainly about the forthcoming constitutional convention and referendum on Commonwealth postwar powers, but Menzies told the conference that 'we should agree first of all on an all-Australian party'. He proposed that a sub-committee meet immediately after the referendum 'to decide ways and means of producing an all-Australian organisation'.[10]

The Victorians were still disunited by the time of the Canberra conference of October 1944, but their various discussions had helped build awareness of the importance of unity within a new party. Five of the twelve federal parliamentary representatives at the conference were Victorians, with seven of eighteen organisations present being Victorian-based: the UAO, the Nationalist Party, the Services and Citizens Party, the Australian Constitutional League, the AWNL, the IPA, and the Kooyong Citizens' Association. The IPA played a nominally non-political role by providing observers rather than delegates. However, one of these was the IPA's economic adviser CD Kemp who, with Anderson, later contributed to the federal and Victorian Liberal Party platforms.

Menzies later paid particular tribute to two delegates from Victoria – Anderson, who with his 'seemingly dry but precise mind' had 'played a great hand at Canberra', and Couchman for her similarly 'clear mind and ... practical grasp of politics'.[11] At the December 1944 Albury conference it was TS Austin, president of the Victorian UAO, who formally moved the formation of the new party.

Building a party

An important precept decided at Canberra was that the Liberal Party would accord maximum autonomy to its state divisions. After Albury, the amalgamating bodies in each state were tasked to establish provisional state executives, form branches, and recruit members.

The Victorians moved quickly. On 29 December 1944 Menzies announced a provisional state executive committee of 22 members, drawn mainly from the amalgamating organisations. Just six had held office with the UAP or the UAO, while there were five from the AWNL and one from the Nationalists. Only one member had parliamentary experience, JA Spicer, a former (and future) senator. Two further members added late in February included the very well-connected financier Ian Potter. It is difficult to resist also noting RE Trickey.

On 5 January 1945 the provisional executive met to appoint interim officer bearers, including Herbert Taylor as its acting chairman, along with members of subcommittees on party organisation, publicity and finance. It also started establishing local branches and building party membership, necessary foundational steps for convening the division's supreme body, the state council. By early March the first office and field staff had been appointed, funds were being raised, and the state parliamentary UAP had belatedly redesignated itself the parliamentary Liberal Party.

Initially the Victorian Division based itself at Penfold House at 116 Queen Street, but soon shifted to nearby 108 Queen Street. Throughout February-March 1945 the mainstream and local press alike were peppered with advertisements for public meetings where 'men and women of good will' could learn how to 'assist in the formation of the Sub-branch nearest to their place of residence'.[12] Menzies, far from being seen as an electoral liability, was promoted as the main attraction at many of these meetings. Advertisements in rural newspapers added assurances of Liberal support for 'decentralisation under which provincial cities and towns might be built up, rural markets stabilised, and national development guaranteed', not to mention 'cheap electric current' and 'running water in every country kitchen and to every farmyard' – an early challenge to the Country Party.[13] As early as April the division claimed 100 branches and 15,000 members.

The interim state council of the Victorian Division convened at Scots Church Hall in central Melbourne on 19 June 1945, with Taylor presiding. In attendance were some 300 party members, comprising mostly one male and one female representative elected from each branch, along with party office holders including Menzies and Hollway. The division was reported to now have no less than 20,979 members and 127 branches, including 60 outside the metropolitan area.

The first council's main purpose was to vote to appoint party office bearers and members of a standing state executive committee. An important early contribution to party culture was provision for equal representation of men and women on the council, the executive and other committees, electoral conventions, and amongst office bearers. Accordingly, the new state executive comprised 15 male and 15 female elected members, plus the divisional president, four vice-presidents and treasurer. At least a third of each of its elected men and women members were to be country delegates. Anderson was elected state president, with two male and two female vice-presidents. A joint standing committee on state policy was created to advise the state parliamentary party on policy, with membership evenly divided between four members elected by the council and four appointed by the parliamentary party. The press reported this and other early council meetings as major events, particularly the pronouncements of divisional presidents.

A sign of the infant division's rapid professionalisation was its speed in establishing a skilled secretariat. In doing so, it demonstrated determination to avoid being a re-labelled UAP by declining, 'after considerable discussion', to appoint the former UAO organising secretary, TK Maltby, as its first full-time general secretary.[14] The position instead went to the accountant and ex-soldier John Verran McConnell, who (with his New South Wales counterpart, John Carrick) became nationally significant as an electoral strategist: a prominent journalist mused that 'it has never been established whether he is known as "Mac" because of McConnell or Machiavelli'.[15] He held his position in Victoria until his death in 1971. By June 1946 the division had six senior staff: as well as McConnell, there was Edith Haynes as secretary of the women's section ('like Churchill', Anderson told the fifth state council, 'but she does not smoke cigars'), RM Berryman as secretary of the Young Liberals, ER Jenner as campaign director, C William Kerry as finance officer, and Kevyn Hume-Cook as publicity officer.[16] The division later added a research department that produced fulsome policy bulletins, and a Liberal speakers' group that helped prepare candidates for parliament by offering tuition in public speaking.

That the party branches were energetic and earnest participants in the early councils is reflected in the remarkable array of resolutions they generated, albeit with a predictable predilection for amending party rules and procedures, and for state level matters such as rural services and local manifestations of creeping socialism. For the first council, 22 branches prepared a total of no less than 54 resolutions. Inner eastern metropolitan branches were the most outspoken. Hawthorn's 14 resolutions ranged from compulsory secret ballots before union strike action, the reservation of all paid positions in the party organisation for returned servicemen or women, to 'a comprehensive all-embracing fitness movement, covering every man, woman and child in Australia'.[17] Camperdown was the most outspoken rural branch, with four resolutions. Branches betrayed a widespread fear of being sidelined: hence Murrumbeena and Prahran sought an assurance of ample time to comment on the draft party platform.

Unlike other divisions, Victoria did not have an annual convention, instead holding its council meetings every four months. The second council, held on 2 October 1945, completed the necessary foundational tasks, notably by approving a state platform (three months before the party's national platform), and agreeing on the division's constitution. The latter gave the council ill-defined yet sweeping power to 'have the general conduct of the business and affairs of the State Division'. This included 'the raising and expenditure of moneys', for which the state executive would appoint a finance committee to act with the party treasurer, while trustees elected by the executive would collect donations.

A more concrete feature of the constitution was the decentralisation of selection of candidates for Lower House seats. However, the specific means of doing so soon had to be re-jigged. Initially, in each electorate a qualifications committee of representatives of local branches and some state executive members would assess nominees, from which just a single preferred candidate would be put to a vote of all branch members in the electorate for endorsement. Such seeming railroading of the party membership contributed to sufficient angst in Toorak and nearby Malvern at the 1945 state election that the state council agreed to a more balanced approach. Henceforth an electorate committee of four members from each relevant branch would present a report on all suitable candidates to a convention of selected branch delegates for their decision by preferential ballot. This successfully produced an agreed candidate out of nine nominees for the March 1946 federal by-election for Henty (which the Liberals won).

A mass democratic party

In building its early membership, the Victorian Division presented itself as a mass party that was neither class based nor otherwise sectional, 'the best cross section of the people that this country has ever witnessed' as Anderson saw it.[18] He even borrowed language from the other side of politics by describing the Liberals as a 'people's party', but in the sense of rejecting Labor's assumption of a society perpetually divided into 'two conflicting camps, employers and employees'. They would instead represent 'metropolitan, country, men, women, employees, employers, shopkeepers, professional men, labourers, artisans. The whole lot'.[19]

Consistent with a personal and party commitment to individualism and self-improvement, Anderson proudly added that his party attracted 'the better class thinking type of Labor man and woman', people 'interested in a home in the outer suburbs, who feel we are offering something the Labor Socialist government cannot'.[20] Liberal interest in upwardly mobile 'battlers' is not a Howard era innovation.

Anderson rejected assertions of the Liberals being beholden to big business, as at least 80 per cent of funds came from people who had never previously contributed financially to politics, clear evidence of being 'truly a people's party'.[21]

Much writing about the early Liberals has noted that party membership included many ex-servicemen and women determined to apply the ideals of their active service to shaping the postwar world. Dick Hamer, an army veteran and a future premier, recalled that in Victoria the party indeed 'attracted a very large number of returned men', who after having 'spent the best years of their young lives fighting for certain principles … wanted to make sure that was reflected in the local scene'. Such ideals, he thought, 'would flourish better under a system of free enterprise'.[22]

Idealism characterises most new political parties, and typically includes the rejection of established party politics. In claiming 'the whole lot', Anderson saw his fledgling Victorian Liberals as 'a true democratic party', unlike the UAP.[23] Although Menzies was effusively welcomed to the early councils, this was not reflective of unthinking loyalty to the leader. The early party instead tried to realise its democratic ideal by decentralising power to its lower levels. Each branch was to elect its own committee and officers, and delegates to the state council. Anderson saw this as deriving from 'the principle that its power lay in the promotion of the maximum concentration of strength in the Branches rather than in its central authority', with 'a well organised Branch of enthusiastic members' being 'the most valuable contribution to a healthy organisation'.[24]

So when in August 1945 the party's federal president, Malcolm Ritchie, asked his state counterparts about progress in drafting platforms, Anderson replied in terms prioritising democratic process over efficiency: 'At our first State Council meeting it was resolved to refer matters of policy back through the Policy Committee to the various Branches which were to call meetings of their members and then submit to the Policy Committee their views'. Now that such feedback had been obtained, the committee would 'formulate a policy and submit this in draft form to Branches, so that Branches will have the opportunity of instructing their delegates to the Council' for debate and, hopefully, adoption.[25]

The reaction of branches to the unexpectedly severe defeat at the federal election of September 1946 reflected their faith in party democracy. At the sixth council held three months afterwards Belgrave proposed surveying every branch for ideas on why the Liberals had done so poorly, and a conference of branch presidents and secretaries on improved campaign methods. These included how 'we should all go more for the women's vote', something that Menzies had raised during the campaign. This seems to have touched a nerve, for Anderson promptly assured delegates that 'the machinery already set up' would do.[26] Branches were allowed a say at council meetings and their resolutions earnestly debated, but their substantive policy and strategy input was ultimately limited.

Public doubts about the Liberals' democratic inclinations, even after years of hard experience, drew angry responses. As late as June 1947 Anderson still proclaimed that 'the trouble is that the Liberal Party is such an example of true democratic control and liberal outlook that suspicious-minded people feel that it is too good to be true'.[27] Yet a state executive of 30 plus members proved too big and diverse to be a practical day-to-day decision-making body. Katharine West in a 1965 historical study saw power within the division as having actually and 'at any time' rested more with the president and a smaller group of trusted advisers, including the vice-presidents, the treasurer, and the chair of the women's section.[28]

A particularly unwelcome legacy of the UAP for the early Liberals was a lingering suspicion of domination by corporate finance. As Anderson told the council in April 1947, 'our opponents always try to say we are financed by big business'.[29] The ideal was for the party to instead be financed by individuals, including membership fees. In practice, such an ideal was not easy to sustain, nor did business donors promptly fill the gap by rallying to the cause.

Fundraising was handled by the finance committee, none of the initial members of which had been on the National Union. It nonetheless included prominent business executives and primary producers, and was chaired until 1957 by William Kirkhope, like Anderson and Taylor a corporate accountant and company director. Anderson said in March 1945 that the division was receiving good funding from business, but there were signs of difficulties just three months later when the treasurer reported to the executive £4,855 cash in hand as against estimated monthly expenses of £1,500. As Taylor cagily confessed to the first state council, the results of the party's appeal were 'somewhat disappointing'.[30]

Perhaps reluctantly, Potter, Kirkhope, Anderson and others were detailed to approach potential donors, again with modest results. Donations over April-October 1945 totalled £11,720 from individuals and companies, and £6,836 from membership subscriptions; the biggest identifiable donors were retailers, banks, and oil and mining companies.

Women, youth and migrants

A distinctive feature of the early Liberal Party in Victoria was its social innovation in encouraging participation by women, youth, and migrants. The AWNL was particularly important in shaping the division's early character, despite the long-term decline in its own membership from an estimated 50,000 in its first decades to about 12,000 by the time of amalgamation. With this still not inconsiderable membership and its venerable status, AWNL support for the new party set an example for other like-minded groups.

Although the AWNL had long encouraged women to stand for parliament, initially it hesitated over absorption into a major political party. Both its Victorian and Tasmanian branches sent representatives to the Canberra conference. All three of its leading figures – Couchman, organising secretary Haynes, and executive member Ivy Wedgewood – supported merger, and proposed this to their members at a meeting on 7 November 1944. Significant opposition led to further general meetings in January and February 1945 before members in July voted 560 to 9 for amalgamation. Menzies told the AWNL's final meeting that 'the Labor Party speaks with one voice from Cape York to Cape Leeuwin, and the Liberal Party could never be fully effective until the same unity was achieved',[31] but an AWNL splinter group held out for some years to come.

The early commitment to equal representation of women throughout the divisional organisation reflected the AWNL's bargaining power. Incorporation of the AWNL gave the division a bigger, wider and more secure membership than it would otherwise have had (although the AWNL's financial assets appear to have been less important). It also added to its organisational expertise in the persons of Couchman and Haynes. Both were dedicated to the political education of women, Couchman being a persuasive speaker and Haynes working tirelessly to encourage established and prospective branches. Comparatively plush former AWNL space in the Howey Court Building on Collins Street was used for conferences and executive meetings.

A separate women's section came into being in December 1945, initially chaired by Mrs A Cairns Officer, former AWNL vice-president, and from 1946 by Nellie Ibbott, also a party divisional vice-president. Haynes served as its secretary until her retirement in 1964. Women's subcommittees dealt with charitable appeals, migration, and parliamentary bills. A health subcommittee followed up a talk on tuberculosis by the Austin Hospital's medical superintendent with representations to the state health minister. When at the fourth council Anderson stepped down during debate on a motion relevant to a personal interest of his, he asked Ibbott to take the chair. The executive resolved in October 1947 that there should be a woman 'on the platform' at all party meetings. By July 1946 over 50 local women's sections functioned in connection with party branches, and 87 by December 1948.

But there is less evidence of women's prominence in determining policy decisions or high strategy. A report to the fourth council by Ibbott referred to organising celebrations for Empire Night, and entertainment for delegates to the party's federal conference held in Melbourne in 1946. The following year, following lengthy deliberations, six silver plates were sent to Princess Elizabeth to mark her marriage. Council minutes suggest that branch delegates were concerned more about the metropolitan-rural balance than that of gender, despite Couchman being a near perennial participant in major council debates.

The November 1946 sixth council agreed to run a female candidate for the Senate at the next national election, as had some other states: Wedgwood duly won a seat in 1949. At state level, there were no female members of the Victorian parliament from any party between 1948 and the election of Dorothy Goble, a Liberal, in 1967. The division only acquired a female president, Joy Mein, in August 1976, just the second female state president of any major Australian political party. (Four months earlier the National Party elected Shirley McKerrow to the Victorian state presidency). Yet the early Liberal Party in Victoria has still been contrasted with the situation facing women in the New South Wales Division, where initially there was 'no longstanding organisational structure and culture to sustain them', leading in 1948 to reforms that followed Victoria's example.[32]

The Victorian Division's youth movement, the Liberal Party's first, was established for members aged between 16 and 25 on 1 August 1945, under the unflattering title of junior activities committee. It was more fittingly dubbed the Young Liberals as from September 1945. Paralleling wider party arrangements, the Young Liberals had their own co-ordination council of two delegates from each of their clubs, and an executive committee. Their first major rally impressed Anderson for producing 'no evidence of the irresponsibility usually associated with young intellectuals'.[33] The Young Liberals grew in number from a reported 1,000 members as of February 1947 to over 2,000 in 1950. They did however prove fractious, and occasionally inconveniently defiant. In 1951 Alan Missen, Young Liberal vice-president and a future senator, publicly opposed dissolution of the Communist Party. When suspension from executive office followed, ten other Young Liberals wrote to the press in his support.

In September 1950 the Victorian Division tried to further broaden its membership through a New Australians' Liberal and Country Movement to attract non-British migrants. A committee of 30 'New Australians' drew up a draft constitution, under which members were to be eligible for full party membership after they had been naturalised. Despite *Labor Call* condemning this 'Tory plan to form a strike-breaking force among New Australians', the movement had eight branches by June 1951 among east and southern European communities.[34] It nonetheless foundered on differing expectations held by the party organisation and the migrants themselves, and limited support from the party's mainstream membership. In 1956 the movement was wound up.

Philosophy

An important way the Liberals differentiated themselves from the UAP – and again emulated Labor – was to proclaim an explicit political philosophy. Based largely on anti-socialism, it was more strongly held and simply stated than laid out as a fully considered set of values. Education of members through printed publications and long exhortations from party leaders extended beyond the practical art of politics to encompass the party's ultimate gaols. Lacking foundational legends to match the Tree of Knowledge or the strikes of the 1890s, the Victorian Division usually expressed its values negatively as alarm over the socialist inclinations of the Curtin and Chifley Governments.

But not always. The divisional newspaper, *The Victorian Liberal*, bore a masthead of youthful members brandishing flags proclaiming Franklin Roosevelt's four freedoms: freedom from fear, freedom from want, freedom of speech, and freedom of conscience or religion. The Victorians added a fifth to the forefront of this image: 'the freedom of the individual to go and come at will, to mould his own career, to rise to the greatest heights or to become a clod – this is his freedom in excelsis'. More upliftingly, this was 'the greatest struggle of mankind', through 'revolt against all forms of physical and spiritual slavery'.[35] The same publication assured readers they were inheritors of a long liberal tradition that extended far beyond Victoria's own Alfred Deakin to include such figures as Herbert Asquith and John Stuart Mill. In his presidential address to the fifth council meeting in July 1946 Anderson added some 'fundamentals of Liberalism', including 'the restoration of the sovereignty of parliament', lately undermined by 'the elevation of the bureaucrat'; and 'the restoration of the rule of law and order', notably by respecting the authority of the Arbitration Court.[36]

Admiration for modern management and campaign techniques imbued much of this. Contrary to later reputations, Menzies and his Liberal Party considered themselves forward looking in ideas and strategy, often drawing on overseas exemplars. The Victorian Division used public polling in imitation of the Gallup polls that predicted United States election results with reportedly uncanny accuracy. Its research officer accordingly distributed to party members in August 1947 the results of polling of public attitudes to such issues as free medical services, factory work hours, and profit sharing.

As a scholar of the Liberal Party wrote in 1978, its stated beliefs, 'though a mere footnote to the history of Western liberalism, are not just gloss; they give the party its sense of integrity'.[37] Belief in a noble struggle of opposing philosophies helped animate much of the party's strategy during its early years. Hence, for example, Anderson in his report to the federal council in August 1947 portrayed proposed amalgamation with the Country Party as an opportunity to create 'one democratic party' to face the 'socialist Labor Party'.[38]

Yet there is little evidence of all this resulting in a discernible climate amongst the party rank and file of lively intellectual debate. Members did not show much predilection for invoking the values of Friedrich Hayek, Ayn Rand, or even Deakin as the doyen of Victorian liberalism, instead preferring familiar denouncements of socialism. *The Victorian Liberal*, dismissed by one branch delegate as being 'far too academic' given its 'three or four columns of essays', ceased publication as early as April 1946.[39]

Intellectual input came more from the IPA's determined promulgation of free enterprise values. Anderson corresponded with Kemp on the division's platform. This unsurprisingly matched its federal counterpart in denouncing socialism, but also included provisions redolent of postwar ideas on a managed economy consistent with the IPA's famed 1944 *Looking Forward* manifesto. It proposed 'the Commonwealth and State Governments adopting a fiscal policy in which they budget for a surplus in years of general prosperity to provide reserves … for lean years, in which they should budget for a deficit'. Even more strikingly, the platform sought 'employer and employee sharing in the fruits of their joint enterprise, through some form of profit sharing or bonus directly related to rate of profit, and in this manner having a sense of common interest and duty'.[40]

Tension between party organisation and parliamentary party

Autonomy left state divisions of the early Liberal Party to resolve their own problems. The formation of the Victorian Division in 1945 went more smoothly than that of its New South Wales counterpart, but was soon dogged by tension between the party organisation and the parliamentary party. Commitment to party democracy obliged the organisation to assume a major role in formulating strategy and policy, while some parliamentarians, including party leaders, were equally convinced of their right to pursue their own choice of initiatives on such matters as battling the disproportionate influence of Dunstan and his Country Party. For all the Liberals' hopes of breaking with the past, the Country Party problem had deep roots that took most of a decade to extract.

Victoria's three-party system had for decades resulted in minority governments and some decidedly improbable alliances of convenience. None of the seventeen governments that Victorians endured from 1924-52 was based on a one party majority in the Legislative

Assembly, and six lasted 124 days or less. (The table at the end of this chapter provides details). The most durable, Dunstan's 1935-43 Country Party government, relied for most of this period on Labor Party support in the Assembly. Labor itself underperformed, producing just two governments that were relatively durable, in 1927-28 and in 1929-32. In 1950 *The Age* was unduly optimistic in welcoming 'the close of one phase of a long, unhappy period of political instability in State affairs'.[41] Not only were the ensuing Country Party governments of John McDonald separated by a four day ministry of Liberal rebels, but even the majority Labor government of John Cain senior that came to power in 1952 was so riven by internal disunity that the party split in 1955.

The main political constant since the early 1920s was that the Country Party, despite being fractious itself, usually held the balance of parliamentary power between Labor and the urban-based conservatives. Its openness to deals with either fuelled instability and distrust. As Brian Costar pointed out, its influence seems incongruous in 'one of Australia's most industrialised and metropolitanised states'.[42] This owed much to electoral malapportionment in its favour that effectively peaked in 1943 when the Country Party held nearly 40 per cent of Assembly seats. The Liberal response to this evolved over several years and was shaped by political events that at times bordered on the bizarre. Four overlapping strategies were pursued at various times by various individuals: amalgamation of the two parties; winning rural seats to reduce the Country Party to a parliamentary rump; a friendly understanding to coordinate electoral strategy and swap preferences; and a temporary unholy alliance with Labor to push through electoral reform, this latter strategy being the subject of occasional flirtations by party leaders that were never quite consummated.

The early parliamentary history of the Victorian Liberals also circulates around the figure of Hollway, leader of the UAP and the Liberals 1940-51, and one of those rare political figures to truly deserve a descriptor overused by biographers and journalists, that of being 'enigmatic'. A lawyer from Ballarat, when Hollway took over the leadership he was widely seen as 'a young man with drive, vigour, and courage.'[43] Subsequent assessments ranged from admiration of his intelligence and personal poise, to growing despair over an autocratic leadership style and seeming obsession with using electoral reform to diminish the Country Party. His contempt for the National Union and public calls for the reinvigoration of the UAP led to public clashes with the UAO, not a good grounding for later navigating the much more capable Liberal Party organisation. Unintentionally, Hollway's provocations helped make the organisation a strong player in determining strategy, including a preparedness to challenge the parliamentary leader.

One outcome of tensions with the Country Party was that the Victorian Liberals developed a stronger rural presence than did their party brethren in other states. Of the division's 237 branches and 41,301 members as of June 1947, 135 and 14,143 respectively were rural. Total membership narrowly exceeded that in New South Wales of 38,498, but rural membership across the border was much lower at 8,450. Another result was that Victorian Liberal anger with the Country Party festered. As late as 1963 Anderson, a onetime Hollway ally, told Menzies that his position on the Country Party was 'an old theme of mine and I've never wavered. It must be destroyed – like Carthage'.[44]

When the Liberal Party was formed, the domineering Dunstan was in coalition with the UAP. In 1944 he had uncharacteristically conceded electoral reform legislation which helped his Country Party lose seats to Labor at the November 1945 election. The Liberals had declined to run against the Country Party in all rural seats, preferring to work towards amalgamation. But in the run up to the election some dissident Liberal MPs launched an irresolute attempt to challenge the Country Party that succeeded only in affirming the power of their party's organisation over the parliamentary party.

The election was precipitated by five dissident Liberals, two independents, two breakaway Country Party members, and the Labor Opposition all combining to reject supply in the Assembly. Deputy Liberal Leader Ian Macfarlan agreed to head a caretaker ministry of himself and the five Liberal rebels pending an election. On 3 October party members at the second state council voted by a large majority to recommend the disendorsement of all six 'Ministerial Liberals', subsequently formalised by the executive. This response, said Anderson, 'unquestionably proved' that the party 'will, if necessary, prefer to sacrifice seats for its principles rather than sacrifice its principles for some seats'.[45] At least as significant was the evident strength of the party organisation, as the pro-Liberal *Argus* concluded:

> The obvious gibe of opponents would be, 'The same old crowd, up to the same old games.' The new Liberal party was bound to make a dramatic gesture to emphasise both its newness and its freedom from old taints. It has made it, and must be congratulated on its probity and firmness.[46]

The executive also set aside its commitment to party decentralisation by dealing firmly with resistance in three electorates to the disendorsements. In one other, Hampden, the sitting Macfarlanite MP was ditched in favour of the obscure 'Mr HE Bolte, young Western district grazier'.[47]

But there was also a catch, which reflected the organisation's still tenuous sway over its capricious parliamentary leader: Hollway seems to have incited Macfarlan's seemingly illogical behaviour. Well before the blocking of supply he secretly agreed with Cain that Labor would support first ousting Dunstan and then passing important legislation establishing independent tribunals for the public service and teaching service salaries and classifications. Kate White references Hollway writing in unpublished memoirs that at the vital moment he declined to vote against the government himself as he felt that the Liberal Party still needed to consolidate its organisation.[48] JB Paul instead claimed in a thesis on Dunstan that the Country Party premier convinced Hollway to pull back. Whatever the cause, an outraged Macfarlan revealed to the press that talks on getting rid of Dunstan had taken place 'in Mr Hollway's office with Mr Hollway in attendance', and 'in the Labor leader's room and Mr Hollway also joined in these'.[49] Hollway responded with a denial and labelling Macfarlan a traitor.

Unsurprisingly, the Victorian Liberals did poorly in their first major electoral test. The Ministerial Liberals won three seats, and the Liberals proper lost three from what the UAP had won at the 1943 state election. It won none of the seven non-metropolitan seats where it challenged the Country Party, including Hampden. Country Party representation in the Assembly slumped from 25 to 18 seats, and Labor formed a minority government with support from two independents.

The Liberals started to increasingly fear that if, like the UAP, they remained largely confined to metropolitan electorates they would be a mere sectional party 'doomed to extinction', elevating the Country Party issue to a matter of survival.[50] Menzies, however, became troubled by what seemed a growing fixation amongst his fellow Victorians. He warned its third state council in February 1946 'not to engage with in a lot of brawls with your prospective allies'.[51]

During 1946 Hollway publicly pleaded with the Country Party for amalgamation, and even offered to surrender the leadership. At the November sixth council, Anderson announced the appointment of six male and five female 'organisers' to assist rural branches, along with the creation of rural district offices. The division also advertised for candidates in rural areas. A more formal approach from Anderson in February 1947 for amalgamation elicited another rejection, followed by threats by the aggrieved Liberals to contest more rural seats.

At the 1947 state election, fought on the issue of bank nationalisation, the Liberals gained eighteen Assembly seats. Hollway became premier, but was shackled to the Country Party in another uneasy coalition that was greatly complicated by Dunstan's unwelcome presence as health minister. Liberal-Country Party contests had occurred in twelve seats, but the fifteen seats left to the Country Party to contest without such opposition suggests continuing Liberal uncertainty on strategy. In June 1948 the Liberals yet again unsuccessfully proposed amalgamation.

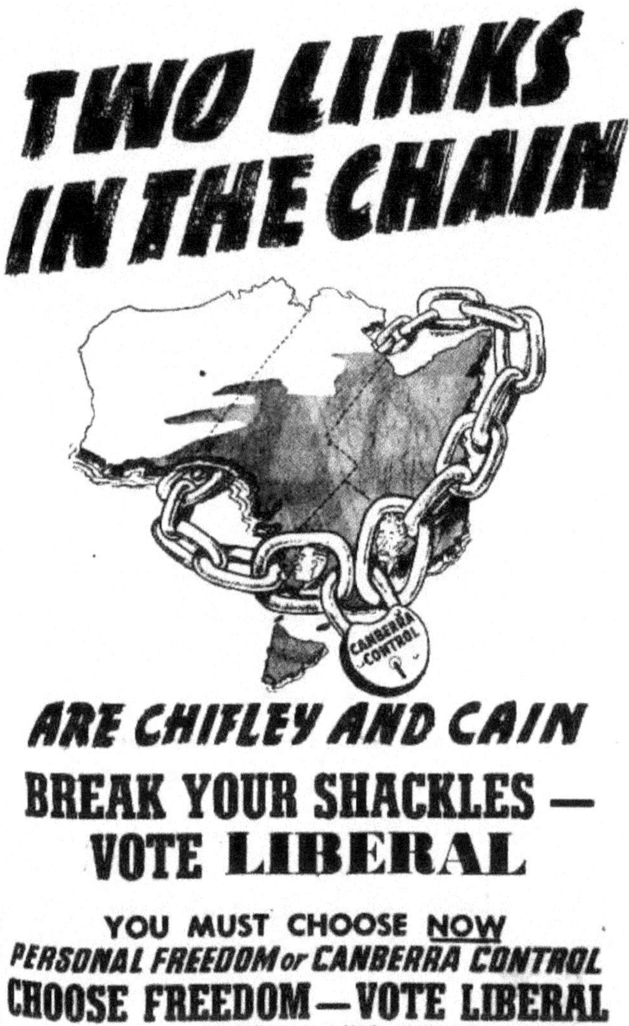

1947 Victorian election advertisement, showing how the Chifley Government's policies were central to the state campaign. From *The Herald* (Melbourne), 21 October 1947, p. 15.

Stabilisation

The 1947 win did not secure an honoured place in Liberal Party annals. A fleeting sense of triumph was dissipated amidst ensuing years of instability and underperformance, ensuring its overshadowing by the election of 1955 that ushered in the Bolte era.

This owed much to Hollway's underwhelming and idiosyncratic performance as premier. Resentment of his reliance on informal advisers external to party and government, including his wife Sheila, along with an increasingly evident drinking problem, earned the disdain of his peers, notably the influential business magnate and state minister Arthur Warner. As a junior minister, Bolte found the parliamentary party 'suspicious of Tom', particularly as he was 'playing around too much with the Labor Party'.[52] Secret negotiations by Hollway late in 1948 to settle a series of strikes cut across the robust response sought by his deputy premier, McDonald. Hollway began demanding that Dunstan leave the ministry, and in December 1948 the Coalition was dissolved, leaving Hollway to soldier on as premier with the help of two dissident Country Party MPs.

Hollway now felt free to pursue neutralising the Country Party. Six of its MPs defected to the Liberals, one of whom helped organise a public meeting in Horsham on 11 February 1949 to establish a new Liberal and Country Party (LCP). Hollway and other Liberals had been negotiating with the founders of this new entity, and before the month was over a merger had been engineered to form a united LCP. As the 1949 federal election approached, Hollway increasingly drew the ire of his federal leader. 'For Heaven's sake', pleaded Menzies, 'encourage our people to go into conference with the Country Party', as 'at Canberra … we all regard a reasonable working arrangement in respect of the Victorian Federal seats as vital' (Menzies's underlining).[53] Undeterred, Hollway sternly warned Menzies 'to watch carefully the activities of some of those in the Country Party who would seek to destroy you politically'.[54]

The party organisation was by this time doing more than the parliamentary leader to keep the party united. Late in 1949, the executive moved to expel from the parliamentary party two MLAs, FL Edmunds and JS Lechte, whose dissent extended to threatening to vote against the minority Liberal government. Hollway and the party room initially opposed intervention in what they saw as a purely parliamentary matter before giving way. In April 1950, the state council barred the LCP from involvement in coalitions. At the 1950 election the following month, Labor gained eight seats, but decided to support a minority Country Party government headed by McDonald.

Tension increasingly centred on Hollway's determination to end the metropolitan-rural electoral imbalance by legislating to apply the 'two for one' formula. Under this, each House of Representatives seat would be divided equally into two Assembly seats, the Commonwealth electorates being less malapportioned. The resulting Assembly boundaries would be adjusted whenever a Commonwealth redistribution occurred. Hollway initially had support from Anderson, the executive and the state council, but many Liberal MPs feared two for one would benefit Labor. Loyalty to the leader initially deterred them from speaking out, but tension grew as he appeared increasingly fixated with two for one, leading to reports that Warner and other members of the parliamentary party were plotting a change of leader. At the September 1950 state council, Hollway's leadership was openly criticised by some branch delegates. Soon after, the parliamentary party decided to oppose two for one, in response to which the executive reminded the MPs that the party's governing body, the state council, supported this strategy. Even more seriously, such growing disunity, failure to consolidate power at the state level, and probably also an inevitable waning of initial enthusiasm, saw party membership decline by 40 per cent from 1948 to 1951.

More broadly, in November 1950 the executive proposed that council decisions be considered binding on the parliamentary party, and even that candidates pledge support for the party platform and council determinations (incongruously reminiscent of the ALP). As an earlier writer on the division, Peter Aimer, concluded, such measures 'reveal the muscle-flexing inclination of the extra-parliamentary section under certain circumstance'. Further proposed constitutional amendments the next month included making clear that the council was to 'determine the Platform and Policy of the Party', and that the executive could disendorse any state MP who failed to support the platform or whatever the council considered 'a decision of major policy'.[55] The main substance of these amendments was embedded into the division's constitution in 1953.

Hollway lost the leadership to Leslie Norman in a closely fought ballot in December 1951, 19 votes to 21, with Bolte becoming deputy leader. The executive's commitment to two for one began to waver, particularly as its implementation required Labor support. In May 1952, after a bitter four-hour debate, the state council voted to rescind support for two for one, a bare majority of party members having accepted Norman's arguments that it risked a future Labor national government fixing the system to help its state counterpart, and that creating more metropolitan seats would favour Labor. The incoming state president, JM Anderson, initially opposed the motion but soon switched to rejecting his predecessor and namesake's support for two for one. The council instead adopted Norman's proposal for a fixed balance in the number of rural, urban, and metropolitan electorates, subject to review every six years. Norman also pronounced that 'the only final answer to the problem of the Country Party is a merger', soon leading to a fruitless approach of his own.[56]

In the wake of Hollway's fall Victorian politics became yet stranger. In July 1952 Labor withdrew its support for the McDonald Government, but the Liberals, after some hesitation, decided to support McDonald. Hollway, meanwhile, resumed secret negotiations with Cain. He proposed that if the McDonald Government could be removed, he would form a rebel Liberal ministry with Labor support solely to legislate two for one, followed by an election. So on 17 September Hollway moved a no-confidence motion against the government, defeated when two Liberals he had been counting on failed to support the motion. On 24 September he was expelled from the parliamentary party. But on 22 October Labor and two other Hollway supporters succeeded in blocking supply in the Legislative Council. McDonald resigned and, concerned that supply would run out before an election could be held, on 28 October the state governor commissioned Hollway to form a government consisting of the eight MPs who comprised his Electoral Reform League. He was defeated the next day in a censure motion, McDonald was commissioned as caretaker premier, and a dissolution was granted.

At the election of 6 December the Electoral Reform League won four Assembly seats, including Hollway reaping a particularly satisfying revenge by defeating Norman in the new leader's own electorate. Cain formed Victoria's first majority Labor government. In August 1953 all the 'Hollway Liberals' were formally expelled by the party organisation. Their cause had not been helped by two of them trying to gatecrash the state council, nor by Hollway making clear that he preferred Labor to another Country Party government.

Hollway's defeat made evident the strength of the party organisation, particularly its ultimate ability to resist a domineering parliamentary leader. JM Anderson later recalled of Hollway and his acolytes that 'we knew we had to get rid of them completely, otherwise we would be out of power'.[57] Memory of the once esteemed Hollway faded as regard grew for the next Liberal premier of Victoria, Bolte. Even his legacy on electoral reform is muddied, for it was the Cain Government that finally introduced two for one late in 1953. As White put it, Hollway, used to UAP organisational laxness, 'neither made the transition to being a strict party man nor learnt successfully to manipulate the party apparatus to consolidate his own support'.[58]

From this long sequence of complex events, two overlapping phases of the early division can be discerned. The first was the attenuated formative period during which Hollway and the tensions of a three-party system intermittently divided the party. The very early Liberals did not define themselves by rivalry with the Country Party: they instead saw their rural counterpart as a philosophical partner, resulting in bafflement followed by growing anger over its continuing refusal to amalgamate into one anti-socialist party.

The Country Party's resolute independence did not entirely invalidate but nonetheless limited the Liberal claim to be a more truly state-wide party than the UAP ever was, and had to be dealt with by other means.

This was followed by a transition that began in late 1949 and was characterised by the party organisation increasingly asserting itself over Hollway and a fractious parliamentary party. Following the short parliamentary leaderships of Norman and Trevor Oldham (the latter killed in a plane crash), Bolte as leader from June 1953 displayed a caution that finally decisively cooled tensions with the organisation and contributed to the narrow Liberal majority won at the election of 1955. JM Anderson recalled the outwardly unprepossessing Bolte as 'always ready to sit down and talk things out', and being 'shrewd but not cunning, forthright without guile'.[59]

Conclusion

The Victorian Liberals would have been gravely disappointed that it took ten years for them to win majority government in their state. A less determined organisation may well have doubted its basic assumptions, management, and membership. Despite some tendency of members to divide over certain major issues, such disagreement did not produce intractably warring factions. Division over two for one did have a philosophical element that manifested itself in disagreement over collaboration with Labor, but also had much to do with tension over strategy and the character of the parliamentary leader. Philosophical differences were insufficiently deep to produce a lasting split.

The foremost defining feature of the Victorian Liberals became that of a strong party organisation that succeeded in being more than a revamped UAP; a close second was its commitment to the equal representation of women in the organisation, if not the parliamentary party. Any suggestion that the Liberals were in awe of the parliamentary leader needs to be qualified by the history of the division's early years. High calibre party managers, some with only limited prior political experience, successfully nurtured a professional party apparatus, a mass membership, and a uniting sense of political philosophy. This provided a sound basis for the young Bolte – cautious, willing to learn, and increasingly politically acute – to emerge as Victoria's most successful postwar Liberal leader.

Even Frederic Eggleston, long a trenchant critic of Victorian politics, conceded in 1953 that despite a continuing lack of interest in ideas, 'the party organisation has been improved of recent years' as 'the party councils have been put on a more permanent basis and a few prominent citizens take part'.[60] As late as 1974 Aimer could conclude that the 'Victorian Liberal politicians thus dominate the organisation less than their colleagues in the other state parties'.[61] In short, the Victorian Division contributed significantly to the Liberal Party of Australia realising Menzies's vision of it becoming Australia's first major non-Labor party to have the benefit of a properly professional party organisation.

Victorian Governments, 1924-1952

Premier	Party or parties in coalition	Dates	Duration in days
Alexander James Peacock	Nationalist	28 April-18 July 1924	82
George Michael Prendergast	ALP	18 July-18 November 1924	124
John Allan	Country/ Nationalist	18 November 1924-20 May 1927	914
Edmond John Hogan	ALP	20 May 1927-22 November 1928	553
William Murray McPherson	Nationalist	22 November 1928-12 December 1929	386
Edmond John Hogan	ALP	12 December 1929-19 May 1932	890

Stanley Seymour Argyle	UAP	19 May 1932-2 April 1935	1049
Albert Arthur Dunstan	Country Party	2 April 1935-14 September 1943	3088
John Cain Snr.	ALP	14 September 1943-18 September 1943	5
Albert Arthur Dunstan	Country Party/ UAP and Liberal Party	18 September 1943-2 October 1945	746
Ian Macfarlan	Ministerial Liberal	2 October 1945-21 November 1945	51
John Cain Snr.	ALP	21 November 1945-20 November 1947	730
Thomas Tuke Hollway	Liberal/ Country Party	20 November 1947-3 December 1948	380
Thomas Tuke Hollway	Liberal	3 December 1948-27 June 1950	572
John Gladstone Black McDonald	Country Party	27 June 1950-28 October 1952	855
Thomas Tuke Hollway	Electoral Reform League	28 October 1952-31 October 1952	4
John Gladstone Black McDonald	Country Party	31 October 1952-17 December 1952	48

1 Blazey, *Bolte*, p. 170.

2 Menzies, *Afternoon Light*, p. 283.

3 'An Overdue Party Revolt', *The Age*, 18 November 1941, p. 4.

'Stir Over Attack on Mr Hollway', *Herald*, 13 November 1941, p. 3.

4 Paul, 'Dunstan'.

5 'Broader Basis of UAP Policy', *The Argus,* 25 November 1941, p. 5.

6 'Services and Citizens', *The Age*, 7 June 1943, p. 2.

[7] 'New Party Aims', *The Age*, 13 April 1943, p. 2.

[8] 'Mr Holt Says Drastic Action is Necessary', *Herald*, 30 November 1943, p. 5.

[9] 'Remodelling of UAP', *The Age*, 11 November 1943, p. 2.

[10] Speech to preliminary unity conference, Menzies papers, National Library of Australia, MS 4936, box 573, file 11.

[11] Menzies, *Afternoon Light*, pp. 289-90.

[12] 'Liberal Party of Australia', *The Argus*,13 March 1945, p. 2.

[13] *Camperdown Chronicle*, 9 March 1945, p. 2.

[14] Minutes Executive Committee, 18 July 1945, Liberal Party of Australia, Victorian Division, 1972.0032, 2/1/1, University of Melbourne Archives.

[15] Whitington, 'Directors of the Liberals', *Nation*, 7 October 1961, p. 8.

[16] Minutes fifth State Council, 26 November 1946, p. 5,

Liberal Party of Australia, Victorian Division, 1972.0032 1/1/1, University of Melbourne Archives.

[17] 'Resolutions', Liberal Party of Australia, Victorian Division, 1972.0032, 1/1/1, University of Melbourne Archives.

[18] Minutes fourth State Council, 4 June 1946, p. 3, Liberal Party of Australia, Victorian Division, 1972.0032, 1/1/1, University of Melbourne Archives.

[19] Minutes sixth State Council, 26 November 1946, p. 3, Liberal Party of Australia, Victorian Division, 1972.0032 1/1/1, University of Melbourne Archives.

[20] Minutes fourth State Council, 4 June 1946, p. 3, Liberal Party of Australia, Victorian Division, 1972.0032, 1/1/1, University of Melbourne Archives.

[21] Minutes fifth State Council, 30 July 1946, p. 4, Liberal Party of Australia, Victorian Division, 1972.0032, 1/1/1, University of Melbourne Archives.

[22] Colebatch, *Dick Hamer*, p. 99.

[23] Minutes sixth State Council, 26 November 1946, p. 3, Liberal Party of Australia, Victorian Division, 1972.0032 1/1/1, University of Melbourne Archives.

[24] Anderson, *The Liberal Party of Australia*, p. 12.

[25] Anderson to Ritchie, 3 August 1945, Menzies papers, National Library of Australia, MS 4936, box 410, file 2a.

[26] Minutes sixth State Council, 26 November 1946, p. 14, Liberal Party of Australia, Victorian Division, 1972.0032 1/1/1, University of Melbourne Archives.

[27] 'The Liberal Party', *The Age*, 30 June 1947, p. 2.

[28] West, *Power in the Liberal Party*, p. 50.

[29] Minutes seventh State Council, 17 April 1947, p. 13, Liberal Party of Australia, Victorian Division, 1972.0032 1/1/1, University of Melbourne Archives.

[30] Minutes first State Council, 19 June 1945, p. 4, Liberal Party of Australia, Victorian Division, 2001.0071 1/3/1, University of Melbourne Archives.

[31] 'AWNL to Wind-Up', *The Argus*, 25 July 1945, p. 3.

[32] Fitzherbert, *Liberal Women*, p. 230.

[33] 'Enthusiasm of Young Liberals', *The Argus*, 14 December 1945, p. 5.

[34] 'Tories Use Foreign Language to Trap New Australians', *Labor Call*, 11 January 1951, p. 1.

[35] 'The Five Freedoms', *The Victorian Liberal*, September 1945, vol. 1 no. 1, p. 1.

[36] Minutes fifth State Council, 26 November 1946, pp. 6-7, Liberal Party of Australia, Victorian Division, 1972.0032 1/1/1, University of Melbourne Archives.

[37] Tiver, *The Liberal Party*, p. 290.

[38] Second annual report to the Federal Council, August 1947, Liberal Party of Australia, Victorian Division, 1972.0032, 1/2/1, University of Melbourne Archives.

[39] Minutes ninth State Council, 3 December 1947, p. 33, Liberal Party of Australia, Victorian Division, 1972.0032 1/1/1/7, University of Melbourne Archives.

[40] *The Platform of the Liberal Party of Australia (Victorian Division)* pp. 5, 7, Liberal Party of Australia Papers, MS 5000, box 141, National Library of Australia.

[41] 'Stability is the State's Need', *The Age*, 27 June 1950, p. 2.

[42] Costar, 'National-Liberal Party Relations in Victoria', in *Essays on Victorian Politics*, p. 157.

[43] 'Upheaval in the U.A.P.', *The Age*, 14 November 1941, p. 6.

[44] Anderson to Menzies, 6 December 1963, Menzies papers NLA, MS 4936, box 1, file 9.

[45] 'Effect of Split on Liberals' Future', *The Argus*, 10 October 1945, p. 3.

[46] 'Painful but Necessary', *The Argus*, 5 October 1945, p. 2.

[47] 'Liberal Surprise', *The Argus*, 23 October 1945, p. 1.

[48] White, 'A Political Biography of Thomas Tuke Hollway', pp. 90-95, 270.

[49] 'More Controversy on the "Political Plot"', *Herald*, 27 October 1945, p. 3.

[50] 'Resume of the Liberal Party-Country Party Position State of Victoria', Menzies papers NLA box 410, file 4, c. 1946

[51] Minutes third State Council, 5 February 1946, p. D13, Liberal Party of Australia, Victorian Division, 1972.0032 1/1/1, University of Melbourne Archives.

[52] Bolte, National Library of Australia, interview with Mel Pratt, 1976, session 1.

[53] Menzies to Hollway 9 March 1949, Menzies papers NLA box 410, file 4.

[54] Hollway to Menzies 17 March 1949, Menzies papers NLA box 410, file 4.

[55] Aimer, *Politics, Power and Persuasion*, p. 168.

[56] State Council 8 May 1952, quoted in West, *Power in the Liberal Party*, p. 22.

[57] Blazey, *Bolte*, p. 51.

[58] White, 'A Political Biography of Thomas Tuke Hollway', p. 271.

[59] Blazey, *Bolte*, p. 51.

[60] Eggleston, *Reflections of an Australian Liberal*, p. 134.

[61] Aimer, *Politics, Power and Persuasion*, p. 183.

6

Queensland Liberalism – The Queensland People's Party 1943–49

Lyndon Megarrity

Observing the wartime dominance of the Labor Party in Queensland, and the demoralisation of the non-Labor side of politics, Brisbane lord mayor and independent state MP John Beals (J.B.) Chandler argued that a new political party was needed to represent the interests of Queensland as a whole:

> Australia must get rid of its inferiority complex and not be afraid of doing big things as America has done. To do these things they must get the best type of men available in the community to enter the Legislature.[1]

Chandler's personal popularity and the efforts of core Brisbane supporters resulted in the formation of the Queensland People's Party (QPP) in 1943. While the Country Party remained the most successful non-Labor party in Queensland, the QPP developed strong branch membership in Brisbane and the regions. It also enjoyed modest success in two state elections. The QPP was similar in outlook to the numerous non-Labor parties in other states that Robert Menzies persuaded to merge into a new party in 1944-45. However, the QPP resisted Menzies's overtures and refused to give up its identity. It was only towards the very end of the decade that the QPP membership chose to formally become the Queensland Division of the Liberal Party of Australia.

This chapter traces the history of the Queensland People's Party within the context of World War II and the collective hope for a 'new world' experienced by many civic-minded citizens. It shows that despite the fact that in state elections, its victories were confined to south-east Queensland, the QPP had a broad appeal for many non-Labor supporters – although not enough to challenge the dominance of the Country Party. Finally, it will argue that despite protestations that it was a 'Queensland' party, it was ultimately moving towards the same general position as the Liberal Party and amalgamation was inevitable.

Non-Labor politics in Queensland 1915-43: The historical context

The unusual enthusiasm for the creation of the Queensland People's Party, especially among non-Labor voters in Brisbane, can only be understood by examining the evolution of Queensland state politics from World War I to the early 1940s. In 1915, the Liberal government of Digby Denham (premier 1911-15) was defeated in the general election by the Labor Party, headed by TJ Ryan (premier 1915-19). It ushered in a long period of Labor rule in Queensland between 1915 and 1957, with the exception of the period 1929-32.

During his time in office, Denham, like most previous Queensland premiers, could rely, at least temporarily, on electoral support from a broad range of rural, urban, metropolitan and regional interests. This had been the case since the emergence of party politics in Queensland in the 1870s and 1880s. While some members of the Legislative Assembly had, for several decades, specifically branded themselves as farmers' representatives, most non-Labor rural MPs had aligned with major parliamentary parties. This status quo was rapidly challenged following the election of the Ryan Labor Government. Changing its name to the Nationalists by 1917, the former Liberal Party became embroiled in internal disputes among non-Labor extra-parliamentary associations jockeying for position in Brisbane. No doubt believing that the metropolitan-focused Nationalists no longer adequately represented their interests, various farming groups formed the regional Northern Country Party (June 1920) and the more state-wide Country Party (July 1920). In the 1920 state election, the combined results of the Country Party (18 MPs) and Northern Country (3 MPs) dwarfed the results of the Nationalists (13 MPs).[2]

The Country Party and the Northern Country Party amalgamated in 1921; the Nationalists, together with a handful of Country Party members, formed the United Party in 1923. While the United Party did slightly better than the Country Party in the 1923 poll (16 to 13 MPs), neither organisation was in a viable position to defeat the Labor Party. Ambitious for office, the Country Party in 1925 merged with the United Party to form the Country and Progressive National Party (CPNP). Under the leadership of farmer and dairy factory owner Arthur Moore, the CPNP defeated Labor in 1929.[3]

The CPNP's victory saw the first woman elected to Queensland parliament. This was Irene Longman, who sat as a backbencher for a single term in the Moore administration. Historian John McCulloch has argued that Longman's advocacy for women and children in parliament helped lead to public reforms, including the introduction of female police officers, 'facilities for disabled children, and for female officials in children's courts.'[4] Until 1966, Longman remained the only woman, Labor or non-Labor, to have been elected as a Queensland MP.

The economic depression undoubtedly had a bearing on Moore's relatively narrow defeat in 1932. After the 1935 election, in which Labor spectacularly trounced the CPNP 46 to 16, tensions within the CPNP reached boiling point. Accordingly, in 1936, the Country and Progressive National Party was dissolved and the Queensland Country Party was reformed. A local branch of the United Australia Party (UAP) was also formed which attracted some metropolitan voters.[5]

After the 1941 elections, however, Labor remained dominant in the 62-seat state parliament with 41 MPs compared to 14 Country and four UAP members. A subsequent attempt at a Country-UAP state fusion, the Country-National Organisation (C-NO) collapsed by October 1943. The Country Party thereafter jealously guarded its separate political identity, although the C-NO did not entirely dissolve as a political organisation for some time.[6]

By 1943, the non-Labor side of politics was at a low ebb. The timing was right for a new political organisation to emerge that could take advantage of the social and cultural upheaval which World War II had created in Queensland and offer an alternative to a Labor government. As the tide of the war began to turn in favour of Allied forces, many electors began to chafe at Labor's wartime restrictions and rationing. Furthermore, the heavy concentration of US and Australian troops in towns like Brisbane and Townsville had placed a strain on local resources and infrastructure. As elsewhere in Australia, the attention of Queensland citizens was moving towards dreams of a post-war world where they would enjoy greater freedoms, and, for many, a chance to reform and improve their community both economically and socially. The federal Labor Party under John Curtin had a vision of post-war Australia which aligned with these goals, but a significant minority of voters were concerned by Labor's plans to expand Commonwealth powers.[7] It was within this context of upheaval and wartime inconveniences that Brisbane Lord Mayor JB Chandler was motivated to form the Queensland People's Party.

Formation of the Queensland People's Party

Born in England in 1887, JB Chandler arrived in Queensland as young man in 1907. He was initially employed as a cane-cutter in Mossman before moving to Brisbane two years later. From 1913, he owned and operated a general store in the central business district, gradually expanding to sell electrical products. He opened a new store in 1923 which subsequently sold radio parts and wireless sets. Chandler's fascination with radio led him in 1930 to start the first commercial broadcasting station in Brisbane, 4BC, as well as several stations in regional towns. While government restrictions on ownership forced Beals to sell all but one of his stations in 1937, his commercial empire was prospering: by 1938 there were branches of Chandler's business in Toowoomba, Bundaberg, Townsville, Rockhampton, Sydney and Melbourne. With a strong interest in civic affairs, Chandler, representing the Citizens' Municipal Organisation, was elected lord mayor of Brisbane in 1940 and held the position until 1952.[8]

Chandler's commercial achievements gave him self-confidence in his ability to make a difference in public life, and provided him with a heightened awareness of both regional and metropolitan Queensland. It might also be speculated that his experience of childhood poverty and his brief period as a manual labourer solidified his conviction that he could represent not only white-collar workers, but all parts of the community as well.

In 1943 Chandler ran as an independent in a by-election for the state seat of Hamilton. He was quickly persuaded by colleagues to spearhead a new political party which would, in the words of Chandler supporter Mrs Annie Tipper,[9] 'work for a higher standard of public life and community service.'[10] To assist with the formation of the new organisation, Chandler tapped into a network of Brisbane businessmen, professionals and community workers, some of whom he had worked with as president of the Queensland Patriotic and Australian Comforts Fund. Prominent among the latter group of volunteers was accountant Tom Hiley, who later recalled that Chandler 'used to be always griping about the Opposition political parties of the day, and they were poor. They were aged and lazy and showed no real competence.'[11]

With Chandler elected as inaugural president, the Queensland People's Party was formed at a crowded public meeting held at Brisbane's Albert Hall on 26 October 1943. While insisting that the new party would cater for the whole community, not just sectional interests, there was an anti-Labor tone in Chandler's speech that night:

> [The QPP] must stand for true democracy. Socialism would destroy one of their most precious possessions – freedom and individualism.[12]

Chandler had been incensed by the Queensland Labor government's decision in 1942 to abolish contingent voting (a form of preferential voting) and replace it with 'first-past-the-post' on the ballot form. As he later proclaimed:

> No greater attack on the people's liberty ever had been made in the history of Queensland than the abolition of the preference vote ... designed to bolster up the sinister political machine and to prevent the free expression of the people's views at the ballot box.[13]

The underlying assumption of Chandler and his supporters was that their new party would be above petty party politics, exemplified in the QPP's idealistic slogan, borrowed from Abraham Lincoln: 'Government of the people, by the people, for the people'.[14] The road to electoral success in state politics could not be built on idealism alone, however. One Labor wag suggested that a more appropriate slogan should be based on the gladiator's address to Caesar: 'We who are about to die salute thee.'[15]

The QPP's first test: the 1944 state election

Assisted by the QPP organiser (and Chandler business associate) VF Mitchell, 31 branches of the party had been formed by February 1944. Most of these branches were located in suburban Brisbane, but there was also growth in regional areas: over the next couple of years branches would be opened in Townsville, Ingham, Mackay, Warwick, Rockhampton, Barcaldine, Gladstone, Bundaberg, Gympie, Toowoomba and numerous other districts.[16] The first test of the party's electoral appeal beyond its membership was the state election held on 15 April 1944. The QPP executive consequently prepared for this contest with a raft of policies designed to attract Queensland electors. A key policy objective was fighting perceived Commonwealth neglect of Queensland, pledging:

> To challenge all or any differential treatment of Queensland by the Commonwealth Government, so as to prevent the neglect of Queensland's interests and the abrogation thereby of the Constitution. To secure just and equitable consideration of the State's needs at all times on

> the same basis as those of the other States, as envisaged by the sponsors of Federation.[17]

Such a policy may have resonated with Queenslanders, who during World War II felt a sense of vulnerability and isolation due to their relative closeness to the Pacific war zone compared to New South Wales and Victoria. It also fed into an ingrained suspicion that the federation served the interests of the larger, more industrialised states at the expense of Queensland.[18]

The QPP's more specific policy agenda for Queensland was outlined by Chandler on 15 March 1944. Notable elements of QPP policy included:

- An emphasis on education and self-improvement. The QPP would raise the minimum school leaving age from 14 to 16; there would be greater investment in libraries; investigations would be made into the possibility of expanding university and kindergarten access; and a conservatorium of music would be considered.
- The need for government to arrange efficient transport of fruit and vegetables throughout the state to prevent waste from gluts in Brisbane.
- An emphasis on the development of secondary industries, which had lagged behind other states: the QPP proposed a new ministry for secondary industries.
- Preference to be given to returned soldiers in terms of employment and promotion.
- A firm preference for compulsory unionism: 'It was essential that they should have an orderly system for the settlement of industrial problems'.
- Improvement of living standards, such as better 'Wages, pensions and social services', along with workplace conditions: the QPP saw the need for 'luncheon rooms, adequate and clean washing and lavatory accommodation, first-aid instruction, and medical inspection of working conditions'.[19]

With such a broad range of policies, it was not surprising that the QPP attracted candidates from diverse backgrounds. They included Fitzroy candidate Harry Weir (teacher at Mount Morgan State School) and Rockhampton candidate JG O'Shannesy (chairman of a brickworks). Among the candidates for Brisbane seats were solicitor and Royal Australian Air Force officer AP Muir, soldier and businessman Major Ken Morris and textile manufacturer Bruce Pie.[20] At least three North Queensland farmers were selected to stand as QPP candidates: Gympie cane farmer NP Damm, N Fitchett of Atherton and Ernie Evans. Although by the next election he had switched allegiance to the Country Party, Evans was sufficiently impressed by the QPP's agricultural credentials to campaign as their Mackay candidate in 1944:

> I stand very definitely for decentralisation – having the factories where the raw materials are produced – benefiting the cities on the coastline.[21]

Among the QPP candidates were two women: Mrs Annie Tipper, endorsed candidate for Fortitude Valley, and Mrs Athena Deane, running for the seat of Townsville. A member of the QPP executive and involved in many women's organisations, Tipper had come to prominence for her extensive wartime volunteer work. She ran canteens for soldiers and had been a member of the committee for the Brisbane Hostel for the Services.[22] Similarly, Deane, a widowed mother of adult children, had become known for her war work, including a stint with the Voluntary Air Observers Corps. Before moving to Townsville, she had worked as a cane farmer in the Lower Burdekin district.[23] Deane had already run unsuccessfully for the federal seat of Kennedy in 1943 with support from the 'Women for Canberra' movement. An advertisement from Deane's federal campaign highlighted the growing sense that wartime service and sacrifice by women had earned them a right to a greater voice in Australian political life:

> Do you think women have played a noble part during the

> war period? Have you or yours benefited by their noble sacrifices? ... Are you prepared to give them more tangible appreciation than mere words ... Are you aware that women feel they have earned the right to representation on all governing bodies? ... Soldiers! Help women as they have helped you![24]

Neither Deane nor Tipper won their seats in the 1944 election. While undoubtedly crying crocodile tears, Queensland Labor Premier Frank Cooper astutely observed that Fortitude Valley and Townsville were 'safe Labour seats ... Can you think of anything more contemptible than putting these two good ladies up in constituencies where they will be politically murdered?'[25]

The 1944 election result for the QPP barely made a dent in Labor's grip on power, but it demonstrated that the party had 'arrived' as a force in state politics. Of the 30 QPP candidates, seven were successful. These men included Bruce Pie (Windsor), barrister Charles Gray Wanstall (Toowong), Tom Hiley (Logan), Ken Morris (Enoggera) and QPP Leader JB Chandler (Hamilton). Significantly, those listed above were either present or future office holders in the QPP organisation, and thus their elevation into state parliament helped legitimate their internal authority.[26]

Nevertheless, the election outcome also indicated that the party had a long way to go before it could claim to have state-wide popularity. The fact that the party could run only 30 candidates for the 62-seat parliament suggests that sources of funding may have been limited. Potential business supporters may have already baulked at the party's resolute support for compulsory unionism, as Pie would later complain.[27] Further, all of the QPP seats were won in the south-east corner, mostly serving constituents in the metropolitan areas, running the risk of earning the organisation the reputation of being a party for Brisbane people, run by Brisbane people.

Menzies rebuffed: the QPP and the formation of the Liberal Party

The Queensland People's Party was invited by federal UAP Leader Robert Menzies to send a delegation to an interstate conference in Canberra of non-Labor parties, to be held in October 1944. The intention of the conference was to begin the process of uniting the non-Labor side of politics under a new party with a fresh set of policies. Unlike most invitees, the QPP declined to attend. Party secretary H Taylor informed the press that:

> the executive of the Q.P.P. felt that the party should first develop unhampered by the prejudices and difficulties associated with other political organisations ... The party believes that it could best serve the peoples' interest by developing and strengthening its present organisation so that when the time came for participation in Federal politics it might be ready to take its share of responsibility.[28]

Having expended so much energy and enthusiasm in creating a new non-Labor party in Queensland, Chandler and his executive were reluctant to oversee its sudden dissolution and merger into what would become the Liberal Party of Australia. This decision would soon create tensions between Chandler and other QPP parliamentarians, who were more inclined towards supporting Menzies's Liberal merger. As Tom Hiley subsequently remembered:

> Chandler was ... still rather concerned to keep his private empire, but Wanstall and I were convinced that it [a merger with the federal Liberals] was all or nothing.[29]

While the QPP chose to be absent, two non-Labor organisations in Queensland did accept the invitation to attend Menzies's Canberra conference: the Queensland Women's Electoral League and the metropolitan-based Country-National Organisation (the remnants of the UAP-Country Party fusion of 1941-43). In a speech at the Canberra conference, Menzies used Queensland's political scene to present a convincing case as to why an Australia-wide united non-Labor party was essential:

> The Government could be defeated at the next Federal election if non-Labor parties took the right course now … [Menzies] told a conference of 80 non-Labour representatives from all States to-day. In Queensland, the Federal United Australia Party members had no United Australia organisation in their electorate. They looked to the Country National Organisation for support, yet the C-N.O. at the last State election did not run any candidates and was, therefore, not a very large organisation, with no State Parliamentary representation. Much more active … had been the new Queensland People's Party, which had some men of marked ability and energy. He regretted that the party had not felt able to be represented at the conference … 'But surely in Queensland we need something more adequate than two quite separate organisations, neither of which undertakes to cover the whole political area,' said Mr. Menzies.[30]

The QPP was also absent from the pivotal Albury conference of December 1944, which helped confirm the general principles and institutional framework of the provisional Liberal Party of Australia (LPA). Menzies was allegedly dismayed by the QPP's absence from Albury, because 'it seems in Queensland to be by far the most promising of the reservoirs from which Menzies can hope to draw that sadly needed commodity to Canberra – new blood – for his 1946 electoral team.'[31] Chandler, believing that his party embodied 'the most progressive political thought of our time', refused Menzies's proposal for the QPP to amalgamate with the Liberal Party.[32]

By way of contrast, the QPP's non-Labor competitor, the Country-National Organisation, agreed to dissolve and take the necessary steps to form a Queensland branch of the Liberal Party in early 1945. A provisional executive of the Queensland Division of the LPA was formed; former director-general of the Commonwealth Department of Civil Aviation Arthur Brownlow Corbett was appointed temporary chairman.[33] Probably feeling politically slighted by this development, the QPP entered into fresh negotiations with the federal executive of the Liberal Party, and by 22 May, Liberal executive chairman T Malcolm Ritchie declared that the Liberals would not enter state politics in Queensland after all. Corbett's provisional Liberal team was effectively sidelined.[34]

Under the agreement reached by the QPP and the federal Liberals, the QPP would retain its separate identity in state politics, an arena in which there would be no competition from the Liberal Party. For federal elections, however, the QPP would 'become the Queensland division' of the Liberals 'for all Federal purposes.'[35] As Tom Hiley explained,

> [The QPP] made an arrangement with them [the federal Liberal Party of Australia] … in terms of which we were to be the Queensland People's Party, agents for the Liberal Party of Australia in the state sphere. We were not an integrated division, we were to [have] our own separate autonomy … [and] run everything. We were to be their agents, do their work for them.[36]

With regard to candidates selected for elections to federal parliament, final approval would be made by the existing 15-member QPP executive, augmented by eight members appointed by the federal Liberals. Despite the fact that QPP subsequently organised campaigns for their candidates, successful MPs sat in Commonwealth parliament as members of the Liberal Party.[37] This turn of events between 1945 and 1946 meant that the Queensland People's Party was politically 'half-pregnant'. As a consequence, the Menzies Opposition would continue to pressure the QPP to fully merge with the Liberal Party of Australia, and for several years, the rank-and-file membership of the QPP would continue to resist the breakup of the party.

The QPP's simultaneous consolidation and decline: 1946–49

Feeling unable to effectively juggle his responsibilities as Brisbane lord mayor, businessman and leader of a political party, Chandler resigned as parliamentary leader of the QPP on 8 March 1946 but remained in parliament until 1947.[38] The new leader of the QPP was party stalwart and businessman Bruce Pie. An uncompromising idealist who vigorously supported the party platform, Pie, like Chandler, believed in industrial harmony between employers and employees. The new leader held fast to the QPP's official commitment to compulsory unionism:

> I know that unions are the greatest protection for the honest employer. I know there are employers who would get away with anything if it were not for the unions. The founders of this party are not connected with the old Tory team.[39]

This commitment to compulsory unionism was an unusual philosophy for a non-Labor party to hold. However, given that Queensland politics in the 1940s was dominated by Labor, this policy may have been partly designed to show Labor-inclined voters that the QPP was the party of employers *and* employees.

Pie also believed in 'higher wages and bonuses' for employees, combined with 'increased production to balance increased wages'.[40] Much to the consternation of the Country Party, Pie and the QPP voted with the Labor government when it legislated for a 40-hour working week beginning from 1 January 1948, replacing the previous 44-hour week. Pie stated:

> We believe the 40 hour week is a desirable and attainable social reform. We believe it should be obtained through the Arbitration Court.[41]

Furthermore, Pie was focused on the notion that the state Labor government had neglected both secondary industry and the regions. Speaking at a time when the potential for post-war northern development was a topical issue, Pie sought to fire up the passions of Townsville voters:

> He asked what had Labour ever done for the people of the North? Had they used their influence to create secondary industries? Had they made a complete survey of the industrial potential existing from Cape York to Coolangatta? The answer … was no.[42]

says—

The Queensland People's Party

is first and foremost a people's party, and above all it is a Queensland party.

ELECT A GOVERNMENT THAT WILL HELP CHECK CANBERRA'S LUST FOR POWER

- **They did it first in South Australia.**
- **Then in Western Australia**
- **And now for Queensland!**

Vote Q. P. P.

For Efficiency, Integrity, and Sincerity in Government

1947 QPP election advertisement, from *The Telegraph* (Brisbane), 30 April 1947.

While Pie was an articulate and energetic party leader, his efforts did not lead to much growth in parliamentary seats. After the state election of 3 May 1947, the QPP was still very much a minority party. In a slight improvement from 1944, the party now boasted 9 MPs, but the Country Party was ahead with 14; Labor, with 35 MPs in the new parliament, remained firmly in power.[43] As in 1944, the party had been unable to win electorates outside south-east Queensland, although businessman Gordon Chalk's victory in East Toowoomba showed that the party had garnered at least some rural support. In addition, the QPP had run a successful campaign for the central Queensland seat of Capricornia in the 1946 federal elections.[44] Still, the 1947 election result provided some substance to Labor Premier Ned Hanlon's attack on the QPP as a Brisbane outfit that wanted 'A better deal for Brisbane.'[45]

There were a number of likely reasons for the QPP's electoral stagnation. The obvious factor was the long incumbency of Labor as the state government. Furthermore, the Country Party had a clearer identity than the QPP as a rural party, hence its higher number of regional seats. Finally, the QPP itself was beginning to have an ambiguous public identity which may have confused the electorate. In 1947, for example, the party's support for compulsory unionism faced heated attack from within its own ranks. 'Compulsory unionism is socialism', new MP Gordon Chalk complained, and attempted to persuade the QPP to drop it from the platform. He was unsuccessful, but the debate indicated that the policy direction set by the early founders of the party was now being questioned by some members of the organisation.[46]

In any case, the QPP's state agenda was at times overshadowed by an increasing emphasis on the same political rhetoric as its Liberal cousins, such as railing against the perceived threat of communism and the federal Labor government's proposed bank nationalisation.[47] Pie's successor as QPP leader (1948-49) Tom Hiley later implied that the public stress on the QPP's anti-communist credentials was not, by itself, a guaranteed vote-winner:

> [Pie] used to fall too much for that, mainly prompted by [campaign director] Charlie Porter, who had a bug about it and he used to write these big speeches for him.[48]

Following the 1947 election, the QPP sought to improve its electoral fortunes by proposing an amalgamation with the Country Party. Ironically, having fought off Menzies's merger overtures in 1944-45, the QPP executive announced in 1948 that the party would be 'prepared to sink its identity and entirely merge its organisation' with the Country Party to 'achieve unity.'[49] The Country Party had a stronger representation than QPP in state parliament, and had a history of underwhelming mergers with metropolitan-based parties in the past. Unsurprisingly, Country Party President Alan J Campbell rejected the offer, stating that the 'Country Party ... was bound by its constitution not to merge into another party.'[50] Alan Hulme (QPP president 1946-49) responded by implying that the proposed amalgamation was a patriotic imperative:

> The Q.P.P. executive awaits your council's favourable consideration of our proposals, and believe it will recognise that in the face of the threat now posed by the socialist forces to the Australian way of life, personal or party considerations can no longer be placed above national considerations.[51]

With amalgamation with the state Country Party a futile cause, some within the QPP questioned whether it was worth holding out against the Liberal Party's continued pressure to join its larger and better resourced organisation. In 1948, federal Liberal President RG Casey attended the QPP's annual convention and pushed heavily for a merger. To emphasise the links between the two parties, Casey at the conference kept repeating the phrase 'We of the Liberal Party, and the Q.P.P.' He returned to Canberra disappointed. Encountering opposition from party founder JB Chandler and other long-term members, a proposal to change the name of the party to the Queensland Division of the Liberal Party was narrowly defeated.[52]

By the July 1949 convention, however, opposition to the name change had diminished. After a lengthy debate, Helen Franklin of the Toowong branch moved for a secret ballot, and as of 8 July 1949, the Queensland People's Party had become the Liberal Party (Queensland Division).[53]

QPP resistance to becoming part of the Liberal family finally broke down because of the changing nature of the party membership. From a small, core membership in 1943-44 focused on Brisbane, by mid-1949 the Queensland People's Party had grown to 20,764 members across Queensland. By then, the organisation had 92 country branches, although sadly for the QPP, this regional growth did not bring about a substantial rise in regional state MPs. The newer members had not experienced the shared passions, circumstances and excitements of the party's formation, and thus they were less likely to be reluctant to dissolve the party in favour of a nationally-based Liberal Party that shared their basic values.[54]

Reflections on the Queensland People's Party era

With the benefit of hindsight, it might be considered that the Queensland People's Party did not achieve tangible political outcomes. Lacking the numbers to form government or even hold the balance of power in state parliament, it was unable to deliver on its political promises. The 1950s and 1960s saw some of the state reforms championed by the now defunct QPP realised, such as expansion of university opportunities, a rise in the school leaving age (from 14 to 15) and better infrastructure for the regions (notably the completion of the Bruce Highway from Brisbane to Cairns).[55] However, credit for these overdue initiatives went to the Frank Nicklin-led Country Party-Liberal Coalition government of 1957-68, a period in which the QPP's successor, the Liberal Party, was the junior partner. It is unclear whether QPP's policies in the 1940s provided any inspiration to Nicklin and his cabinet.

The QPP nonetheless provided a political training ground for ambitious men and women, often in their thirties and forties, seeking to make a contribution to post-war Queensland. Some had served in the armed services in World War II, and many others had volunteered their time as part of the war effort. If the QPP had not been created by Chandler during a time of low morale for non-Labor politics, a number of key Queensland Liberal figures may not have emerged. Future state Liberal ministers who began their political careers as Queensland People's Party MPs or organisers included Gordon Chalk, Tom Hiley, Charles Porter and Ken Morris. Commonwealth Liberal ministers who entered political life with a QPP background included Alan Hulme (minister for supply 1958–61; post-master general 1963-72) and Senator Annabelle Rankin, minister for housing (1966-71).[56]

Rankin's victory in the 1946 federal election was the QPP's only successful attempt to place a woman in parliament. The party paid lip-service to the idea that wartime sacrifice had earned women a place in politics, but in the post-war period it would appear that the QPP heavy-weights were not entirely comfortable with this idea. For example, in 1946, a motion was passed at the QPP convention approving 'the principle of equal status for men and women in employment' and making this, along with 'equal pay for equal work for males and females', a part of the QPP constitution.[57] At the 1947 convention, the mover of the original motion, Mrs R Maloney, found that the motion had been left out of the 1946 convention minutes, and the motion had to be moved (successfully) again.[58]

The hard truth was that like all political parties of the time, the QPP was a very masculine-oriented party. While QPP candidate for Bulimba Mrs Hilda Brotherton claimed that wives and mothers could contribute much to politics because, unlike male breadwinners, they were more aware of 'the more personal and intimate life of the community',[59] the QPP was more focused on the future of returned male soldiers than women's issues.

More positively, ordinary membership of the QPP provided many community-minded people with an outlet to discuss local, state and international matters of the day. Annual conventions brought delegates from across Queensland, allowing them to feel part of the formal political process by proposing and voting on resolutions such as advocating 'the completion of a bitumen surfaced all-weather coastal road from Brisbane to Cairns ... in the interests of Queensland's expanding tourist industry.'[60] Party organisers also arranged social activities such as a Queensland young people's club, women's luncheons and get-togethers, and the chance to hear guest speakers.[61] In 1949, for example, the Townsville branch of the QPP hosted a visit by British Conservative MP, Anthony Nutting, who gave a public address on the importance of the British Commonwealth in the post-war world.[62]

The Queensland People's Party, for the most part, aligned with the aims and purposes of the Liberal Party of Australia, which in 1949 won the federal election and stayed in office until 1972. It was only a matter of time before the QPP amalgamated with the larger party. The fact that it took several years suggests that Chandler and many party members had a conviction—perhaps somewhat unrealistic—that Queensland political issues could best be resolved by the grassroots efforts of a Queensland-based party.

---

1 'Chandler Heads New Political Party', *Morning Bulletin*, 27 October 1943, p. 3.

2 See Megarrity, *Robert Philp and the Politics of Development*, p. 19; Hughes and Graham, *A Handbook of Australian Government and Politics*, pp. 503-19. The Queensland Legislative Council was abolished in 1922, and during its existence, members of the Legislative Council were appointees rather than elected representatives.

3 Hughes and Graham, *A Handbook of Australian Government and Politics*, pp. 520-2; Costar, 'Arthur Moore', pp. 184-5.

4 McCulloch, '100 Years of Women's Suffrage in Queensland 1905-2005', pp. 63-4.

5 'Unity First Need', *Courier-Mail*, 10 June 1935, p. 11; Hughes and Graham, *A Handbook of Australian Government and Politics*, pp. 522-3; Costar, 'Arthur Moore', pp. 205-6.

6 Hughes and Graham, *A Handbook of Australian Government and Politics*, pp. 524-5; 'State Opposition Fusion Ended', *Townsville Daily Bulletin*, 25 October 1943, p. 1.

[7] Bongiorno, *Dreamers and Schemers*, pp. 202–3; Bolton, *The Oxford History of Australia Volume 5*, pp. 10–26; Bolton, *A Thousand Miles Away*, p. 336.

[8] See Laverty, 'Chandler'; 'Chandler Managers' Dinner', *Courier-Mail*, 30 August 1938, p. 11; 'Mr. JB Chandler: A Busy Man', *Townsville Daily Bulletin*, 28 October 1939, p. 7; 'New President: Chamber of Commerce', *Queensland Country Life*, 6 October 1938, p. 2.

[9] Mrs Annie Evangeline Tipper née Huxley frequently appears in 1940s newspapers as 'Mrs. HC Tipper' following the then standard practice of wives being referred to by their husband's names. Sometimes she is referred to as 'Mrs. AE Tipper'.

[10] 'Lincoln's Slogan for People's Party', *Courier-Mail*, 27 October 1943, p. 3.

[11] Hiley Transcript.

[12] 'Chandler Heads New Political Party', *Morning Bulletin*, 27 October 1943, p. 3.

[13] 'Honesty, Integrity, and Justice: Queensland People's Party', *Queensland Times* (Ipswich), 16 March 1944, p. 3. Preferential voting was reintroduced in Queensland through the *Elections Act Amendment Act 1962*. See also Hughes and Graham, *A Handbook of Australian Government and Politics*, pp. 501, 503.

[14] 'Lincoln's Slogan for People's Party', *Courier-Mail*, 27 October 1943, p. 3.

[15] 'Truth to Tell', *Truth* (Brisbane), 26 December 1943, p. 14.

[16] 'Q.P.P. Extending to Country', *Courier-Mail*, 13 December 1943, p. 3; 'Q.P.P. Convention Next Month', *Morning Bulletin* (Rockhampton), 26 October 1946, p. 1.

[17] 'Queensland People's Party: Our Objective', Queensland People's Party pamphlet dated 25 November 1943, held at John Oxley Library.

[18] See Megarrity, *Northern Dreams*, pp. 57–9.

[19] 'Honesty, Integrity, and Justice: Queensland People's Party', *Queensland Times* (Ipswich), 16 March 1944, p. 3.

[20] '2 More Q.P.P. in City Seats', *Courier-Mail*, 1 March 1944, p. 3; Williams, 'Pie'; Stevenson, 'Morris'.

[21] Ernie Evans, quoted in 'Mackay Election', *Daily Mercury* (Mackay), 1 April 1944, p. 44. Evans was later to become a minister in the Nicklin Coalition Government.

[22] 'Mrs. Tipper for Valley', *Telegraph* (Brisbane), 29 February 1944, p. 2; 'The Late Mrs. HC Tipper', *Brisbane Telegraph*, 28 December 1949, p. 6.

[23] 'The Federal Elections: Mrs. Athena Deane', *Cloncurry Advocate*, 6 August 1943, p. 6; '147 Candidates for State Polls: 6 Unopposed', *Courier-Mail*, 4 March 1944, p. 3.

[24] '"Women for Canberra" Movement', *Longreach Leader*, 7 August 1943, p. 8.

[25] 'Premier Claims Q.P.P. Unfair', *Courier-Mail*, 8 April 1944, p. 4.

[26] Hughes and Graham, *Voting for the Queensland Legislative Assembly*, pp. 205-10.

[27] 'Q.P.P. Leader Says: I Will Not Break Faith with the People', *Morning Bulletin* (Rockhampton), 22 September 1947, p. 5.

[28] 'Unity Conference: Q.P. Party Attitude', *Cairns Post*, 9 October 1944, p. 2.

29 TA Hiley, Sir Thomas Hiley Transcript, Box 5321, OM Acc 974, 1974, John Oxley Library.

[30] 'Menzies See Federal Win by Non-Labour', *Courier-Mail*, 14 October 1944, p. 3.

[31] 'Menzies Gets a Break', *Sunday Mail*, 17 December 1944, p. 5.

[32] 'Chandler Won't be a Liberal', *Smith's Weekly*, 3 February 1945, p. 1.

[33] Ibid.; 'Split Threat in Q'land Non-Labour', *Courier-Mail*, 4 April 1945, p. 3.

[34] 'Liberals Agree on QLD for QPP', *Telegraph* (Brisbane), 22 May 1945, p. 3.

[35] 'Q.P.P. Control Liberal Pact', *Courier-Mail*, 25 May 1945, p. 3.

[36] Hiley Transcript.

[37] In the 1946 federal elections, there were four QPP/Liberal elected (two in both the House of Representatives and the Senate). Hughes and Graham, *Australian Government and Politics 1890–1964*, p. 377; 'Q.P.P. Control Liberal Pact', *Courier-Mail*, 25 May 1945, p. 3.

[38] Laverty, 'Chandler'; 'Chandler Reigns as Parlt. Leader', *Courier-Mail*, 9 March 1946, p. 1.

[39] 'Q.P.P. Leader Says: I Will Not Break Faith with the People', *Morning Bulletin* (Rockhampton), 22 September 1947, p. 5.

[40] 'Large Crowd Attends to Hear Mr. Bruce Pie', *Townsville Daily Bulletin*, 17 July 1946, p. 3.

[41] Lack et al., *Three Decades of Queensland Political History*, p. 315.

[42] 'Large Crowd Attends to Hear Mr. Bruce Pie', *Townsville Daily Bulletin*, 17 July 1946, p. 3.

[43] Hughes and Graham, *Australian Government and Politics 1890-1964*, pp. 526–7.

[44] Ibid., p. 377.

[45] 'Big Money Brought New Pie', *Courier-Mail*, 10 April 1947, p. 3.

[46] 'Q.P.P. Leader Says: I Will Not Break Faith with the People', *Morning Bulletin* (Rockhampton), 22 September 1947, p. 5.

[47] 'QPP-Liberal Party: Bundaberg Rally', *Morning Bulletin*, 14 February 1946, p. 2; 'Q.P.P. Leader Says: I Will Not Break Faith with the People', *Morning Bulletin* (Rockhampton), 22 September 1947, p. 5.

[48] Hiley Transcript.

[49] 'Queensland Party Wants Merger', *Newcastle Morning Herald*, 20 November 1948, p. 3.

[50] Ibid., p. 3.

[51] 'Points on Unity by Q.P.P.', *Courier-Mail*, 1 December 1948, p. 5.

[52] 'Party Name Move Again', *Brisbane Telegraph*, 8 October 1948, p. 8.

[53] 'Q.P.P. Changes to "Liberal Party"', *Courier-Mail*, 9 July 1949, p. 3; 'Q.P.P.'s Name Died Hard', *Brisbane Telegraph*, 9 July1949, p. 11.

[54] 'Q.P.P.'s Name Died Hard', *Brisbane Telegraph*, 9 July1949, p. 11.

[55] Fitzgerald, Megarrity & Symons, *Made in Queensland*, pp. 154, 164.

[56] Rankin was the first woman to represent Queensland in the Commonwealth parliament. See Coltheart, 'Rankin'.

[57] 'Mr. Alan Hulme New Q.P.P. Head', *Sunday Mail*, 10 November 1946, p. 3.

[58] 'Q.P.P. Leaders' Fighting Speeches at Annual Convention', *Morning Bulletin*, 19 September 1947, p. 7.

[59] 'Candidate Backs Woman Members', *Telegraph* (Brisbane), 28 January 1947, p. 5.

[60] 'Q.P.P. Leader Says: I Will Not Break Faith with the People', *Morning Bulletin* (Rockhampton), 22 September 1947, p. 5.

[61] 'Fight Against Socialisation', *Courier-Mail*, 1 November 1947, p. 8; 'Home Help "Too Little, Too Costly"', *Courier-Mail*, 2 February 1946, p. 4; 'Q.P.P. Leaders' Fighting Speeches at Annual Convention', *Morning Bulletin*, 19 September 1947, p. 7.

[62] 'Empire Unity Will Secure Democracy', *Townsville Daily Bulletin*, 23 February 1949, p. 2.

7

South Australia's Liberal and Country League in the Formation of the Liberal Party of Australia

Baden Teague[1]

When Robert Menzies called together the Unity Conference in Canberra in October 1944, there were representatives from all the Australian states. The most cohesive group and the one most ready for the new Liberal vision was the delegation from South Australia. For more than thirty years they had learnt and re-learnt that political *union* of liberal, conservative and rural interests were necessary for electoral success. They were all members of the one party, the Liberal and Country League (the LCL), and it was not long before their party became the South Australian Division of the new Liberal Party of Australia (LPA).[2]

Seven South Australian delegates attended the foundational Canberra conference and all of them were the established leaders of the LCL. Thomas Playford MP had been the state premier already for six years and he would go on to be premier for the next twenty. Douglas Gordon had been the LCL president since 1943 and Hon Alexander Melrose MLC, sitting next to him, served as the LCL president for the seven years prior to that. Mrs Doris Rogers was the active president of the LCL's women's council[3] and Mr AS Dunk was the LCL's experienced general secretary since 1935 and he would continue until 1952.

There were two more SA delegates and both were already Menzies's personal friends and strongest supporters. Senator George McLeay had already served as a Menzies minister and in 1944 he was the United Australia Party leader in the Senate. Finally, but foremost, was the Honourable Philip McBride, a minister under Menzies and the leader of the SA Liberal Senate team at the recent 1943 federal election. McBride, a wealthy pastoralist, had the warmest friendship with Robert Menzies and, from the outset, he was the most active South Australian at the foundation of the LPA's federal executive and federal council. Later, McBride became Menzies's minister for defence in the 1950s and then the federal president of the LPA in the 1960s.

The seven South Australian delegates were a single cohesive team. In contrast, the other seventy delegates comprised seventeen groups across a wide spectrum of political backgrounds. Also, the seven South Australian delegates came with a positive readiness to support Menzies's Canberra conference. The lacklustre response of others, namely the Queenslanders, turned out to be rather underwhelming.

Of course, as is well known, Menzies's experience in the politics of the 1930s and 1940s led him to know how very essential it was for any nationally-unified Liberal Party of Australia to build and maintain a strong coalition with the Country Party. Even at the lowest point politically, at the 1943 federal election, the Country Party had won nine seats while the United Australia Party had won fourteen seats.[4] Curtin's Labor had won 49 seats. In his planning for the Unity Conference of October 1944, Menzies in his wildest hopes still wondered if the Coalition partners might yet form *one* united party. However, the Country Party refused to countenance any kind of amalgamation. Thus, as the journalist, Edgar Holt, put it: 'The Country Party of one-eyed horse traders did not come to the fray but remained in their own stables'.[5] Menzies in 1944 was realistic enough to know that a Country Party merger was a bridge-too-far, but he continued to emphasise to all his Liberal colleagues that the health of the Liberal and Country Coalition would always be of great importance.

It was in this respect that the South Australians had already achieved a unity which was then unique in Australia and this would not be possible to attain in the emerging LPA. After all, the Country Party had been permanently disbanded in South Australia twelve years earlier when the Liberal and Country League had been formed in 1932.

It is useful now to recall how this Liberal and Country amalgamation in South Australia had happened in 1931 and 1932. Actually, it was even earlier, in 1927, that this breakthrough had begun. The Liberal Federation (LF) led by Richard Layton Butler (SA premier, 1927-30 and 1933-38), carefully pursued the goal to win over the CP members, urging them to join the much larger Liberal group. Malcolm McIntosh MP (Albert, 1921-59) came over in 1927 and Butler appointed him one of his six ministers. In 1928, Frederick McMillan (Albert, 1921-33) joined the LF; as did Edward Coles (Flinders, 1927-30) and Reginald Carter (Burra Burra, 1927-30) who became 'oncers' but Liberals nevertheless. All these parliamentarians shared the objective not only to gain the best outcomes for their rural electorates, but also to ensure that they won elections against Labor by being disciplined and united.

The onset of the Great Depression from October 1929 led to massive unemployment, much misery and the loss of government by the Liberals. The LF's opponent in the 1930 SA election was Labor's Lionel Hill. His disingenuous, campaign slogan was 'Work for the Workless, Land for the Landless, and Equitable Taxation for All.' In contrast, the Liberal premier was truthful in warning the public that, with the drought and the depression continuing, much suffering lay ahead.[6] Unsurprisingly, Labor romped to victory in 1930 but it was only a year or two later, when Labor's incompetence had been clearly revealed, that the public realised that Labor had duped them. The SA public put the Liberals back into government as soon as they could and kept the Liberals in office for the next thirty years, for all eleven state elections from 1933 right up until 1962-65. It is true that many independents, mostly country farmers, won seats in 1933 but, after succeeding Butler as premier in 1938,

Playford successfully wooed these independents (and the voters who had elected them) to support his own increasingly-achieving Liberal and Country League. It needs to be understood that Playford's unifying premiership had been fundamentally built on the foundations for unity that had already been significantly achieved in 1931 and 1932.

This early unity in South Australia had flowed from developments in federal politics through the SA Liberal response to the Scullin-Lyons crisis of 1931. Two senior Labor ministers, Joe Lyons MP and James Fenton MP, resigned in January from the Scullin Government to protest Labor's wrong-headed approach to the Depression. Two months later, six Labor members, led by Lyons and Fenton, crossed the floor to support the Opposition's motion of no-confidence in the Scullin Government. Two of these six were South Australians, Moses Gabb MP (Angas, 1919-34) and John Price MP (Boothby, 1928-41). The motion narrowly failed, but it left Scullin mortally wounded, and he staggered on inconsequentially until Labor's defeat at the December 1931 federal election. What is significant here is the way the SA Liberal Federation positively responded to this crisis.

Charles Hawker MP (Wakefield, 1929-38) and Walter Duncan MLC successively served as presidents of the Liberal Federation, 1927-30 and 1930-32 respectively. Hawker grasped the importance of unity for the coming election, put together a brilliant plan, and then he persuaded Duncan to make his plan work. Hawker's friend was Dr Archie Grenfell Price, master of St Mark's College and a University of Adelaide lecturer in geography. Price was not a member of any political party and thus he was ideally placed to establish a united approach among Liberal-leaning groups to contest the coming crucial election. The plan was to maximise the seats to be won by supporters of the newly emerging United Australia Party.

This UAP was the merger that year (1931) of Lyons's group of six with the Latham-led Nationalist Party. Grenfell Price was the best person to convene the unity ticket because, not least, he had in March that year published his own booklet to solve the economic crisis of the Depression, and 30,000 copies had sold in just a few weeks. The public perceived Grenfell Price as an expert with the best economic solution to the misery of the Depression.

With Hawker's and Duncan's full support, Grenfell Price convened a meeting of all the leaders of the Liberal-leaning organisations in SA. At its first meeting it was unanimously decided to call this group 'the emergency committee' and to adopt the objective to win federal seats in support of the election of a Lyons-Latham United Australia Party Government which would pursue an orthodox economic policy consistent with the Premiers' Plan and with the published views of both Lyons and Latham. (At this time Menzies was the attorney-general of Victoria but he already had the political clout to be the principal and successful advocate that persuaded Lyons rather than Latham to lead this new UAP.) Also, at this first meeting of the emergency committee, Grenfell Price was confirmed as the committee's chairman and as the campaign director for the upcoming election.

Grenfell Price, with advice, negotiated a full slate of candidates for the seven SA seats in the House of Representatives and for the three SA Senate seats. These ten candidates included four sitting Liberal members (Hawker in Wakefield was one of them), two former Labor sitting members (Gabb and Price who had crossed the floor) and four brand new candidates (including McBride, Stacey and Badman[7] who were successful).[8] The emergency committee unanimously endorsed Price's lists of candidates, and Grenfell Price went on superbly to manage the election campaign. This crucial federal election was held on 19 December 1931 and it became an immense triumph for the emergency committee's team. Nine of the ten federal seats were won and all nine of these members of parliament supported the UAP government, with Lyons going on to be prime minister from January 1932 until his death in April 1939, and Menzies becoming prime minister after that. Federally, yes, this was a triumph, but equally significant was the immediate repercussion for state politics. This triumph was like an electric shock that energised all of the politics of South Australia.

OUR NATIONAL FLAG
OUR NATIONAL LEADER
OUR NATIONAL HOPE

THE HON. J. A. LYONS

Emergency committee advertisement authorised by Grenfell Price. From *The Advertiser* (Adelaide) 18 December 1931.

The success of the emergency committee led directly to the unification of SA's Liberal Party and Country Party to form 'The Liberal and Country League' which flourished from 1932 for the next forty years. These state-based negotiations for unity were conducted swiftly and successfully by Richard Butler (leader) and Walter Duncan (president) for the Liberal Federation, and by Archie Cameron (leader) and Oliver Badman (president) for the Country Party, and by Keith Wilson (president) for the Liberal Reform League. Cameron stopped being a thorn in the LF's side and he was assured of soon becoming the federal member for Barker.[9] Badman was already a UAP senator but he was allowed by the rules that were negotiated when the LCL was founded, to choose to sit in the Country Party room in Canberra, and he did.[10] Wilson transitioned from being a separated liberal reformer to being a progressive insider who was given the crucial task of chairman of the organising committee in the new party, and very soon he was elected as a senator for the LCL.[11] Butler's reward for the unity achieved was to become SA premier again, 1933-38. Duncan was promoted to serve as president of the Legislative Council, 1944-62. Meanwhile, the successful visionary, Charles Hawker, continued in the House of Representatives held in the highest esteem and with the highest integrity by his friend, Robert Menzies,[12] until Hawker's untimely death in the Kyeema airplane disaster on 25 October 1938. Butler was knighted in 1939, Duncan also in 1939, McBride in 1953, and Wilson in 1959.

And so it was that, when Menzies initiated the Canberra Unity Conference of October 1944, the South Australians were already united. The political union of liberal, conservative and rural interests had already helped deliver them electoral success at the state level. They had established a strong, unified and forward-looking party, ready to become an exemplar of the emerging nation-wide Liberal Party of Australia. For example, the LCL had already adopted the strong principle of raising the party's finances partly through grassroots membership subscriptions and partly through donations which strictly had to have no strings attached. Menzies's August invitation to the Unity Conference was happily received and the response was immediately positive. The original group of seven SA delegates were essentially the leadership group of the LCL. Ten months later when all the implementation steps had been completed, the inaugural federal council of the LPA met in Sydney in August 1945 and the SA delegates were the same group of leaders: that is, except for Mrs Rogers's absence seriously ill, and with the addition of Archie Cameron MP[13] and Dudley Turner, the LCL treasurer and a foundation member of the LPA's finance committee.[14] Dudley Turner was a close friend of Grenfell Price and was the chairman of the finance committee of Price's St Mark's College. He had already served as the very successful treasurer of the emergency committee in 1931[15] and he became the treasurer of the LCL.

The South Australians who attended the Unity Conference in 1944 greatly admired Robert Gordon Menzies, his skill as a speaker, his depth intellectually to understand the battle of ideas, his humour and patience in chairing a meeting, and, above all, his inspiring vision to see established a truly national and united Liberal Party. While the premier, Tom Playford, recognised these skills in Menzies, he always remained quiet about his colleague's qualities because he knew that he would need to negotiate with him, particularly about federal grants for South Australia's advantage. The South Australians were not alone, both at the Canberra Conference and at the subsequent ratification Conference in Albury, to regard Menzies as the right person at the right place at the right time to lead the formation of the Liberal Party of Australia.

Not many of the South Australians had the capacity to explore the 1940s' philosophers of freedom, Hayek, Popper and Rand,[16] nor did many articulate the growing economic orthodoxy of Keynes.[17] If anyone did, it may well have been John Duncan-Hughes[18] as well as the reforming lawyer then politician, Keith Wilson. The third scholar-politician, Archie Grenfell Price,[19] was the one best placed to articulate the ideas of freedom to the interested parliamentarians. In this context, the South Australians were inspired by the depth of Menzies's own understanding of liberal and democratic principles, such as the views Menzies most clearly had set out in his broadcast of May 1942, *The Forgotten People*.[20]

By late 1944, Menzies had translated his political and economic philosophy into his draft for the ten objectives of the Liberal Party of Australia. He presented his draft to the Canberra Unity Conference which warmly accepted it as the new Liberal Party's basic creed. The South Australian delegates warmly endorsed it. In summary, the party's ten objectives were as follows:[21]

- Loyalty to the British Crown and to the Commonwealth of Australia.
- The security of all Australians,
- Defence, a universal duty, and patriotism fostered,
- An intelligent, free and liberal Australian democracy, with parliament, the law, and freedom of speech, religion and association, where citizens are free to choose their own way of life, where the people are protected from exploitation, and where individual initiative and enterprise are encouraged,
- Generous repatriation benefits,
- Industries and markets promoted, country life improved, and where decentralisation is encouraged,
- Full employment with good wages,
- Cooperation and common interest for employers and employees, with a steady rise in living standards,
- Social provision for superannuation, sick benefits, widow benefits, and unemployment relief that is made on a contributory basis, and medical services for all,
- Education for children and adults expanded, with true citizenship,
- Family life recognised as fundamental to everyone's wellbeing, where every family lives in a comfortable home at a reasonable cost, and with adequate community services.

The South Australian delegates not only welcomed the party's objectives, they also helped to define the party's organisational structure. There would be a federal council, executive and secretariat, but the state divisions (such as the LCL in SA) would continue to have 'substantial autonomy' regarding state matters, finance, preselection and campaigning. One aspect of genius was Menzies's insistence that the LPA would be financially autonomous.

The new party was established during the first months of 1945. In all states the public responded so very positively that by August at the inaugural LPA federal council meeting there were, Australia-wide, about one hundred thousand subscribed members of the party. The membership numbers were as follows:[22]

NSW Division	230 branches	33,000 members
VIC Division	130 branches	25,000 members
QLD Division	71 branches	5,200 members
SA Division	245 branches	25,200 members
WA Division	38 branches	4,000 members
TAS Division	57 branches	5,000 members
Total	771 branches	97,509 members

At this time there were seven million people in Australia and 4.5 million voters. South Australia at this early stage had the most LPA branches and a membership second only to New South Wales, in part because the SA Division was already so strongly established, and in part because the whole idea of this new Liberal Party of Australia was so well received by the South Australian people.

The three most significant federal parliamentarians from South Australia during the 1940s, Philip McBride, George McLeay and Archie Cameron, all supported Menzies in the formation of the new nation-wide Liberal Party. It is useful to expand about their positive relationships with Robert Menzies and about their willing efforts to see the new party successfully established.

Philip McBride was elected to the House of Representatives in 1931, three years before Menzies transferred in 1934 from being the attorney-general of Victoria to being the attorney-general of Australia and deputy leader (to Prime Minister Lyons) of the UAP. McBride was two and a half years older than Menzies. In 1940, Menzies appointed McBride minister for the army and for repatriation and a little later moved him to be minister for munitions and for supply and development. The World War meant Australia was engaged in a priority military effort and McBride was in the thick of this effort every day. From 1937-44 McBride was a senator[23] but being in the 'other House' did not diminish his continuing close teamwork with Menzies, both in and out of government. McBride was chosen by the SA LCL to lead the Senate team of candidates into the 1943 federal election. This election was a disaster for the UAP and every Liberal was shocked that McBride, their 'best candidate,' failed to win. This zero-outcome for the UAP Senate teams happened in all the other five states as well, under what was effectively a winner-takes-all system.[24] Robert Menzies was so deeply shocked that he wrote this warm-hearted letter to his friend:[25]

> Senator the Honourable P A McBride   30 August, 1943
>
> My dear Phil,
>
> At every election some losses are almost good and some seem unbearable.
>
> The greatest loss that our side of politics has suffered in this election arises from your defeat in South Australia.
>
> If high ability and strong character and a real instinct for truth and fair dealing were the qualifications for political success you would have been returned easily at the head of the poll.
>
> I should hate you to go out of politics and not know that one man at any rate, who is in some position to judge, values these superb qualities of yours and your great services to Australia.
>
> Yours sincerely,   Robert Menzies

As it turned out, McBride was re-elected to the House of Representatives at the next election in September 1946. He used his time-out for the two and a quarter intervening years to work wholeheartedly to establish Menzies's Liberal Party of Australia. During these same years, besides managing his pastoral interests, he also found time to be chairman of Elders and a director of the Bank of Adelaide, the Wool Board, Adelaide Steamship and Wallaroo Fertilizers. Travelling anywhere in Australia at his own expense was no trouble for him. When McBride retired from parliament in 1958, he went on to be elected the first South Australian to serve as the LPA's federal president.[26]

George McLeay was born into a farming family on Yorke Peninsula and he became a self-employed accountant then merchant, as did his brother, John, who also became a federal parliamentarian. George joined the Liberal Party aged 30 and for the next dozen years was very active in the senior offices of the party before being elected to the Senate in 1934. George McLeay was exactly the same age as Robert Menzies and they brought complementary skills to the teamwork of government. Menzies knew the law and politics, while McLeay knew the world of commerce and politics. They had the same values. They became the two ex officio parliamentarians who led the Liberal Party of Australia from the very start. Back in 1938, Lyons as prime minister had appointed McLeay vice president of the executive council, but Menzies promoted him to be minister for commerce and leader of the government in the Senate. Menzies again promoted him to be minister for trade and customs and then postmaster-general, keeping him as Senate leader both in government and in Opposition. Menzies and McLeay were a professional partnership, they trusted each other and they became firm friends.

In the mid 1940s they together led in the building of the nationwide Liberal Party of Australia. After the great Liberal victory in 1949, McLeay served as minister for shipping, fuel and transport until he died in office in 1955. George's brother, Sir John McLeay, became speaker after Archie Cameron died in office in 1956.

Archie Cameron was the third significant federal parliamentarian in the 1940s and 1950s from South Australia. He was a fiery Scottish Australian from the bush, a farmer and battler, who plainly spoke the truth as he saw it. He was, within a few weeks, the same age as Menzies and McLeay but it was Archie who had served at

Gallipoli and in the trenches of the Western Front. He served as a soldier alongside his best friend, Tom Playford, and they remained closer than brothers until the end of their lives. Both Archie and Tom were tall, strong men, both were teetotal and non-smokers who had rescued their fellow diggers from the whores of Cairo. Playford was saturated with his own family's Baptist culture while Cameron became with the fullest enthusiasm an adult convert to the Catholic Church. Such a difference was of no consequence to Cameron and Playford; rather, they were united by their shared experiences and by both of them *not* being part of the establishment. They both despised 'entitlement'. They were simply glad to be alive and to have the chance to serve the public in parliament all their days. The mark of their service was their unimpeachable integrity.[27]

In September 1939, for just one year, Archie Cameron (SA) became the leader of the federal Country Party, displacing the failed Page (NSW), outvoting the ambitious McEwen (VIC), and being a year or two ahead of the gregarious Fadden (QLD). Thus, from March 1940, Cameron became de facto deputy prime minister to Menzies and a member of the Advisory War Council, as well as minister for commerce and minister for the Navy. Cameron worked well with Menzies; in fact, so well that, when tensions soon arose for Cameron within the Country Party,[28] he quit them forever to be loyal to Menzies during the final years of the UAP and then from the beginning of the Liberal Party of Australia. Cameron was the *only* non-Labor South Australian in the House of Representatives to win his seat in the disastrous election of 1943. Thus, he served continuously as the member for Barker for 22 years, from 1934 until his death in 1956. Menzies, after the great Liberal victory of 1949, arranged for Cameron to be speaker. Cameron famously served well in this elevated office. Menzies left him out of cabinet to avoid difficulties arising in the Coalition from having the ex-Country-Party Cameron serving in cabinet with his old rivals from the Country Party, Page, McEwen and Fadden.[29]

There were two important political developments, one in April 1943 and the other in August 1944, where in parliament the strong alliance between Menzies and these three South Australian leaders, McBride, McLeay and Cameron, was of crucial significance. The first was Menzies's formation of the National Service Group, and the second was Menzies's huge opportunity to oppose and defeat Labor's socialist referendum which attempted to gain 'Fourteen New Government Powers' at the expense of the states and of the people of Australia.

Menzies formed the National Service Group together with 16 of his UAP colleagues including McBride, McLeay, Cameron and Wilson.[30] In fact, this group included all ten of the South Australian LCL/UAP members and senators except for the one LCL/CP member from SA, Badman, who stayed apart.[31] The group emerged quite suddenly, just four months before the August 1943 election. It was the group's wake-up call to the then UAP leader, the old survivor, Billy Hughes MP. Hughes had 'filled the gap' after Menzies had been deposed in 1941, but for two years he had stood idly by while the UAP as a party had deteriorated until it no longer had any credibility. The UAP was about to be overwhelmed by the Curtin Labor landslide. The spur to the formation of the National Service Group was Curtin's inadequate reform of Australia's defence capability. It was the middle of the World War and the Army of the USA led by General MacArthur was defending Australia from the Japanese aggression, having driven the enemy back from the Coral Sea and on from New Guinea northwards and westwards through South-East Asia. MacArthur had criticised Curtin because American conscripts were dying in Asia but Australian conscripts were not allowed by Australian law to be deployed there.

Curtin was too cautious. He did not want to offend his Labor colleagues who were slow to allow wider deployments. Hughes had already declared himself and the UAP as supporting the prime minister's inadequate position. The 17 MPs in the National Service Group threw down the gauntlet to Curtin but also to Hughes. Menzies (from the backbench) and the group argued that Australia was in a World War and that the Australian troops should be able to be deployed *anywhere in the world* that they were required in order to win the war. However, Curtin with Hughes's support had the numbers. Clearly, the National Service Group was also a ginger group rallying a new political approach, more effective than Hughes would ever be. After Hughes's election loss in August 1943, Menzies was elected the leader of the Opposition with the full support of all the members of the National Service Group who had survived.[32] This step, his becoming the leader of the Opposition, was the crucial step for Menzies to propel the formation, one year later, of the entirely new party, the Liberal Party of Australia.

The enormous failure of Labor's 'Fourteen Powers' referendum on 19 August 1944 followed Menzies's successful leadership of the 'Vote No' campaign. This referendum result became the political launching pad that propelled Menzies to establish the new party. All the principles and policies and processes had been prepared by then. The referendum result gave Menzies the political authority to act. It was the South Australian leaders, his loyal friends, McBride, McLeay, Cameron and Wilson, who urged him to grab this opportunity with both hands and to run with it. Before August was over, Menzies had written all his letters, inviting all the Liberal-inclined leaders from all the states to come to the Unity Conference in Canberra in mid-October. Menzies's letter of invitation summed up the politics exactly:

> The Referendum campaign showed clearly that a great body of public opinion in this country is liberal and progressive, but distrusts and resists excessive government control of and interference in the productive and business activities of citizens, and is not prepared to accept socialism as the pathway to human happiness. Events have shown that this opinion is not confined to existing political parties or organisations, but is represented by many new bodies which are dissatisfied with existing

> parties, but are in no sense supporters of the present Government's activities, or inactivities. ... [So that] a nation-wide movement with a liberal policy and approach and an effective popular organisation may be discussed without reservations from any point of view, I propose, as Leader of the Opposition, to invite organisations in [each] State to send representatives to a conference ... to examine the position ... and to seek earnestly for a common basis ... and, if possible, to begin a new and comprehensive movement.[33]

Menzies had already published his own 'liberal democratic philosophy' in a radio broadcast that he gave a few days before his colleagues elected him leader of the Opposition. He totally rejected socialism. He advocated new and fair principles for industry and commerce. His objective was full employment with good wages. He wanted government to be compassionate and supportive of Australians in difficult circumstances. Of course, he wanted security through strong defence in which everyone contributed. He was articulate about parliamentary democracy and the rule of law. His vision was even more inspiring when he spoke about human freedom and the capacity of every individual to improve their skill and be rewarded for effort. He said:

> The essential driving force in human progress is to be found in the natural instinct to look for a reward for enterprise or skill or endurance. ... In a successful and happy community, it is the individual who matters; that you cannot make a powerful State out of weak men; and you cannot enjoy independence as a nation unless you have encouraged independence among your citizens. ... Democracy lies in its elevation of the ordinary man, and its recognition of the fact that there are amazing possibilities in every boy and girl.[34]

These are the principles that the South Australian friends of

Menzies believed should become the principles of the new party. They knew what Menzies stood for not only from knowing him in parliament but also from his public speeches and writings. The South Australians remained confident that these principles, in one form of words or another, would become the basic creed of the Liberal Party. And in 1944 they did.

A study of the minutes of all the meetings of South Australia's Liberal and Country League organisational wing during 1944-46 shows a steady, positive enthusiasm for both Menzies's leadership and for the nation-wide formation of the Liberal Party of Australia. For example, at the LCL annual general meeting in September 1945, the president and state executive reported in these glowing terms:

> By far the most important development on our side of politics in this country during the year, has been the successful formation of the Liberal Party of Australia which was finally launched at the inaugural meeting of the Federal Council in Sydney on August 28th, 29th and 30th. The Liberal Party is now firmly established in each State of the Commonwealth, and many of the early difficulties have been ironed out, and the way paved for the smooth and efficient working of the organisation throughout Australia. South Australia is represented by Mr P A McBride on the Federal Executive and on the Federal Committee on Policy; and by Mr D C Turner on the Federal Finance Committee; and by the General Secretary, Mr A S Dunk on the Federal Constitution Committee.[35]

It was in May 1945 that Philip McBride had reported that the LPA had decided to name the state organisations of the party as 'divisions' instead of the earlier name, 'branches'. The word 'branch' would be reserved for the most local organisation of the party in each town and suburb. Thus, from this time the alternative public name for the Liberal and Country League became the South Australian Division of the Liberal Party of Australia. This was accepted, but the LCL kept on using its older name for the next thirty years, while its federal members always used the newer name and always sat in the Liberal Party room in Canberra. It was in 1974, when the Playford era was well and truly over, that the LCL adopted a reformed constitution and a brand-new state policy platform, both of which gained a new popular appeal and an improved organisational effectiveness.[36] It was at this significant fresh start in 1974 that the party announced itself as 'The Liberal Party of Australia (South Australian Division)'. Ever since then, this has been the only name used in all contexts for the Liberal Party in South Australia.

The Liberals in South Australia fully took on the name of the new Australia-wide party which its members in 1944-45 played such a key role to establish.

---

[1] Dr Baden Teague, Liberal historian, Liberal state councillor 1973-2024, and Liberal senator for seven Australian parliaments, 1978-96; BA honours in History and BSc (Adelaide), and PhD in Philosophy (Cambridge).

[2] The writer of this chapter thanks three particular friends and scholars for reading my draft and for kindly making significant suggestions for improving amendments: Bruce Edwards, Hon Stephen Wade and Professor Don Markwell.

[3] At the Liberal Party headquarters in Adelaide there is an honour board which lists successive presidents of women's council. Three names stand out in this list: Mrs EA Mayfield (1911-24), Mrs CG Rogers (1942-47) and Lady Wilson (1952-69). This honour board was erected in 1952 'in memory of Doris C Rogers in appreciation of her outstanding service to the Liberal and Country League, 1920-1952'.

[4] These 14 UAP seats comprised 6 in Victoria, only 4 in NSW, 2 in Tasmania, 1 LCL seat in SA, and 1 in Queensland.

[5] Holt, *Politics is People*, p. 22.

[6] Teague, *The Liberal Story*, p. 69.

[7] Oliver Badman at this time was the new president of the Country Party in SA. During the next year, 1932, in the negotiations that in SA formed the united party, The Liberal and Country League, he agreed to disband the Country Party permanently, and he became an assured LCL foundation senator instead.

[8] The full list of ten and their political backgrounds are set out in Teague's book, *The Liberal Story*, p. 74.

[9] Archie Cameron MP was one of the two state members for Wooroora, 1927-34 (CP until 1932 and LCL thereafter) and then he was elected the federal member for Barker, 1934-56 (LCL until 1944 and then LPA and LCL thereafter). He was a minister under Lyons and Menzies, and from 1950 he was elected by the House of Representatives as the speaker, serving until his death in office in 1956.

[10] Oliver Badman, an EC and LCL senator, and Philip McBride, the EC and LCL MP for Grey, both began as parliamentarians at the 1931 federal election. However, at the end of Badman's six-year term, Badman and McBride agreed to swap places. Thus, at the 1937 federal election, Badman was elected the LCL member for Grey and McBride was elected as an LCL senator. At the disastrous (for them both) 1943 federal election, Badman left parliament forever, while all LCL Senate candidates were defeated. This meant that McBride devoted the greater part of his time and all his talents to the building up of the Liberal Party of Australia during the three years, 1944-45-46. At the 1946 federal election McBride was elected as the LCL and LPA member for Wakefield, and he served as a close ministerial colleague of Menzies thereafter, 1946-58.

[11] Senator Keith Wilson's wife, Betty Wilson, was the daughter of the lord mayor of Adelaide, Sir Lavington Bonython and the granddaughter of one of the federation founders, Sir Langdon Bonython. Betty Wilson, for the next fifty years and more, became perhaps the most active Liberal in SA, serving as president of the LCL women's council, 1952-69 and thereafter as party vice-president. Ian Wilson, son of Keith and Betty, founded the Young Liberal movement of South Australia in 1951, graduated in Law, became a Rhodes Scholar to Oxford, and was elected the federal MP for Sturt, 1966-69, 1972-93. Sir Langdon Bonython's impressive portrait hangs today in the entrance to the Legislative Council because it was his donation that made possible the completion, during the 1930s, of the State Parliament House (and another of his donations built the Bonython Hall at the University of Adelaide).

[12] See Martin, *Robert Menzies*, Vol. I, p. 125.

[13] Archie Cameron MP, Member for Barker, was the **only** non-Labor member from SA in the House of Representatives between the federal elections of 1943 and 1946. He also happened to be Playford's earliest best friend and, increasingly, he was one of Menzies's supporters.

[14] At the 1945 inaugural council meeting there were eight South Australians among the 44 delegates. There were seven delegates for each of the six states, plus the federal parliamentary leaders, Menzies for the House and McLeay (a South Australian) for the Senate. The crucial friendships here were between Menzies, McBride and McLeay. They had become battle-hardened political colleagues. All three were Presbyterians, Australians with a Scottish heritage.

[15] Dudley Turner proved vital to the success of the emergency committee in 1931 because he was a marvel at raising funds. When the LCL was founded in 1932 Turner went on to be the LCL treasurer as well, and in 1944-45 the

foundation representative for South Australia on the LPA's finance committee. See Kerr, p. 98.

[16] One of Malcolm Fraser's favourite books when he became prime minister in 1975 was Ayn Rand's novel, *Atlas Shrugged* (1957), but Rand's fame as a philosopher of freedom was established already with her novel, *The Fountainhead* (1943).

[17] Keynes's economic orthodoxy guided Western democracies in the 1940s and 50s, until modifications taught by Milton Friedman and others, such as in monetarism, price theory and applied macroeconomics, became widespread by the 1970s, 80s and 90s.

[18] John Duncan-Hughes MC served as the MP for Boothby, 1922-28, then as a senator, 1931-38, and finally as the MP for Wakefield, 1940-43. He had graduated in arts and law from Cambridge. He served on the personal staff of the Prince of Wales (the future King Edward 8th) when the prince toured Australia in 1920, and then was appointed personal secretary to the Governor General Munro Ferguson. He owned one of the best libraries in South Australia (6,200 books, eventually donated to the National Library). He was the brother of Walter Duncan MLC. 'Jack' added 'Hughes' to his name in order to inherit his great uncle's magnificent mansion, 'Hughes Park' in the Skillogalee Valley near Watervale in SA's rural mid-North. This great uncle, Sir Walter Watson Hughes, had owned the Moonta copper mine and his statue stands at the front of the University of Adelaide in recognition of his original benefaction to establish this university.

[19] Archie Grenfell Price attended Magdalen College, Oxford, on the recommendation of his headmaster, Canon Henry Girdlestone, a graduate of Magdalen himself. Archie then recommended Magdalen to several South Australians including Don Laidlaw, Jim Forbes and Ian Wilson, all of whom attended Magdalen before becoming Liberal parliamentarians. Malcolm Fraser also attended Magdalen College and John Gorton was at Brasenose.

[20] Robert Menzies was no longer prime minister nor even the leader of the Opposition during this 1942 year. He used this 'sabbatical' to good effect by thinking through and writing about his own developing principles of freedom and democracy, on which he believed both the quality of life and the prosperity of the people depended. He became focused on the necessary political foundations that would be needed for post-war reconstruction. Menzies's writing that year led to him giving a series of 105 radio broadcasts to Australia from January 1942 to April 1944. His most remembered broadcast was titled *The Forgotten People*. Menzies published this and 36 other broadcasts as a book in 1943, each ranging from five to ten pages long. Menzies's political and economic philosophy was already clear, well before his approach became reinforced by CD Kemp's *Looking Forward*, a book published by the Victorian Institute of Public Affairs in August 1944. Menzies warmly commended *Looking Forward* at the Canberra Unity Conference and the delegates ordered thousands of copies.

[21] This version by the writer is briefer than the original document but it sets out a fair summary of it. The complete document can be found in Henderson, *Menzies' Child,* pp. 81-2.

[22] Hancock, *National and Permanent,* p. 59.

[23] McBride's service as a senator for South Australia was from 21 October 1937 to 30 June 1938, and then from 1 July 1938 to 30 June 1944. The former period of eight months covered the remainder of Badman's term, and the latter period was the normal term for all senators elected at the 1937 federal election. It is significant that McBride was part of the parliament during Menzies's first eight months as leader of the Opposition. McBride voted for Menzies in the party room. McBride was still in Canberra and he kept up a regular conversation with Menzies for most of the period leading up to the October 1944 Unity Conference.

[24] It was at the 1949 Senate election that the voting procedure for Senate elections was changed. The former 'winner-take-all' approach was changed to become the much fairer proportional voting system for Senate elections.

[25] This letter is on file in the McBride family archive in South Australia.

[26] Sir Philip McBride served as federal president, 1960-65, which included Menzies's final five years as prime minister. There have been two other South Australians to serve as federal president: the Hon Jim Forbes MC, 1982-85, and the current federal president, the Hon John Olsen who began in 2020.

[27] For a description of the worlds of Cameron and Playford, see Teague, *The Liberal Story,* pp. 81-5.

[28] After the September 1940 federal election, the Coalition was returned to government. Menzies continued as prime minister and Cameron expected to continue as leader of the Country Party and deputy prime minister. However, the Country Party room at its first meeting following the election insulted Cameron by deciding to open the CP leadership to a fresh election. Cameron refused to participate, choosing instead to resign from the Country Party. He also resigned as a minister. He joined Menzies's United Australia Party room immediately, kept up a degree of 'Scottish Highland' animosity towards some of his old colleagues, and looked entirely to the future and to the emerging Liberal Party of Australia, which all but one of his LCL colleagues in South Australia (Badman) also supported.

[29] One fortunate outcome of being the speaker of the House of Representatives was that Cameron was, of course, invited to attend the Coronation of Queen Elizabeth II on 2 June 1953. It meant a splendid visit not only to the UK but also to Europe as well. Archie and Margaret Cameron travelled together with Tom and Lorna Playford via Italy where Playford (as Premier) was in a position kindly to arrange for Mick O'Halloran (his own Labor counterpart in SA) to meet the Pope and where Playford and Cameron had this one chance to revisit France where together they had fought at the front line 35 years earlier.

[30] Starr, *The Liberal Party of Australia*, pp. 63-4.

[31] The National Service Group had seventeen Members, all of whom signed the one letter addressed to Hughes on 1 April, 1943. The ten South Australians were the six senators McLeay, McBride, Wilson, A McLachlan, J McLachlan and Uppill together with Cameron, Duncan-Hughes, Grenfell Price and Stacey. The three Victorians were Menzies, Leckie and Spicer. The one West Australian was Collett and the one from NSW was Harrison.

[32] The one NSW member of the National Service Group, Captain Eric Harrison MP, became deputy Liberal leader to Menzies in April 1944 after Hughes was ousted for re-joining the Advisory War Council. Menzies was himself a Victorian and, all other things being equal, it was sensible to have a loyal supporter from the biggest state, New South Wales, as the deputy.

[33] Starr, op. cit., page 66. This extract of Menzies's significant letter of August 1944 twice here includes the word 'liberal'. Starr incorrectly has a capital L, despite his source having a small l for both uses of the word liberal. Starr's source is the *Sydney Morning Herald*, 30 August 1944, p. 3. Also, it is clear from the context that Menzies was here referring to liberal public opinion and to liberal policy, whereas The Liberal Party of Australia was only given this name two months later.

[34] Menzies's radio broadcast, following the 1943 federal election and a few days before he was elected the leader of the Opposition. See Kemp, *A Liberal State,* pp. 284-5.

[35] South Australian State Library Archive, Liberal Party, SRG 168.

[36] For a description of the SA era of modern reform for the party, 1966-75, see Teague, *The Liberal Story*, chapters 6, 7 and 8.

8

The Wild West: Formation of the Liberal Party of Western Australia

Sherry Sufi

As geographically the largest and economically the most resourceful state, Western Australia has played a crucial role in Australia's national development. Yet its isolation and the belated onset of democracy has meant that Western Australia developed a unique political culture and took some time to grow into its true national importance.

The Liberal Party of Australia has likewise been a latecomer to the Australian political scene, coming into existence after both the Australian Labor Party and the Country/National Party. But while many have celebrated Menzies's watershed victory in the 1949 federal election, few now remember that the Liberals first achieved a change of government at Harvest Terrace in 1947.

The poll would make Ross McLarty WA's 17th premier and the party has since produced the stalwart Liberal governments of Sir David Brand (1959-71), Sir Charles Court (1974-82), Richard Court (1993-2001) and Colin Barnett (2008-17), each of whom significantly shaped the state's development and prosperity. On the momentous occasion of the party's 80th anniversary, this chapter reflects on the political landscape in Western Australia before the formation of the Western Australian Division of the Liberal Party of Australia (at times referred to as the Liberal Party of Western Australia). It highlights the distinctive aspects of Western Australia's political culture, the role of its women's organisations and the key constituencies of the early centre-right tradition. It also looks at the initial challenges and successes of the Liberal Party in Western Australia shortly after its conception and formation in 1944.

Western Australia: isolated and exceptional

As the British settlement of the island continent of Australia began in 1788, its initial focus was on the east coast. Western Australia didn't come into the picture until 1829. When it did, it was under direct British rule. Although Western Australia was established as a free colony, such was its stagnation that it soon requested convict labour as necessary for its development. Convict transportation commenced in 1850 well after it had become the subject of sustained opposition in the eastern colonies.[1] Western Australia took no part in the campaigns of the Anti-Transportation Leagues – the first political campaign to unite the other colonies in a manner which presaged the later federation – and this was arguably the earliest manifestation of WA's political separatism.

Convict transportation in Western Australia stopped as late as 1868.[2] A direct result of this was the delayed advent of democracy. While the other colonies started achieving self-government in the 1850s, Western Australia was the last colony to do so in 1890.[3] This was partly because a high concentration of ex-convicts were not trusted with the franchise, but also due to the colony's small European population concentrated in the south-west corner of such a vast territory. Perth was geographically isolated from much of Western Australia, let alone the rest of the continent, and this has gone on to play a significant role in shaping the political culture and collective mindset of this unique state.

By the time Western Australia did gain self-government, it was reluctant to join the federation for a variety of reasons. Not the least of which was that the first federal convention where the proposal was to be discussed came in March and April 1891, only a few months after the first WA election held in December.[4] There was a widespread view at the time among many Western Australians that joining a federation so soon after becoming independent might mean that the state simply changed from being under direct British rule to direct Commonwealth rule. Naturally, the idea of remaining autonomous was an attractive one. In the early years, conservatives across Western Australia were also concerned about the economic implications of federation. They feared that removing tariffs would reduce state revenue and harm local industries, which were not as developed as those in the eastern states.[5] Despite these concerns, Western Australia held a successful referendum in 1900 to join the federation.[6] Its success was driven partly by demographic changes and the sudden influx of settlers during the 1890s to regions such as the goldfields. Coming predominantly from the eastern states, these settlers were naturally pro-federation.[7] Concessions, such as allowing WA to charge excise on imports until 1905 nevertheless proved vital in swaying the decision.

Left-right divide in early days

In the midst of this, the Western Australian Labor Party emerged in 1899, at a time when WA's political culture remained in a fledgling state. The embodiment of socialism and trade unionism, the birth of the party was largely fuelled by the social and economic upheavals of the gold rush and growing discontent with financial elites among the working class. Due to its advocacy for the rights of workers, fairer wages and improved social welfare, Labor values naturally resonated with the expanding urban and mining populations. Labor's early successes were underpinned by its ability to organise effectively and its commitment to legislative reforms that were perceived to be benefiting the working class. This early momentum not only secured significant electoral victories, but also laid the foundations for a robust political force that would shape WA's political destiny for decades to come.

While the ALP would first contest what was just WA's fourth election in 1901, a prevailing liberal political class had nevertheless established itself by then, largely centred around (later Sir) John Forrest, premier from 1890 until federation. Its members argued that Labor's socialist objective threatened individual freedoms and economic progress by advocating for the redistribution of wealth and increased government control over industries. They feared that unionist activities would disrupt economic stability, leading to strikes and reduced productivity. At the same time, Marxist thought, with its call for class struggle and revolution, was seen as a direct threat to the social order and the interests of business and property owners. These latent anti-Labor sentiments provided fertile ground for the emergence of organised conservative and liberal movements which sought to protect individual enterprise, economic liberalism and limited government intervention.

Compared to the other colonies, Western Australia had experienced a rapid transition from an all-independent state parliament in the 1890s to a chamber where, by 1905, all 50 members of the Legislative Assembly (MLAs) represented either Labor (spelt 'Labour' at the time) or what was then known as the Liberal (Ministerial) Party. One might view this as a somewhat amorphous prelude to a well-defined two-party system in the contemporary sense. The early 'liberal' movement in Western Australia primarily represented commercial and property interests. With the ALP gaining electoral success from 1904, a bloc of 'liberals' crystalised in opposition to them.

One of several precursors to the modern Liberal Party was the Liberal League of Western Australia. Formed in 1906, at the same time George Reid was fighting his famed 'Anti-Socialist Campaign' in response to the adoption of the 'socialist objective' in the ALP federal platform,[8] the league focused on championing individualism and opposing governmental control or national ownership of industries. Its platform as laid out in *The West Australian* newspaper on 7 August 1906, called for:

> Defence of personal, industrial, and political individualism; and opposition to governmental control or national ownership of unprivileged industries. Opposition to all forms of class legislation, or the domination of any one

> section of the community. Opposition to the imposition of a federal land tax. Fiscal peace, subject to the removal of proved anomalies. Maintenance of State rights. Retention of the control, by the State, of its lands, railways, debts, and borrowing powers. Continuance of the Braddon Clause, and retention of the Book-keeping Clauses, at least for this State. Promotion of a real union with the rest of Australia, and defence of the Commonwealth by railway communication. Removal of the Federal Parliament from State influence.[9]

To appreciate the backdrop that paved the way for the eventual establishment of the Liberal Party of Western Australia, it is crucial to wrap our heads around some of the key political rifts that existed at the time. Besides protectionism versus free trade and socialism versus capitalism, the other key rift pervasive through the early federal period was centralism versus federalism. Centralism emphasises the importance of a strong central administrative body to manage the affairs of its various constituent units. Federalism on the other hand emphasises the importance of empowering the various constituent units to run their own affairs as autonomously as possible and of consequently limiting the federal apparatus to a minimum of intervention. In a state like Western Australia, that was not only geographically the most distant from the rest of the country, but also the most resourceful, the temptation to go its own way had always been there right from the start. This partly explains why in its federation referendum held on 31 July 1900, the WA 'Yes' vote was 69.47 per cent which is lower than the average of the six colonies of 75.52 per cent.[10]

Following a merger in 1907, the National Liberal League was formed to unify the efforts of the Liberal League with the slightly older and slightly more conservative National Political League. After this, a separate women's organisation, the Australian Women's National League of Western Australia, emerged under the leadership of

Miss Lina Wilson in 1910. This new league operated independently but aligned itself with the National Liberal League. By 1911, both leagues resolved to unite forming a single entity across the state. Challenges in forming separate branches led to a joint conference in February 1912, where the men's and women's leagues affirmed closer cooperation for unified operations. The Women's League proposed renaming itself the Women's Liberal League of Western Australia, reflecting on-going constitutional changes aimed at consolidating their influence within the Liberal movement. This consolidation aimed to streamline operations and enhance effectiveness, marking a significant development in WA politics.[11]

After six years of Liberal government, the ALP won a major victory 34:16 under John Scaddan in 1911, dominating pastoral, mining and metropolitan districts. Ironically, it was the electoral loss which saw the term 'Liberal Party' gain relevance in everyday use – before this the NLL's parliamentarians had largely been referred to as 'Ministerialists'.[12] By 1912, this Western Australian Liberal Party had undergone significant organisational changes in an attempt to become more responsive to the priorities of those opposed to socialism and the caucus pledge. Yet it must be noted that this movement still lacked an effective party machine for fundraising and candidate preselection. At the subsequent 1914 election, Labor was reduced to 26 MLAs, losing metropolitan seats to the new WA Liberal Party. In the same timeframe, the first separate Country Party was established in WA in 1913. It ended up winning 8 seats in 1914, mainly from the Liberals who lost most of their conservative rural strongholds. This Country Party is the predecessor to the modern National Party of Western Australia. In his book *Menzies' Child*, Gerard Henderson notes that:

> Although Labor governed in Western Australia from 1904 to 1905, in the early years after Federation the Liberals were predominant. In 1911, however, Labor won the State election and John Scaddan was premier until 1916. The following year Scaddan went with the con-

> scriptionists, and the party split. A National Coalition led successively by Henry Bruce Lefroy, Hal Colebatch (for a month only) and James Mitchell was in power from 1916 until 1924. Labor won the 1924 election, remaining in power until 1930. From 1930 until 1933, Western Australia was led by a National-Country Coalition. Labor won again in 1933, remaining in office until 1947.[13]

Despite these challenges, liberalism attracted diverse voters who supported free enterprise, individual freedom and a prosperous future for Western Australia. Initially, the original WA Liberal Party was a business and coastal party with limited support from primary producers outside the extreme south-west. Over time, the liberal platform evolved to reflect the interests of various constituencies. In 1916, the WA Liberal Party ousted the Scaddan Labor Government, and by the 1917 election, Labor was heavily defeated due to a split over the issue of conscription. But non-Labor itself remained somewhat fractious, with its 34 electoral districts divided among the Country Party, Nationalists, National Liberals and National Labor marking the formation of anti-socialist and anti-trade union blocs in WA politics without a formal organisational structure. Notably, from 1916-24, there was no formal Nationalist-Country Party coalition, but successive Liberal/Nationalist premiers included Country Party ministers in their cabinets. Internal tensions led to the resignation of three Liberal/Nationalist premiers between 1916 and 1919.

By 1917, the WA Liberal Party would be dissolved and succeeded by the new centre-right Nationalist Party (alternatively referred to as the National Party) which resulted from an odd merger between what was then the federal Liberal Party and the short-lived National Labor Party. This Nationalist Party had evolved from the Liberal League and upheld principles like the unity of the British Empire, White Australia and preferences for returned soldiers –

which both its conservative and ex-Labor supporters could agree upon. Its stance on states' rights and parliamentary responsibility reflected a more explicating liberal commitment to local governance and individual freedoms. This Nationalist Party would eventually become the United Australia Party (UAP) in 1931. In Western Australia, there was no official merger, the Nationalist Party simply adopted the name UAP for federal elections.

Nationalist Party leader James Mitchell served as premier until 1924. At that election, the Country Party split between coalitionists and those seeking a distinct identity, contributing to the ALP's return to office. The period from 1924-47 saw Labor dominance. In 1930, the Nationalist and Country parties formed a Coalition cabinet led by Mitchell, with each party providing four ministers. This government, though stable, lost the 1933 election due to the economic hardships of the Depression, reducing the Nationalists to eight of 50 districts. The party faced the on-going problem of reliance on metropolitan seats that were vulnerable to Labor in adverse times. After 1933, in a Legislative Assembly where small mining districts enjoyed the greatest weighting, the Country Party held more seats than the Nationalists and formed the official Opposition.

A great deal of conservative activism from 1930-33 was diverted towards the Dominion League that was promoting the secession of Western Australia from the rest of the Commonwealth. Drawing on the support of many key Nationalists, it caused serious internal dissent. Secession was put to a vote in WA and received 68 per cent support in a referendum held concurrently with the 1933 state election.[14] The rejection of the pro-secession Mitchell Government in favour of an anti-secession ALP ministry, which only gave lukewarm support to the Dominion League's London delegation, ensured the failure of secession. Many voters appeared intent on a generalised protest rather than a clear mandate for independence.

The creation of the UAP would itself involve the Nationalists merging with what was known as the Australian Party and the All for Australia League – however the Nationalist name was retained by the organisation which would be invited to attend Menzies's Unity Conferences in 1944. As a result of some of the key ideological rifts discussed so far, WA political history before the end of World War II had come to develop some distinct features. The state's political culture is no doubt unique due to its geographical and political isolation. This isolation came to foster a sense of exceptionalism and a shared perception of neglect by the national government.[15] The physical distance from the eastern states also helped shape a political identity marked by a combination of parochialism and a strong sense of independence. This backdrop helps us appreciate the context out of which the Liberal Party of Western Australia would eventually be born.

The role of women's organisations

Besides the political ideologies, movements and parties explored in the previous section, it is important to look at the role of women's organisations which played a disproportionately large role in mobilising the WA centre-right tradition before the birth of the Liberal Party of Western Australia as we know it.

As early as 1899, women in WA had already gained the right to vote, making it the second colony/state after South Australia to achieve this milestone. The Western Australian Women's Suffrage League founded by the Women's Christian Temperance Union in 1896 and the Women's Franchise League established in 1899 played key roles in the enfranchisement of Western Australian women. The efforts of Lady Margaret Forrest and Edith Cowan were significant in achieving legislative change. Notably, the government believed that enfranchising women would balance the radical votes from the male-dominated goldfields[16] – in part because of the conservative connotations of the temperance movement.

As a result of this early enfranchisement, women participated in the July 1900 referendum on joining the Commonwealth. After securing the vote, women's organisations continued to shape WA's political culture, advancing causes for women and children. It was the Women's Service Guild (WSG) founded in 1909 that had the principal responsibility for promoting civic education and political representation for women while maintaining a non-partisan stance.[17] In 1911, Lady Edeline Strickland (the wife of the governor) initiated the creation of the National Council of Women of Western Australia (NCW) which coordinated women's groups and lobbied for legislative changes. It was Bessie Rischbieth, a prominent campaigner, who led the WSG and founded the Australian Federation of Women's Societies (AFWV) in 1921 which was a national umbrella group for women's organisations with a focus on constitutional reform and publishing *The Dawn* journal. Continuing to reach beyond the boundaries of WA, she also co-founded the British Commonwealth League of Women in 1925.

The Australian Women's National League (AWNL) established in Western Australia in 1909 significantly shaped centre-right politics by promoting conservative values such as loyalty to the throne, opposing state socialism and advocating for women's political education and home life protection. By 1913, the AWNL in WA had merged with the Liberal League discussed earlier, with women's branches outnumbering men's and playing a central role in supporting the subsequent war effort. With 250 branches across WA, this strengthened the movement and helped ensure that women's issues received due attention. By 1915, there had emerged 271 branches as well as the first Young Liberal societies.

The sustained efforts to enhance women's political participation came to fruition when WSG founding member and endorsed Nationalist candidate Edith Cowan became the first woman elected to an Australian parliament in 1921 (with the backing of the otherwise non-partisan Rischbieth and her organisation). Florence Cardell-Oliver, herself serving as a Nationalist/Liberal in the WA parliament from 1936-56, was also known for her independent views and lively debates, becoming the first woman to achieve full cabinet rank in Australia as minister for health 1949-53. Her consecutive electoral victories as the member for Subiaco were a notable achievement at a time when the few women who did get elected to Australia's parliaments generally only served one term.

The emergence of the Liberal Party of Western Australia

World War II had a profound social, economic, political and cultural impact on the entire world, and this was certainly true of Western Australia. Australia had entertained its share of political anxieties right from its beginnings as a society, and as a long-standing fear of the so-called 'yellow peril' became manifest with the threat of Japanese invasion, Australian electors sought security and the protection of government.

As a relatively unified and well organised party of big government, Labor benefitted from the situation. They also benefited from the fact that popular Labor Prime Minister John Curtin himself represented a WA seat. With the centre-right weakly organised and lacking in popular leadership, the result was landslide Labor victories when WA went to the polls in both state and federal elections in 1943. Henderson notes that 'In Western Australia, the Country Party was the main non-Labor organisation, winning 15.2 per cent of the vote to the Nationalists' 13.4 per cent. At the 1943 federal election the ALP won every seat in Western Australia'.[18]

One silver lining for the Nationalists/UAP was the emergence of a charismatic Senate candidate by the name of Jim Paton, who would go on to become the founder of the WA Division. A Tasmanian-born World War I veteran who had obtained the rank of lieutenant-colonel, Paton had subsequently enjoyed a successful career as an accountant. An athletic man who had succeeded at hockey and basketball, Paton was a founder and life member of the WA Surf Life Saving Association. He had first risen to political prominence as the president of the Perth Chamber of Commerce.

In November 1939 he had been one of several prominent Western Australians, including the premier and Opposition leader, to sign off on a statement demanding that the war must usher in a new era 'built on principles of honesty, unselfishness and brotherhood.'[19]

This liberal internationalism carried over into the speech Paton delivered to launch his Senate campaign, in which he advocated for Australia's active role in the global community, warning against isolationist tendencies. Paton critiqued economic theories promising unrealistic benefits and called for responsible governance to safeguard against societal decay. He concluded with a vision for inclusive governance and fair treatment for all Australians, emphasising the importance of historical lessons and integrity in policy-making.[20]

Despite failing to win a seat at a time when the lack of proportional representation made Senate elections an effective 'winner-takes all', Paton's campaigning earned him the respect of his party and he was subsequently elevated to become president of the Nationalists in May 1944.[21] A man of deep thought and principle, he was then involved in the printing of a detailed pamphlet outlining 'The National Party's Mission' in eloquent and liberal terms. This reflected a widespread wartime desire to articulate a clear political philosophy or 'faith', which could act as the blueprint for a better world:

> Its fundamental principle is its insistence on the reasonable freedom of the individual, and on the value and responsibility of the individual, as such, in the work, wellbeing and progress of the nation. This freedom is the freedom that allows others equal freedom; it is freedom of religion, of thought, of speech, of movement, of choice of occupation; it involves equality of opportunity, equality before the law, and the freedom of government to legislate, not as the agent or at the direction of any organisation, but according to justice for all sections of the nation.[22]

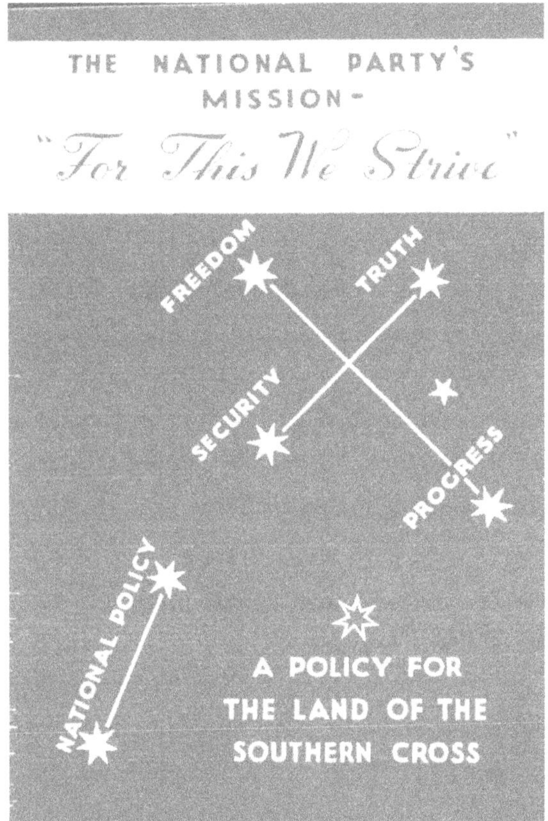

'The National Party's Mission', pamphlet from Menzies's Papers in the National Library of Australia.

To this day, party elders in the Liberal Party in WA often speak of how magnanimous and statesman-like Paton was, not only towards factional rivals in his own party but towards political opponents. For instance, in a display of goodwill in 1945 Paton as president of the Liberal Party conference, moved a resolution expressing heartfelt sympathy towards Prime Minister Curtin amidst his severe and ultimately terminal illness. This gesture, unanimously endorsed by conference delegates, transcended political divisions in a display of WA solidarity. Paton's note to the acting prime minister, Frank Forde, included a message from the Liberal Party of Western Australia pointing towards a resolution passed unanimously by the delegates to the Liberal Party conference:

> That this conference expresses to the Prime Minister, Mr. Curtin, its sympathy with him in his illness, following the strain and responsibility of his office in time of war, and trusts that he will be speedily restored to health.[23]

But just because he was thoughtful doesn't mean that Paton was not a fighter, and this would come out during the 1944 'powers' referendum which sought to greatly expand the scope of the Commonwealth government in a manner that was an anathema to the long WA tradition of seeking to maintain the state's autonomy. As president of the Western Australian Constitutional League, Paton played a significant role in running the 'No' campaign in his state.

Paton's involvement in the campaign had major implications for what was to come, as party elders often emphasis. Firstly, the campaign lifted Paton's profile within the WA centre-right community and core decision-making circles. Secondly, it provided him with tangible experience of running political campaigns. Thirdly and perhaps most beneficial in the long run was the fact that the campaign actually fell short, with WA becoming one of only two states that ended up voting 'Yes', albeit narrowly with 52.2 per cent – meaning that Paton could not rest on his laurels, and had to continue to seek to hone his methods. As Henderson notes:

> Except for Western Australia and South Australia, Dr Evatt's referendum had proved a fizzer for Labor. For non-Labor, however, Evatt's embarrassment was Menzies' opportunity. Not only did it provide the spark for the formation of a new unified non-Labor party. It also helped define the political debate for many years to come.[24]

The overall rejection at the national level no doubt underscored a deep-seated wariness of centralised control and socialist policies. Yet the fact that WA, a state otherwise known for its exceptional disdain for the Commonwealth ended up voting 'Yes' was a strange wake up call for the forces of the centre-right. Jim Paton, who was at the centre of it all, knew that with non-Labor forces about to be united nationally, Western Australia needed to be brought on the journey to become an integral part of one united voice against socialism.

The irony was that the most committed and energetic display the WA centre-right had mustered in recent memory was in the secession campaign of the Dominion League. As resident historian and party elder Jeremy Buxton often mentions, several Liberal Party activists had cut their teeth as Dominion League campaigners. Sir Charles Court remarked on this many years later, noting the overlap between the contribution of Cyril Dudley among others to the 1947 state election victory.

Despite having the furthest to travel, Paton and five other Western Australian delegates readily accepted Menzies's invitation to attend the first Unity Conference held in Canberra in October 1944.[25] These were: Leader of the WA Nationalist Party Ross McDonald; senator and former Menzies Government minister Herbert Collett; Mr Stanley Wesley Perry and Mr Grant McDonald of the Constitution League; and Paton's Nationalist Party colleague Mr James Bartington. Building on his experience in producing the pamphlet explaining the Nationalist Party's mission, Paton and Bartington would notably serve on the committee on name and objectives. While the name 'Liberal Party' was swiftly adopted, Paton would later dub it the 'Freedom Party'.[26]

On leaving the conference, McDonald would praise what he saw as its three core principles which he felt gave it a strong chance of achieving enduring unity:

> the whole political structure shall be democratically controlled by the individual members; that States will remain autonomous in respect of State political affairs and selection of Federal candidates for Parliament; that the Federal Council of the party to which all States will

> have equal representation, shall administer that party's activities in the Federal sphere on behalf of component States.[27]

Despite its reputation for separatism, WA would play a prominent role in the latter. In August 1945, the WA Liberals would face their first electoral test in contesting the by-election for John Curtin's seat of Fremantle. While the sense of tragedy surrounding Curtin's death in office meant that the Liberal candidate, Brigadier Donald Cleland, had little chance of succeeding, just days later he would be appointed the first federal director of the newborn Liberal Party of Australia. Cleland took up his office in Sydney[28] and founded the Liberal federal secretariat.

Because the WA Nationalist Party was relatively intact compared to some other state organisations, Paton took over as provisional president of the Liberal Party council almost by default, and would go on to be the first division president. While the Nationalists had only nominally adopted the UAP monicker, this time they embraced a full name change, in part because 'the word Nationalist had been discredited, not merely by National Socialism but by right-wing, anti-Jewish European "Nationalist" parties that were often Nazi fellow-travellers. This was a real concern to the growing number of "new Australians" in the post-war electorate.'[29] In answer to the question what does the new party stand for?, Paton explained that:

> We will preserve personal freedom whilst crushing exploitation. We desire to recreate and build up the dignity of the home and the individual. We will restore moral standards and the practice of the simple Christian and social virtues of truth, courage, mutual help and real effort. We will do this by revitalising education, by restoring the truth in its application to the real problem of living instead of prostituting knowledge to the makeshift demand of material gain.[30]

On the negative side, Paton denounced:

> Socialism and communism as preached today in Australia and to the extent that it is in operation is nakedly fascist in its effect. Regardless of such good intent as exists such methods offer a form of living death because it will produce nothing but a cruel and selfish declining material prosperity, the pulling down of proven values, and the substitution of propaganda and a doctrine of infallibility for truth. Therefore its advocates are in the forefront of the forces of anti-freedom. We stand for freedom, the most important right of the individual in this life.

Following Paton, Edward Frank Downing QC would take over as president in 1947. The initial leadership team included notable figures like Margaret Battye and Sir Don Cleland, both of whom were among the earliest vice-presidents. Other influential leaders included James Bartington, Clive Palmer (not the contemporary Queenslander, but the general secretary of the Liberal Party of Western Australia), Hal Colebatch, Charles Simpson, Harold Daffen, Stanley Wesley Perry and Herbert Collett, each contributing significantly to the party's foundation and early development.

These leaders worked tirelessly to ensure that the new party's vision would align with Western Australia's unique political and economic landscape. Advocating for private enterprise and economic growth aligned well with the state's resource-rich economy, highlighting the need for policies that promoted industrial development and innovation. A focus on scientific research and national defence also resonated with WA's strategic importance and potential for growth. By integrating these state-specific interests into a cohesive national strategy, the aim was to ensure that Western Australia would benefit from and contribute to a united, centre-right political movement.[31] In those days, many of the newly recruited Liberal Party members were ex-servicemen, opposed to growing socialism, union influence and Labor's clumsy handling of demobilisation. Former Lieutenant-Colonel Charles Court and former Captain Bill Grayden are leading examples.

The formation of the Liberal Party attracted growing support and enthusiasm. In October 1945, David Brand became the first WA Liberal to win a seat, taking Greenough from the ALP in a by-election victory that boosted party morale.[32] The first conference of the Liberal Party in Western Australia, held in July 1945, set the pattern for the party's internal machinery. This conference was significant in establishing the organisational framework that would support the party's growth and electoral success. This included the recruitment of paid field officers. The Nationalist extra-parliamentary organisation had greatly decayed with only a few remnant branches. Although Senator Allan MacDonald (UAP/Liberal 1935-47) had been the full time employed general secretary of the Western Australian Nationalist Party from 1930, in the early days, most of those around the party management tended to be volunteers working towards the party's growth and electoral success.

In formalising an organisational structure for the newborn party, women's divisions and the 'legion of liberty' which later became the Young Liberal movement played significant roles. The inclusion of women and youth in the party's organisational structure ensured a broad base of support injecting fresh ideas and energy into the party's activities. The women's divisions were particularly active in grassroots campaigning, voter education, and community engagement. Their efforts were crucial in building a strong support network for the Liberal Party within the state. With big shoes to fill as the successors to Edith Cowan, the Liberals would succeed in securing the election of WA's second federal female parliamentarian in Agnes Robertson in 1949. Robertson had been mentored by Rischbieth and was a long-time servant of the Liberal women's council. Despite being a staunch anti-communist who gave strong defence to the so-called 'horror budget' of 1951, she failed to secure the party's reindorsement in 1955 (due to concerns over her age), and would instead stand successfully for the Country Party – becoming its first female senator.[33]

The Young Liberal movement also played a vital role in engaging younger voters and giving the Liberal Party a sense of looking towards the future that its predecessors had often lacked. Officially launched in WA in March 1948 as the 'legion of liberty', one of the YL's prime activities was the mobilisation of anti-socialist sentiment on university campuses, recruitment of students as Liberal Party members, vital debate training at various on campus politics clubs, assisting on campaigns with pamphlet dropping among other things, as well as fundraising. Hancock notes one occasion when 500 young people were invited to a ball dinner, 400 became YL members with a committee elected.[34]

The establishment of the Western Australian Division of the Liberal Party resulted in growing momentum in membership and branch expansion. We can see from the figures below the rapid rate at which the newborn party grew in the state of Western Australia.

- March 1945: 2000 members, 15 branches.
- April 1945: 2500 members, 31 branches.
- August 1945: 4000 members, 38 branches.
- June 1947: 6695 members, 62 branches.
- September 1950: 21,415 members, 156 branches.[35]

Facing the polls

With all this momentum and a by-election victory under its belt, the WA Liberal Party hoped to reap dividends at its first full electoral test, the 1946 federal poll. The Liberal Party sought out effective candidates, mostly with an ex-service background and generally new to politics. Candidates like Bill Grayden, Gordon Freeth, Gordon Hack, Paul Hasluck, Seddon Vincent and Malcolm Scott brought diverse experiences and strong credentials to the party – though the pool of talent proved deeper in 1949 than 1946, in part because ex-servicemen were still finding their civilian feet.

Paton likewise did not wish to be confined to an organisational role, hence he once again stood as a candidate in 1946, this time for the Lower House seat of Perth. While Paton was successful in securing electoral cooperation with the Country Party,[36] the fact that the president was focused on a single seat rather than the overall campaign was controversial (he was alleged to have been parachuted in ahead of five pre-existing nominees)[37] and arguably backfired. The party's campaign focused on addressing post-war economic challenges, advocating for reduced taxation and promoting industrial growth. But for the moment the message failed to resonate. The centre-right's only victory would be in the seat of Swan where Country Party candidate Len Hamilton achieved a 3.2 per cent swing, eclipsing the required 3 per cent by the narrowest of margins.

What is truly remarkable is how quickly the party was able to recover, for in less than six months it would achieve the first full scale Liberal election victory of any state. Paton had learnt his lesson, and this time he would be focused on helping the party as a whole.

The 1947 state election exemplifies the WA Liberal Party's strategic approach in targeting key seats, recruiting candidates, and forming electoral alliances with the Country Party. The ALP had held office for 14 years. Since 1945 it had been led by Premier Frank Wise, who known for his general competence despite lacking charisma. The Liberal Party faced a challenging landscape with only 8 seats, fewer than the Country Party. The party focused its campaign on criticising the state government's record – particularly its weak submission to a centralising federal government. McLarty's policy speech called for the states to take back income taxing powers whilst simultaneously reducing taxation levels, decentralisation and water conservation to encourage development outside the metropolitan area, and concentrated efforts to raise homeownership.[38] On the latter issue, the Liberal leader claimed that the ALP ignored 'one of the basic causes of our housing, hospital and other problems, namely the excessive taxation that has crippled incentive and production'.[39]

The Liberals shrewdly concentrated their efforts and resources on winnable seats, often where ALP incumbents were retiring. Of the 29 ALP seats, 15 were uncontested, while the Liberal Party instead focused on backing just 10 additional candidates alongside its eight incumbents. It did not contest Country Party incumbents but competed with the party in three seats.

The election outcome hinged on tight preference flows, resulting in Labor losing six seats – four to the Liberal Party and two to the Country Party. Additionally, the Liberal Party secured a crucial rural seat adjacent to metropolitan areas, previously held by an independent aligned with the Country Party, tipping the balance to form a Coalition government. With 13 seats for the Liberals and 12 for the Country Party, Ross McLarty assumed office as premier leading a Coalition ministry. In reflecting on the victory, Paton emphasised the youth of the party and its active members, as well as the fact that Labor 'stands for the abolition of State Parliaments' and that its members in those parliaments were content to be 'yes men' for Canberra.[40] McLarty admitted that he had benefitted from Labor's complacency, and that the Liberals still had a way to go if they wanted to match their opponents' organisational rigour.[41]

On the back of the victory Paton announced that he would ride off into the political sunset, and not recontest the presidency. But the party he would leave behind would go from strength to strength. In September 1947, the Chifley Government's controversial policy of bank nationalisation sparked widespread political opposition, galvanising the Liberal Party further.

On 10 March 1949 in Perth the Liberal Party faced a critical decision regarding a proposal for federation with the Country and Democratic League (CDL). The CDL had presented an offer aimed at unifying the parties, which was deliberated by the Liberal Party's state executive. Despite careful consideration, the Liberal Party declined the proposal, as explained by Mr Frank Downing, president of the state branch, citing unresolved concerns within the party about the CDL's formula which would confine the Liberals to being an exclusively metropolitan entity. The decision highlighted the party's commitment to seeking substantive and practical solutions to resolve inherent issues, rather than accepting incremental changes that did not address fundamental objections.[42]

The early pioneers of the Liberal Party of Western Australia faced the challenge of balancing grassroots movements with organisational strength. The McLarty-Watts Government demonstrated close Liberal-Country cooperation in dismantling socialist controls and facilitating industrial development. On the back of this, a meeting held in the wheatbelt town of Beverley 133km south-east of Perth renewed the push for a unified anti-socialist party, which it ushered in by merging the local Liberal and Country branches, resulting in the advent of the Liberal and Country League (LCL).

In May 1949, the WA Division of the Liberal Party ceased to exist independently and merged with the newly formed LCL. This decision, made during a council meeting attended by representatives from about 70 branches, marked a turning point in the region's political landscape. Despite initial resistance from some CDL quarters, the formation of the LCL laid the groundwork for integrating political identities. Mr Frank Downing, president of the Liberal Party's West Australian Division, expressed disappointment over opposition from certain CDL factions but remained optimistic about broader support.[43] Under the leadership of Mr AL Barrett-Lennard, a former CDL leader, the LCL sought to consolidate its position by inviting the CDL to join under similar conditions.[44] The council meeting also endorsed candidates for upcoming elections, such as Mr W Grayden and Mr HA Leslie, indicating preparations for a unified electoral campaign against socialist influences in the region's politics. But in the end the Country Party chose to maintain its identity – which has since become increasingly distinct from the WA Liberal Party.

Nevertheless, the McLarty-Watts Government laid the groundwork for long-term influence in Western Australian politics. Integral to this evolution was the active participation of women and youth within the party, fostering modernisation and inclusivity. Margaret Battye, a pioneering female lawyer and inaugural chair of the Liberal state women's council, played a crucial role in shaping policies and strategies. Her leadership, alongside other women leaders, was instrumental in the party's growth and development. The initial policies of the Liberal Party centred on economic growth through reduced taxation, increased industrial production, and education reform focused on smaller class sizes, enhanced teacher training, and expanded facilities. Healthcare reforms aimed at constructing regional hospitals, improving nursing services, and modernising transport infrastructure were also key priorities. These comprehensive policies underscored the party's commitment to fostering economic stability and addressing critical social needs, marking a transformative period in Western Australian governance.

The 1949 Federal Election

In preparation for the 1949 federal election, the Liberal Party crafted a compelling platform focused on restoring discipline in industrial relations, reducing government bureaucracy, and championing free enterprise. This strategic emphasis resonated widely, leading to significant electoral gains as voters responded positively to the party's stance on economic management and individual freedoms. The cultural mood had shifted from a wartime desire to embrace government, to a peacetime desire to be free of its unnecessary strictures.

In parallel, the early state election campaign (which would lead to McLarty retaining office at the March 1950 poll) saw the Liberal Party addressing local concerns with practical solutions. Key policies included infrastructure enhancement, expanded educational opportunities, and improved healthcare services, all aimed at building a robust support base among voters attentive to everyday issues.

In the lead-up to the 1949 federal election, significant changes in electoral representation and candidate selection set the stage for a transformative political landscape in Western Australia. The adoption of proportional representation for Senate elections marked a significant shift, coinciding with a substantial expansion of federal parliament that granted Western Australia three additional House of Representatives seats. Among these new seats, Canning and Moore emerged as strongholds for the Country Party, while Curtin, though initially leaning towards Labor, was poised as a probable gain for the Liberals. Perth and Swan, which had evolved into predominantly suburban constituencies, were reinforced in favour of the ALP.

The Liberal Party strategically sought out candidates with military backgrounds and limited political experience, aiming to strengthen their electoral appeal. Bill Grayden, a former state parliament member, resigned to contest Swan, while Gordon Freeth, a 35-year-old ex-RAAF flight-lieutenant and solicitor from Katanning, was selected for Forrest. Gordon Hack aged 45 was a respected hotelier who had served as deputy controller of the Australian Catering Corps during the war, who was chosen for Perth. Meanwhile, Paul Hasluck, aged 44 was a distinguished academic at the University of Western Australia with a diplomatic background (working for Evatt of all people), who was actively recruited for the seat of Curtin. Senate candidate Seddon Vincent, a 41-year-old barrister from Kalgoorlie with wartime service in the RAAF, represented the Liberal Party's strategic focus on key mining regions. Malcolm Scott, a 39-year-old prominent farmer from Bridgetown with diverse business interests, including pearling and mining, was endorsed after a brief stint with the Labor Party, reflecting his disillusionment over bank nationalisation. Additionally, Bill Snedden, a 22-year-old law clerk and Young Liberal state president, contested Fremantle, displaying youthful enthusiasm despite being too young for significant wartime service.

The WA Division of the Liberal Party executed a robust campaign leading up to the December 1949 election, achieving notable success despite financial challenges. Hancock records that the division faced a fundraising target of £50,000 for 1948-49, of which only half was met due to the party's policy against accepting donations from umbrella groups such as trade associations.[45] Instead, contributions were sought from the interstate headquarters of companies with branches in Western Australia, a practice sustained over subsequent years.

Since 1947 when the terms of senators elected in 1940 had expired, Western Australia lacked Liberal representation at the federal level. Yet at the 1949 federal election, the Liberal Party won three out of eight WA seats, alongside two won by the Country Party, with three remaining under Labor, securing a comfortable 53:47 two-party-preferred split for the Coalition in WA. Notably, Paul Hasluck secured the seat of Curtin with 61.2 per cent of the vote, reflecting a swing of 12.5 per cent from the previous election. In Swan, Bill Grayden garnered 52.4 per cent of the vote, benefiting from a 9.6 per cent swing driven by his popularity in the blue-collar eastern suburbs. Gordon Hack achieved a swing of 11.3 per cent in Perth, narrowly defeating his Labor opponent with 49.9 per cent of the vote, although the joy of the victory would be mellowed by his premature death in 1951. Gordon Freeth faced strong competition in Forrest from Country Party candidate Brigadier Arnold Potts but secured victory with 52.8 per cent of the vote, bolstered by preferences from both independents and the Country Party. Meanwhile, Kalgoorlie and Fremantle, traditionally safer ALP seats, witnessed swings of 9.3 per cent and 8.3 per cent respectively in favour of the Opposition.

The Country Party's anticipated victory in Moore, assisted by Liberal preferences, and the competitive performance of Bill Gillespie in Canning further underscored the dynamics of the election. The Coalition's success extended to the Senate, where they polled 49.2 per cent of the vote and secured four out of seven vacancies, electing Senators Robertson, Vincent, and Scott to represent Western Australia's interests in federal parliament. To sum up, the 1949 federal election in Western Australia not only redefined electoral boundaries and representation but also highlighted the strategic campaigning and candidate selection strategies employed by the Liberal Party. By leveraging military backgrounds, academic credentials, and regional affiliations, the party successfully navigated a shifting political landscape to achieve a significant electoral outcome.

Conclusion: the road beyond

As leader of the 'corner party' of Anti-Socialist Protectionists, WA's Sir John Forrest had been central to the founding of the original Commonwealth Liberal Party in 1909, and only narrowly missed out on succeeding Alfred Deakin as its leader in 1913.[46] Although in the 35 intervening years, WA's centre-right had pushed for secession, they would nevertheless play another prominent role in the founding of the Liberal Party of Australia.

While the division can boast of providing the first federal director in Donald Cleland, its greatest claim to fame is in proving liberalism's electoral viability at the 1947 state election. The victory was an unlikely triumph reflecting the sustained efforts of men like Ross McDonald, Ross McLarty and Jim Paton. As other state divisions would openly advertise, the success would have national reverberations, acting as the beginning of a 'swing to liberalism' across the continent.[47]

In the decades that followed, the Western Australian public witnessed several productive eras of the Liberals in power. Not the least of which were the governments of Sir David Brand and Sir Charles Court. Brand oversaw significant development in Western Australia, including lifting the iron ore export ban in 1960, fostering major industries in mining and refining, and securing funding for key infrastructure projects like the Ord River dam and the east-west railway. His tenure saw the state achieve financial independence from the Commonwealth Grants Commission by 1969, coinciding with his appointment as KCMG.[48]

As a central figure in Western Australian politics, Court became the Liberal Party leader in 1972 and premier in 1974. His tenure was characterised by a strong focus on economic development, particularly in the mining and resources sectors. Court played a significant role in establishing the Northwest Shelf natural gas project, which became a cornerstone of the state's economy. He was also instrumental in the development of major infrastructure projects, including the Ord River Irrigation Scheme and the expansion of port facilities in Dampier and Port Hedland.[49] Court's administration emphasised the importance of decentralisation and regional development, aiming to boost economic opportunities outside of Perth.

The key to these leaders' success was the way they actively demonstrated the core Liberal message: that it was in giving people the freedom to flourish, as opposed to dictating to them via what Paton dubbed the 'dead hand of dull government', that you would generate true national progress and prosperity.[50]

---

1 National Museum of Australia, 'Convict Transportation Ends', Defining Moments, accessed June 30, 2024, https://digital-classroom.nma.gov.au/defining-moments/convict-transportation-ends

2 Babette Smith, *Australia's Birthstain*, p. 518.

3 Moon and Sharman, 'Western Australia', p. 183.

4 de Garis, 'Western Australia', in *The Centenary Companion to Australian Federation*, p. 286.

5 Black, *The House on the* Hill, p. 77.

6 'Road to Federation: Western Australia', Museum of Australian Democracy, accessed 3 June 2024, https://getting-it-together.moadoph.gov.au/western-australia/road-to-federation/index.html

7 Western Australia Museum, 'The Roaring Nineties', accessed 3 June 2024, https://museum.wa.gov.au/explore/wa-goldfields/life-on-fields/roaring-nineties

8 See Gorman, 'George Reid's anti-socialist campaign in the evolution of Australian liberalism'.

9 'Liberal League of Western Australia', *The West Australian*, 7 August 1906, p. 5.

10 'State Referendums, Past Referendums, 1900 Popular Referendum on Australian Federation', Western Australian Electoral Commission, accessed 4 July 2024, https://www.elections.wa.gov.au/elections/state-referendums/past-

referendums/1900-popular-referendum-australian-federation

[11] 'The Liberal Party', *The Argus* (Melbourne), 10 April 1912, p. 6.

[12] de Garis, 'Western Australia', in *The Emergence of the Australian Party System*, p. 341.

[13] Henderson, *Menzies' Child*, p. 55.

[14] Harrop, 'The Republic of Western Australia', p. 327.

[15] Moon and Sharman, 'Western Australia', p. 184.

[16] Fitzherbert, *Liberal Women*, p. 90.

[17] Davidson, *Women on the Warpath*, p. 17.

[18] Ibid., p. 62.

[19] 'Moral Rearmament', *The West Australian*, 10 November 1939, p. 16.

[20] 'Senate Campaign', *Kalgoorlie Miner*, 5 August 1943, p. 4.

[21] 'Outsiders Vote at Nationalist Conference', *Sunday Times* (Perth), 7 May 1944, p. 4.

[22] 'The National Party's Mission', pamphlet from Menzies's Papers in the National Library of Australia.

[23] 'Anxiety about Mr Curtin', *Sydney Morning Herald*, 5 July 1945, p. 1.

[24] Henderson, *Menzies' Child*, p. 67.

[25] 'Wide Appeal Aim of Non-Labour Unity Movement', *The Argus* (Melbourne), 14 October 1944, p. 5.

[26] 'Liberal Party', *The West Australian*, 20 December 1944, p. 4.

[27] '3 Factors for Unity', *The Daily News* (Perth), 27 October 1944, p. 7.

[28] The Liberal Party of Australia Federal Secretariat moved from its temporary location in Sydney to be permanently in Canberra from late 1951.

[29] Buxton, *Commemorating 70 Years: Electoral History*, p. 4.

[30] 'Liberal Party', *The West Australian*, 20 December 1944, p. 4.

[31] 'Mr Menzies Appeals for Non-Labor Unity', *The Herald (Melbourne)*, 13 October 1944, p. 5.

[32] 'Greenough by-election' *Geraldton Guardian and Express* (WA), 3 November 1945, p. 3.

[33] Birman, 'Robertson, Agnes Robertson (1882-1968)'.

[34] Hancock, *National and Permanent?* p. 109.

[35] Figures from Hancock, *National and Permanent?* p. 39.

[36] 'C. and D. League-Liberal Pact', *The West Australian*, 13 April 1943, p. 13.

[37] 'Five Candidates Wiped Oat To Make Way For Mr. Paton', *Sunday Times* (Perth), 23 June 1946, p. 4.

[38] 'Liberal Party Policy', *Kalgoorlie Miner*, 21 February 1947, p. 6.

[39] 'State Election', *The West Australian*, 28 February 1947, p. 17.

40 'The Liberal Party', *The West Australian*, 26 March 1947, p. 11.

41 Ibid.

42 'W.A. Liberals Reject Federation Offer', *The West Australian*, 11 March 1949, p. 2.

43 'The State Liberal Party', *Kalgoorlie Miner*, 4 May 1949, p. 4.

44 'Liberal & Country League Views', *The Dowerin Guardian and Amery Line Advocate*, 12 May 1949, p. 8.

45 Hancock, *National and Permanent?* p. 114.

46 Gorman, *Joseph Cook*.

47 See the NSW chapter.

48 Black, 'Brand, Sir David (1912–1979)'.

49 Jamieson, *Charles Court*, pp. 150-3.

50 'Liberal Party', *The West Australian*, 5 July 1945, p. 6.

9

Conservative Arcadia: Non-Labor Parties in Tasmania, 1903 to 1950

Stefan Petrow

Of all the Australian states, arguably Tasmania was the most politically fertile for non-Labor parties, who should have dominated political contests in the first fifty years of the twentieth century. Tasmania was rabidly pro-Empire, pro-Crown, and did not have a militant work force or union movement. An isolated island with isolated, barely educated communities scattered around it and struggling to survive, its people preferred the comfort of the status quo to any changes that might upset the natural order of things in what federal Labor politician William Morris Hughes called in 1909 an 'Anti-Socialist paradise'.[1] Tasmania's residents could rely on the most conservative Legislative Council in Australia to block radical measures, and on dominant conservative newspapers to support non-Labor parties against the unexpected rise of the Labor Party from 1903, by denouncing its allegedly socialistic policies. Raising the spectre of socialism was a scare tactic rather than an accurate reflection of those policies, as Tasmanian Labor would prove itself to be comparatively conservative, fitting in with the temperament of the island. The upshot was that non-Labor parties securely held government for most of the period 1903-34, and when a moderate and broadly supported Labor Party did hold office (1914-16, 1923-28 and 1934-50) it introduced social and fiscal measures that even staunch opponents found difficult to attack as socialism or on other grounds.

This chapter will begin in section one by developing these points and provide more discussion of the demographic, social, and constitutional features that shaped political culture in Tasmania. In section two I proceed to explicate the chequered history of various non-Labor parties and organisations, which were marked by constant changes, leadership spills and at times divisions between 1903-44 that benefited the Labor Party. The final section charts the early years of the Tasmanian Liberal Party from 1944-50 as it aspired to learn from the mistakes of its predecessors and form a modern political party intended to match if not surpass Labor in organisation, membership, wide-ranging and progressive policy development, and candidate preselection.

Essentially conservative: political culture in Tasmania

In the nineteenth century conservative interests of different kinds held a strong hold over incipient progressive forces in Tasmania. In the penal period to 1853 the autocratic lieutenant-governors and their powerful convict bureaucracy gave little scope to opponents seeking political rights and refused to share power with a section of wealthy landowners and merchants.[2] The anti-transportationists, led by the redoubtable journalist, the Reverend John West, forced the end of the convict system, but politically they were motivated by a desire to end autocracy and decentralise power among grasping wealthy landowner families. From 1856 when self-government began, those families opposed extending the powers of the colonial government and dominated an expanding local government system that operated in their vested interest rather than for benefit of the colony more broadly.

Between 1901 and 1947 Tasmania had by far the lowest population of the Australian states. In 1901 the population was 172,475, rising to 257,078 by 1947, about half of the second lowest, Western Australia, with 502,480.[3] A characteristic of Tasmania from the mid-nineteenth century had been an exodus of population seeking advancement and prosperity in the other colonies, but from 1900-26 alone Tasmania lost by migration 'one fifth of its average population', or around 38,000 people.[4] The loss of 'many of the more intelligent and vigorous of the younger generation', argues Townsley, 'acted as a safety valve and reduced the effectiveness and even the likelihood of a radical protest'.[5]

A further contribution to the essential conservatism of Tasmania was the even spread of its small population over a large area of the island, with 'no sharp contrast between rural and urban interests' and 'no clear-cut distinctions in the distribution of wealth'.[6] This resulted in well-known names and personalities being more dominant than 'issues and party politics'.[7] The low incidence of political and industrial conflict can partly be attributed to how disputes were handled 'at a personal level'. The spread of population resulted in a relatively low level of urbanisation, with the two major cities of Hobart and Launceston having small populations in Australian terms but big in Tasmanian terms, and Tasmania had a higher ratio of rural workers than the Australian average according to the 1933 census.[8] Before World War II industrialisation was minimal, unemployment was typically high and poverty was widespread, all contributing to quiescent stability.[9]

Despite its small population, Reynolds has identified five diverse economic and geographical regions in the nineteenth century that remained relevant into the twentieth century.[10] These were the Midlands, where the most wealthy pastoralists had settled and many pastoral families exerted much conservative political influence; the north-west and north-east with a varied agricultural population of hard-working and egalitarian small farmers, who were more liberal than the pastoralists; the southern Huon and Channel fruit-growing region with its proliferation of orchardists also more inclined to liberalism; the rugged West Coast, where much of Tasmania's mineral wealth was developed and where some radicalism found a conducive home amongst young local and migrant miners eager to form unions to protect their interests; and the two competing cities of Hobart, the political capital, and Launceston, the commercial capital, which tended to be more open to new ideas than its rival and had a more assertive Trades Hall up to 1940.[11] Political parties had to take regional differences and regional political traditions into account when formulating policies and appealing to electorates in the twentieth century.

Discussion of personalities and politics was mostly undertaken in the three dominant daily newspapers based on regional readerships of long standing: *The Advocate* in the north-west, *The Examiner* in the north and *The Mercury* in the south.[12] All three newspapers leaned conservative and greatly favoured non-Labor parties and organisations. Labor ideas were discussed first by the radical *Clipper* and then in turn by the more moderate *Daily Post*, *World* and *Voice*, all Hobart-based and all critical to some extent of the Labor Party's policies or inaction.[13] After its establishment in 1890, the University of Tasmania was too small in staff and student numbers (the lowest proportion of young people to attend university in Australia) to have much influence on political life before 1945, but academic economists did advise governments on how to deal with their perennial budget deficiencies.[14] Although Tasmania was the state most dependent on Commonwealth financial grants, generally Tasmanian politicians of every stripe fiercely opposed any 'Commonwealth interference in the government of their state'.[15]

The political system replicated mainland states with a bicameral parliament of a House of Assembly and a Legislative Council established in 1856. The *Constitution Act 1900* introduced manhood suffrage for the House of Assembly and the *Constitution Act 1903* enfranchised women, but they were not eligible to stand for parliament until the *Constitution Act 1921*.[16] Tasmania differed from the other states in that its ultra-conservative Legislative Council had the most restrictive franchise and, with the power of veto, could reject or amend Bills sent to it by the Assembly. Moreover, the Tasmanian constitution did not include a double dissolution of both Houses. Tasmania's Legislative Council therefore had more power than most other Upper Houses.

The *Constitution Act 1900* required electors to the Legislative Council to own freehold estate of £10 per annum or to be an occupier of property worth £30.[17] The *Constitution (War Service Franchise) Act 1920* extended the Council franchise to anyone who actively served in World War I. This was extended again by the *Constitution Act 1941* to anyone under twenty-one years who actively served in any war. The *Constitution Act 1946* reduced the value of property occupied to £26 per annum for electors and extended the right to contest Legislative Council elections to anyone aged twenty-five and over. More than 'a house of review', most Legislative Council members felt they had a duty to resist reforms or what some members regarded as 'dangerous innovations' whether attempted by Labor or non-Labor parties.[18] Voting became compulsory for both Houses by the *Electoral Act 1928* and the turn out for the House of Assembly elections was normally 95 per cent.[19]

Focusing now on the House of Assembly, where governments were formed, the *Constitution Amendment Act 1906* reduced the thirty-five single member districts to five districts with six candidates each following the boundaries of the five Commonwealth electoral districts – Bass, Darwin, Denison, Franklin and Wilmot. A significant related stage was the modification of the Hare-Clark 'variant' of proportional representation for Assembly elections in the *Electoral Act 1907*.[20] In 1909 the five electorates averaged 19,157 electors, almost eight times the 1906 average.[21] The larger electorates encouraged co-operation between candidates and made 'coherent party organisation' advantageous.

The first election when the five electorates and the Hare-Clark system was employed in 1909 saw Labor's seats increase from seven of thirty-five to twelve of thirty.[22] While Hare-Clark seemed to benefit Labor, one drawback was that candidates from the same party were battling each other as much as their opponents to gain first preference votes and some sitting members were replaced at every election. As most elections under Hare-Clark did not result in an emphatic victory, if one member moved to the opposing side it could cause the downfall of a government. A party which won most of the votes overall might still not gain the majority of seats because 'the quota was based on an even number of vacancies'.[23] Independents also were a factor in the Hare-Clark system. In eight of the fifteen elections between 1909 and 1950 independents were elected, with a total of eighteen overall. Independent influence will become apparent in the next section on the history of non-Labor parties in Tasmania.

Non-Labor parties in Tasmania

We now turn to the characteristics of the party system before the formation of post-war Liberal Party in 1944. According to Joan Rydon's statistics, of all the Australian states, Tasmania was the most evenly divided between the Labor and non-Labor parties with Labor in office 46 per cent of the period 1918-40 and averaging 53 per cent of the seats.[24] She stressed that 'personalities were as important as parties' and that state politics were 'very divorced from federal questions'. Outside Rydon's 1918-40 period, we should note that from 1909-17 non-Labor was in government for six years and, often with the support of independents, Labor for two years and from 1941-50 Labor was also in power and remained so until 1969. Despite the dominance of Labor from 1934, non-Labor, notes Townsley, 'always appeared in sufficient strength in Parliament to foster hope and preclude demoralisation', in terms of seats won at least.[25] Both Labor and non-Labor parties placed much more emphasis on 'interests' than on 'doctrine' and tried to appeal to a broad spectrum of voters by focusing on 'bread and butter politics'.[26]

Scott's research on the background of candidates and elected members of the House from 1909-59 shows that Labor drew from 'a wider cross-section of the community than other parties' and was not 'an exclusively working-class party'.[27] Labor's members tended, especially in the 1930s and mid-1940s, to be younger and intent on making 'a professional career of politics', while non-Labor party members tended to regard politics 'as a part-time occupation' and entered parliament after establishing themselves in other careers. Surprisingly, only four per cent of Labor members were trade union officials, over 37 per cent came from the employer classes and significant numbers from farmers and orchardists. Labor's spread of hydro-electricity into rural areas won electoral support, which partly explained 'the exceptional conservatism of the Tasmanian party'.[28] Non-Labor members were drawn mainly from farmers, the professions, business managers and merchants, who collectively made up 82 per cent of non-Labor members, and, as to be expected, very few from the employee classes and no trade union officials.[29]

By far the most studied party in Tasmania has been the Australian Labor Party mainly due to the herculean research of Richard Davis, who detailed the organisational structure and branches, divisive issues between the political and union wings, policies, elections, limited finances, party organisation, women's involvement and personalities that defined the party from its formation in 1903.[30] The Tasmanian Labor Party survived defections at times of stress in Australian history and remained stable for most of the period 1903-50. Further to the left was the Communist Party, whose candidates stood at some state and federal elections, but with a very low number of votes and with no impact on political life in conservative, non-militant Tasmania.[31]

The socialism of the early Labor Party was restricted to taking over monopolies, but from 1910 radicals at some party conferences forced debate on the socialisation of the means of production, distribution and exchange.[32] In a 'brief socialist flutter', Tasmanian delegates were directed to vote for the socialisation objective at the 1921 Brisbane federal Labor conference, which passed in a watered down version after an amendment by Maurice Blackburn stated that the socialisation objective was limited to preventing exploitation. The Blackburn amendment was accepted by Tasmanian Labor in 1922, but a sizable proportion of the party and practically all subsequent Labor leaders adhered to 'the old formula'. While the acceptance of the Blackburn amendment gave 'the appearance of radicalism', the Labor Party was too conservative to attempt the implementation of socialisation.

The history of non-Labor parties in Tasmania is more complicated and has not been subjected to close scrutiny. The first important step, taken after the suffrage was extended in the early twentieth century, was the formation of the Reform League, which organised branches and developed a ten-point program that candidates who sought its endorsement at the 1903 elections had to subscribe to.[33] The Reform League was not effective and ended in September 1903, but did set 'a precedent and a model for widespread electoral organisation in Tasmania'.

In April 1904 conservative forces formed a National Association 'to oppose "class and socialistic legislation"' and support candidates representing 'the producing, manufacturing and trading interest of the state'.[34] Weller sees the National Association as a response to the Propsting Liberal-Democrat ministry (1903-04) and the formation of a federal Labor government rather than to 'the isolated and small' Tasmanian Labor Party, which secured only three seats and 10.7 per cent of the vote at the 1903 elections. The National Association appointed a full-time organiser to form branches throughout Tasmania and elected a state council with northern and southern representatives, but membership was small, the most 'active' branches were dominated by women, and meetings resembled 'social gatherings'.[35] The Association suffered reputational damage from its close association with the liquor trade and its domination by 'a conservative clique'. Women exercised the vote for the first time at the 1906 elections when Labor's 'enthusiasm and vigour' was criticised by conservatives for adding 'a new and unsporting element into politics', which increased Labor's seats to seven and had to be countered.[36]

The National Association tried to forge 'a more positive and dynamic' image by reforming itself as the Southern Tasmanian Progressive League in January 1907.[37] While it still opposed socialism, it now supported 'progressive legislation'. Despite forming branches, appointing an executive and developing an organisational structure, the Progressive League still resembled a social and not a political group. Progressive League candidates were only united by their 'anti-socialist views' and it disappeared after the 1909 elections. Weller regarded the association and the league as representing unsuccessful attempts to form 'an electoral body with continuity of existence'. Members of parliament did not run or form these two bodies and the league was willing to endorse candidates, but not 'to dictate to MHAs', a common philosophical tenet of non-Labor organisations.

At the 1909 elections, as noted earlier, the Labor Party increased its seats in the Assembly to twelve out of thirty, which exacerbated anti-socialist concerns.[38] Some members of the Farmers and Stockowners' Association (avowedly non-political) realised that the various non-Labor organisations had failed because they had not developed strong ties in country areas. Partly due to the association's efforts a state-wide conference in August 1909 formed the Tasmanian Liberal League (TLL), whose objectives included states' rights, preserving 'the individual and collective rights of the people' and fighting socialism. The TLL formed a state council, an electorate committee and local branches, whose delegates sat on the two bodies.

The TLL differed from earlier organisations in making Premier Neil Elliott Lewis its chairman and including four MHAs on its state council, but parliamentarians were not required to vote for the TLL platform.[39] Lewis had been involved with the earlier organisations. Some MHAs thought Lewis was too conservative to lead the Liberal Party and threatened to withdraw their support if he did not agree to their demands. When he failed to act, five Liberals rebelled over a finance bill and brought down the Lewis Government. The moderate Earle Labor Party formed its first government in October 1909, which lasted only a week until the Liberals re-united under Lewis. But the rebellion showed that the Liberal Party was 'a fusion of groups with varying ideas' and differences could surface at any time.[40] Consequently, Lewis tried to pacify his moderate opponents and neutralise Labor by formulating, the 'Charter of the Working Man' and passing Tasmania's first 'comprehensive' *Factories Act* and *Wages Board Act*.

The TLL spent the next two years perfecting its 'internal structure' and appointing three organisers to form branches (132 by May 1912).[41] By 1912 it had established 'a "modern" non-Labor organisation' with 'continuity of existence, a sound participating branch network and effective co-ordination of the units of the party organisation'. Liberals now had a party machine to match Labor's, but the TLL resolutely opposed interference in party matters. Aided by the party machine, the Liberals secured victory in the 1912 elections with 16 seats and 54.48 per cent of the vote compared to Labor's 14 seats with 45.52 per cent.[42] Despite his election victory, Lewis realised that his support was dwindling and he resigned, handing the Liberal Party leadership to a more 'energetic', younger leader Albert Edgar Solomon.[43]

Having to deal with the discord that remained after Lewis's departure and the unpredictable behaviour of Liberal Joshua Whitsitt, Solomon lost a no confidence motion called by the Labor Party in April 1914.[44] The governor called on Earle to form a Labor government, which he maintained by eschewing 'party differences' wherever possible and avoiding social reform because of the war until April 1916.[45] Labor was then defeated by the Liberal Party led by Sir Walter Lee, but outside events soon caused more disruption. The conscription plebiscites split federal Labor led by Billy Hughes, who formed a new party he called the Nationalist Party to obscure its sectional character.[46] This created problems for Lee because his Liberal Party was reluctant to join a party led by a former Labor prime minister and preferred to work alongside the newly-formed National Federation, which was 'the only extra-parliamentary Nationalist organisation' to survive to the 1940s.[47]

For a time much confusion reigned on the non-Labor side of politics. The Liberal Party remained the main non-Labor party in parliament, but the National Federation was gaining supporters in different electorates for the formation of a Tasmanian branch of the Nationalist Party.[48] Women branches of the TLL agreed to dissolve and fight for the Nationalist cause in the second conscription plebiscite. In a series of by-elections held in 1917 in some electorates Liberals stood and in others Nationalists.[49] But in 1919 the Nationalists dominated the elections winning 16 seats (55.20 per cent of the vote) to Labor's 13 seats (41.44 per cent of the vote) and 1 independent, who favoured the Nationalists.[50]

By 1922, however, conservative newspapers and the Legislative Council were criticising the Lee Government for inter alia financial mismanagement and disunity.[51] This particularly upset rural interests and led to a new force in non-Labor ranks, the Country Party, which had not featured much in Tasmanian non-Labor politics. In 1922 frustration at slow economic growth resulted, with the support of the Tasmanian Farmers, Stockowners and Orchardists' Association, in the formation of the Country Party.[52] In 1923 the Country Party won five seats (two of its members had been Nationalists) out of thirteen candidates standing in its name and held the balance of power much to the chagrin of the Nationalist government. Disunity again surfaced in October 1923 when three Nationalist members voted against the Lee Government, enabling the Lyons Labor Party to assume office, 'an unexpected and almost miraculous bonus' writes Davis.[53] Lyons was able to retain office later in October when six Nationalists and one Country Party member voted against a no-confidence motion.

In 1925 the Country Party dissolved after four of the five Country Party MPs decided to join the Nationalists to fight against the Labor Government; only two of the four were re-elected as Nationalists and Lyons secured Labor's first election victory.[54] According to Legislative Councillor Joe Darling, a Country Party founder, the one achievement of the Country Party was to drive the National Union of Melbourne, 'a secret body, controlled to a great extent by the wealthy combines of Australia', out of Tasmania.[55] Lyons secured victory because he was 'a credible alternative' who sought to solve Tasmania's financial difficulties rather than trying to implement Labor policies. At his policy speech at Deloraine he spoke as 'a Tasmanian Premier rather than a Labor official'. The term 'deloraining' thereafter signified how a Labor premier consciously walked away from his party's policy to hang on to government and signified a threat to non-Labor parties too.[56] The president of the once hostile Chamber of Commerce, WH Cummins, declared that Tasmania, due to Lyons's leadership, was in 'the happy position of knowing no party; there were two united parties in Parliament'.[57]

Inclined towards consensus, Lyons co-operated closely with the Nationalist Leader John Cameron McPhee and effectively ran 'an informal coalition ministry' that was decidedly not socialist. But in the 1928 election campaign the Nationalists, worried that they were solidifying Lyons in office, abandoned all pretence at co-operation and attacked Lyons 'vigorously and unfairly' for doing things they had once praised him for doing but also for a rise in unemployment.[58] The onset of the Great Depression further disrupted Tasmanian non-Labor politics. At the federal level, with the support of Melbourne business interests, Joseph Lyons and another Tasmanian Allan Guy left the Scullin Labor Government over differences in economic management of the Depression and joined with some Nationalists to form the United Australia Party.[59] Some modern commentators have been less than fulsome about the UAP, with Lonie probably reflecting the general view that it was 'a fractious coalition of cabals' only held together by the leadership of Lyons, who, influenced mightily by his wife Enid, became one of the most successful conservative Australian prime ministers.[60]

In Tasmania the Nationalist Party did not support the UAP and preferred to continue the existing two-party system.[61] The Nationalist Party was crucially supported at election time and in fund raising by the Australian Women's National League (AWNL), formed in 1928 with the help of the powerful Victorian AWNL, 'the largest conservative political organisation in Australia' according to Sawer and Simms.[62] The Tasmanian AWNL sought to combat socialism and the nationalisation of industries, educate women in politics and 'promote the welfare of women and children'. By February 1931 it had formed fifty-five branches throughout Tasmania. At the

May 1931 elections the Nationalists won 19 seats to Labor's 10 and 1 independent seat (a former Labor MP). This was the worst defeat since the Hare-Clark system was introduced and a Labor split seemed likely.[63]

While the Nationalists and the AWNL worked effectively in tandem, the non-Labor landscape was complicated by the appearance of three new political groups with different concerns – the Reform League, a Tasmanian branch of the All for Australia League (AFAL) and the Young Nationalists Organisation (YNO), all formed in 1931.[64] In essence, the Reform League wanted to cut state parliament costs by reducing the number of members and their salaries, the AFAL wanted to unite Australians to fight the economic crisis of the Depression and other national problems, and the YNO aimed to spread the Nationalist message among younger Tasmanians. Many Nationalists did not want to support the UAP when it included ex-Labor member Lyons and his sidekick Guy. The situation was further complicated by differences in viewpoint between the northern and southern wings of the Nationalist Party over whether to support the UAP.

In October 1931 the AWNL, the YNO and the National Federation decided not to accept 'loss of party identity' and refused Lyons and Guy immunity from electoral opposition because they were not Nationalist members.[65] As Lyons was leader of the UAP, the AFAL and the Reform League insisted that he be supported. The AWNL soon broke ranks and decided to support Lyons, but the National Federation endorsed its northern-based state secretary, George Gerald Pullen, who felt personal animosity towards Lyons, to stand against him in Wilmot. The AFAL, YNO, AWNL and the Nationalist Party denounced the actions of the National Federation. Despite the division of non-Labor organisations, the UAP won all five Tasmanian seats and Lyons easily beat Pullen to become the first and only Tasmanian prime minister.

In the 1930s non-Labor remained divided. In Tasmania the federal elections were contested by the UAP, while in state elections the Nationalist name was resolutely retained.[66] When they combined organisationally in 1935, they still retained their separate names as the United Australia and Nationalist Organisation (UANO). The AWNL was the only other non-Labor organisation to survive the 1930s and in 1936 decided to abolish its divisional councils and form a state council of delegates from the different branches.[67] The AWNL became 'a definite influence' throughout Tasmania and actively supported all non-Labor candidates at state and federal elections, but the Nationalist Party could not break Labor's stranglehold on state government after McPhee lost office to Labor's energetic, decisive and modernising Albert Ogilvie in 1934.[68] In 1939 Ogilvie died unexpectedly and was replaced by the highly conservative Robert Cosgrove, who became the longest serving premier in Tasmanian history. Non-Labor remained weak until the mid-1940s when Labor faced a more determined and organised, but still fallible opponent in Menzies's Liberal Party.

Formation and early years of the Tasmanian Liberal Party 1944 to 1950

In the wake of the 1943 UAP federal election disaster, the UANO in Tasmania considered following the New South Wales example by dissolving the organisation and merging with other bodies to form 'a Liberal-Democratic Party'.[69] Some members of the UANO realised that it should adopt a platform with 'a wider appeal to all sections of the people' and elect officers on 'a different basis'. The strongest push came from the Bass-Wilmot divisional council, whose younger members, believing that the UAP had 'outlived its usefulness', wanted the party to be 'completely swept away' and to establish 'a totally new party which will represent all non-Labor interests'.[70] They wanted the new party to embrace 'liberalism and democracy'. *The Examiner* wanted the new party to be 'a virile, constructive and united non-Labor party' that did not 'champion any sectional interests', but had 'a policy for the nation'.[71]

Events took a decisive turn when Robert Menzies seized the initiative, espousing the idea of forming 'a progressive liberal party' devoid of reactionary elements and calling for a unity conference of all political organisations 'opposed to Socialism and believing in Democracy' in October 1944.[72] Tasmanians were well represented at the conference: the Leader of the Opposition Nationalist Party Henry Seymour Baker, a lawyer, who gave 'a rousing speech', but was not on the frontline of national debate; representatives of the AWNL, Tasmanian branch President Mrs Florence Mary Parker, Hobart secretary Mrs Effie Millicent Baker (Henry's wife) and Miss Amelia Martha 'Millie' Best, a Launceston businesswoman; two Tasmanian representatives of the Australian Constitutional League, Reginald Charles Wright, a lawyer who had been a member of the YNO, and Cyril Carrington, a company manager; and representatives of the UANO Harold Bushby, a lawyer and strong supporter of Menzies, William Frederick Mills, an insurance manager, Arthur Ernest Wadsley, a businessman, and the honorary secretary, Frank Alfred Allen, an insurance manager.[73] The Bakers, Parker, Wright, Wadsley and Allen represented southern Tasmania, and Best, Carrington, Bushby and Mills northern Tasmania.[74] Northern-based Nationalist Senator Burford Sampson also attended.[75]

Interestingly, in his conference address, Menzies, referring to the UANO and the AWNL, noted that on his visits to Tasmania he was 'always struck by the want of cohesion which exists between the Southern centres of the Island and the Northern centres', something he clearly wanted to avoid in the Liberal Party: 'a common organisation outside Parliament is absolutely imperative'.[76] Although hard evidence is elusive, it appears that Menzies was popular in Tasmania. In July 1941 the state conference of the UANO supported his leadership when it was coming under fire even from his own side of politics.[77] During the 1943 federal election and the 1944 federal referendum campaigns, he faced his share of interjectors, but was received enthusiastically by large audiences throughout Tasmania, especially in Hobart.[78]

The conference closed on 16 October by unanimously agreeing to form a new non-Labor political party called the Liberal Party of Australia, and to submit the adopted ten-point policy to state organisations for 'ratification'.[79] The new party adopted a federal structure to avoid marginalising any particular state. A federal executive would have equal state representation – of particular importance for the smallest state.[80] A provisional executive committee, including Baker and Bushby from Tasmania, was formed to carry out the decisions of the conference and suggest a time and place for the next conference.

When Baker returned to Hobart he told *The Advocate* that, once the conference decisions were implemented, there would be 'a powerful Federal Party, with branches in each state, and with a permanent staff to carry out a vigorous plan'.[81] He felt that the conference decisions would be accepted by state organisations 'without serious qualification'. The Tasmanian representatives 'emphatically supported union of all bodies within a Federal type of organisation'. When Reg Wright returned to Hobart, he told his daughter Alison, 'Well, we've elected Bob Menzies as leader, I think we've done the right thing', hardly a ringing endorsement.[82] On 29 October at a meeting of the state council of the UANO and the Tasmanian Constitutional League the decisions of 'the unity conference' in Canberra were 'unanimously accepted'.[83] The meetings appointed delegates to attend the next conference at Albury in December, which would endorse the constitution and objects of 'the new Liberal Party of Australia'.

Of the six delegates appointed to represent Tasmania at Albury, Henry Baker, Reg Wright, Mary Parker, Harold Bushby and Cyril Carrington had attended the first conference.[84] The sixth representative was Burnie auctioneer John Clement Leary, representing the Darwin divisional council of the UANO. In summarising the Albury conference proceedings, Baker was inspired 'to put into practical operation a constructive policy based on liberal and progressive thought, as opposed to the sterile doctrine of socialisation'.[85] His immediate task was to establish a provisional executive committee and an 'autonomous' Tasmanian branch of the Liberal Party. Former non-Labor organisations would be dissolved and all who believed in the new movement would become 'original members on an equal footing'. The new party would not only prepare to fight elections, but also investigate 'the economic aspects of current problems'. A permanent secretariat of 'well qualified men' would be charged with providing information and assisting the Liberal Party and its parliamentary representatives in each state branch.

The Tasmanian branch of the Liberal Party wanted to move quickly to build a strong party organisation in preparation for the state and federal elections due towards the end of 1946.[86] In mid-January 1945 the provisional committee was mostly formed while Menzies was in Hobart and he reportedly 'discussed aspects of the organisation with leaders of the movement'. The first task was to establish sub-branches, which would elect members to the state council, and then permanent officers would be appointed.[87] The state council would take over from the provisional committee, 'control the affairs of the organisation' and appoint seven members to represent Tasmania on the federal executive. *The Advocate* thought restoring 'the old name of "Liberal", honored in other years, is a good omen' and forming a 'broad-based' party was 'essential if it is to gain support as a democratic institution'.[88] While the federal party would develop its own policies, 'the Tasmanian policy will be that of the Tasmanian section'. A significant sign of support for the new party came on 1 February 1945 when the AWNL decided to dissolve eighteen years after its formation.[89] The AWNL president, Mary Parker, said they had decided to present 'a united front' and members would become 'individual members of the Liberal Party'.

On 3 February provisional committee elections resulted in Reg Wright being elected president and Dame Enid Lyons, Mrs Joyce Heathorn, importer Arthur James Beck, Harold Bushby and John Leary vice-presidents.[90] Member of the Constitutional League, Edwin Russell 'John' Cottier, became the state secretary and Cyril

Carrington honorary treasurer. Delegates present at the meeting came from a wide geographical area – eight men from Hobart, five men and eight women from Launceston, two males from Burnie and one male from Devonport, Latrobe, Longford, Penguin and Wynyard. Full of his usual zest, Wright announced that the Liberal Party aimed at achieving 'a true liberty for the individual in business and in pleasure' and in return expected every individual to do his 'duty in the defence of the country which shelters him'.[91] The party also aimed to secure the right for 'all classes to enjoy social and economic justice' and supported 'arbitration in industry', improved education, and most importantly would maintain agriculture 'on equal proportions with city life' and urge 'preference for servicemen and women'.

While Wright gave a taster of the Liberal Party's policies, more revealing was the Tasmanian Liberal Party's first meeting, held at Hobart Town Hall on 13 February, where the deputy leader of the federal Opposition, Eric Harrison, spoke. In moving thanks to Harrison, state Opposition Leader Henry Baker, noted that the Tasmanian UAP had 'never previously been linked with any form of Australian party political organisation', which had 'weakened and impoverished' its work and caused it to lose 'touch with the people' and disintegrate as 'a fighting force'.[92] This explained why 'those opposed to the socialistic trend' of the ALP supported a new party with 'a positive political creed and an active, re-vivified type of organisation' based on the 'democratic government of the party by members'. As the federal constitution laid down, the party finances relied on member contributions, 'rank and file support', and not on 'a few large contributions'.

Baker explained the differences between the Liberal Party and its non-Labor predecessors. The Liberal Party provided machinery to keep contact between state and Commonwealth representatives and the organisations through a policy committee and thus enable members to keep contact with their parliamentary representatives.[93] Women were expected fully to participate in 'the control of the organisations' and conduct their own 'special activities by a woman's section'. Baker envisaged the party headquarters to be 'a centre of interest to all members', providing 'an information service' to parliamentarians and members interested in political problems and building a reference library. He supported holding 'discussions and debates on current affairs' at monthly luncheons and forming a speaker's class and youth section. While Baker was concerned by Labor's principle that 'all means of production, distribution and exchange should be socialised', he declared that the Liberal Party was 'not opposed on principle to community ownership in all circumstances', but regarded it as 'a practical question, to be dealt with on its merits in each case'.

Other speakers were keen to correct misimpressions. President Wright made it clear that the Liberal Party was 'not a fusion of existing bodies nor an uneasy partnership of old associations'.[94] It was, in fact, 'a new party which would draw its members direct from the electors who subscribed to the objectives of the party'. Launceston businessman James McDougall Fotheringham made it clear that regional rivalries would have no place in the new party: 'There would be nothing of the "north and south feeling" because there could be no division in achieving the party's objectives'. When Baker returned from a meeting of the provisional federal executive in March, he was impressed by Menzies's suggestion that 'a certain proportion of the committees of sub-branches should be new members under 30' and welcomed contributions from 'the younger generation' more amenable to 'a radical approach' to problems such as peace in industry, agriculture and the agricultural worker, education, health, housing and slum clearance, all weighty matters for Tasmanians.[95]

Clearly, the Tasmanian leaders of the Liberal Party wanted the electorate to understand the newness of the party in terms of policies, party organisation, leaders and membership, but not all onlookers were convinced. 'Think Well' doubted a real change had occurred and alleged that Liberals were 'still being led by the same old "stagnation" leaders who have changed their party name four times since 1910'.[96] A proponent of bank nationalisation called 'Justice' thought the anti-nationalisation Liberal Party was 'actually the re-organised mouthpiece of the big financial institutions', which the Labor *Voice* newspaper named as the Institute of Public Affairs, 'a secret body of rich men'.[97]

Such commentary hardly registered as the Liberal Party continued to enhance its presence in Tasmania. Indeed, Baker predicted 'a great liberal revival throughout Australia, which will re-build parliaments to a line of sanity and a real path to democracy'.[98] With federal Labor's plans to nationalise the banks and the airways, now was the time for 'an uprising of a party built on democratic lines' like the Liberal Party. Wright had called branches 'strongposts for liberties for the common man among electors' and travelled the state to attend the formation of new branches.[99]

By the provisional state executive meeting on 26 May, 34 branches had been formed with 2,200 members.[100] That meeting resolved that the state council be elected by the branches, with each branch electing two representatives 'of whom one should be a man and one a woman'. Such 'equal representation' gave women 'their rightful place in politics' and rewarded their hard work at elections and in maintaining 'political activity'. Member of the provisional executive of the Northern branch, Millie Best, described Liberal women as 'co-administrators' with 'a moral obligation' to serve the Liberal Party and, once the party had been 'properly constituted', to discuss issues of 'vital importance' to women such as housing, 'the lot of country women and children, hospitals and medical work'.[101]

The message about what the Liberal Party stood for certainly permeated into the branches. In June 1945, when the influential Central Hobart branch was formed, vice-president of the provisional committee, Alderman Arthur Beck, called the Liberal Party 'a "people's party" in every sense'.[102] It would not be 'dominated by a few men, as was the case in the organisations it superseded, but would be controlled entirely by its membership'. Channelling Menzies, Beck called it 'a new political force', which 'brought new hope to the "forgotten people" of the set-income middle class' and salary and wage earners. He declared that some people in the Liberal Party 'would walk out if it proved a "big business party"'.

President of the Sandy Bay branch, rising lawyer Stanley Burbury, spread a similar message to members of the New Town branch. He believed the Liberal Party would protect 'the rights of the common man against exploitation of any kind, whether it came from "big business" domination or trade union domination' and would not let control of the party 'fall into the hands of the unprogressive conservatives. The principles of liberalism are not reactionary and unprogressive'.[103] Vice President Harold Bushby was concerned about another form of domination. He told the Lilydale branch that the state council will be 'the voice of the members' and will 'conduct the business and affairs of the party' in Tasmania: it will not be controlled by the politicians.[104] The branches also defined the beliefs informing Tasmanian Liberalism. For example, in February 1946 the East Launceston branch set down three principles, which were endorsed by the state executive and sent to state council: 'democracy can best be fulfilled by decentralisation of political power'; 'respect for observation of the law is the first duty of citizenship'; and 'the State exists for the individual'.[105]

The first conference of the state council was held at Launceston on 21 July with 51 branches represented by 100 delegates. Provisional committee chairman, Reg Wright, told delegates that he was impressed with the 'pace' at which the branches had developed, with a total of 55 and over 4,000 members, and stressed that the branches 'must be kept alive' to ensure victory in the state and federal elections.[106] To stop the growth of communism spreading its 'tentacles into movements which supported Labour', they must stabilise politics by forming 'a strong party'.[107] Wright told delegates that the provisional committee had organised itself into three sections – southern, northern and north-western – which had formed branches in their areas under the co-ordination of the state office in Hobart. The provisional committee had held women's afternoon meetings, lunch hour forum talks and published the party journal called *The New Beacon*, which seems not to have survived for long. It was now ready to hand control over to the state council, which the conference would form.

The conference agreed to elect four vice presidents from the four electoral districts other than the president's division.[108] The executive would consist of the president, four vice presidents, a treasurer and twenty members elected from state council, and would 'exercise all the powers of the council', except the 'special duties' of electing members of the policy committee and federal council and amending the constitution. The executive was empowered to form local or special committees 'for such purposes as it might think fit'. On the motion of Mrs Dorothy Edwards (Launceston, East), men and women would be equally represented on the executive and the conference agreed to another motion that four members of the executive should be chosen from the five electoral districts. Equal representation of men and women branch delegates on the executive and the state council continued until 1962.[109]

The election of state council members proceeded with Wright elected as president and Burbury for Franklin, Bushby for Wilmot, Fotheringham for Bass and Lyons for Darwin elected as vice presidents.[110] Carrington was elected treasurer. For the five electoral divisions the following were elected: Denison (Mrs Joyce Heathorn, Miss Joy Piesse, Arthur Beck and Horace Theodore Kench); Franklin (Mrs Quentin McDougall, Mrs Ronald Bilton Denholm, Douglas Fairfax Calvert, and Stephen Carlos Woolnough); Bass (Mrs H Bearup, Mrs Dorothy Edwards, Thomas Dove Wardlaw and Sinclair Jeavons Thyne); Wilmot (Mrs David Taylor, Mrs R Brown, Denham Henty and George Hogarth Napier); and Darwin (Mrs AR Balon, Mrs P Williams, John Leary and M White).

The conference decided to follow the party constitution and

appoint a joint standing committee on state policy consisting of four members of the state parliament and four non-parliamentary members presided over by the leader of the parliamentary party.[111] The policy committee would be charged with drafting 'a state policy for submission to the council'. On a motion by Burbury, four extra members would be elected to the state policy committee to formulate policies to take to the next election. On Wright's motion, the conference unanimously agreed to continue to work with the state Opposition.

As for electing parliamentary candidates, this would be the responsibility of 'a committee constituted by the delegates to the state council from the electoral divisions for which the election is to be held'.[112] For the Senate election, candidates would be selected by a committee comprised of seven Tasmanian members of the federal council and seven members of the state council chaired by the state president. The seven Tasmanian representatives elected to the federal council were Enid Lyons, Joyce Heathorn, Harold Bushby, John Leary, George Hogarth Napier and Sinclair Jeavons Thyne. The seven state council members elected were Mrs McDougall, Millie Best, James Fotheringham, Trevor Max Payne, Arthur Beck, M White and Harry Gillett.

The Examiner, a strong supporter of the new Liberal Party and impressed with its 'rapid expansion', identified some possible members who were holding back, 'fearing that it will turn out, after all, to be just the old anti-Labour set-up in a new guise'.[113] It pointed out that policies had yet to be formulated and those with 'progressive ideas' should join to shape those policies and influence 'the character and outlook of the party'. One Liberal, HG Woodford of Campbell Town, warned members not to follow previous 'anti-Labour forces' by taking 'their privileges for granted' and advised that, 'unless we are prepared to be as "militant" as Labour', the Liberal Party would not win the next elections.[114]

One point of division after the election of office bearers was the 'general desire among the rank and file to cut the painter, so far as possible, from control of the movement by members of Parliament'.[115] The only sitting member of either the federal or state parliaments to be elected to the executive was Enid Lyons even though 'several prominent MPs sought office'. Lyons was also the only member of parliament of the seven elected to represent Tasmania on the federal executive. This gave hope to supporters of the new movement that 'there will be an infusion of new ideas into the future policy of the party'.

The Examiner also identified ructions caused by the recent elections of the state executive. It reported on 'a lack of harmony' between the newly-elected state executive and members of the parliamentary Opposition, who criticised the executive for not working with them and for not allowing them some representation on the executive.[116] A conspicuous absentee from the executive was Leader of the Opposition Henry Baker, who had served on the provisional committee to establish the Liberal Party and was so enthusiastic about its prospects. This weakened the unity that the Liberal Party was seeking to build. Some members resented 'the tendency to "cold shoulder" or "drop" former stalwarts of the UAP organisation', who had kept the organisation going. Some stalwarts allegedly threatened 'to organise a breakaway movement'.

Senior figures moved quickly to scotch the rumours of division. State president of the UANO and president of the Central Launceston branch of the Liberal Party, Senator Burford Sampson, rejected the notion of 'a breakaway movement'.[117] The UANO had decided not to dissolve until the Liberal Party was placed on a firm foundation, elected its officers and adopted a 'definite constitution'. After all this was done on 21 July Sampson asked the secretary of the Tasmanian UAP, Frank Allen, to call a state council meeting at Tunbridge on 15 September formally to dissolve the body. The Tunbridge meeting agreed to dissolve from 30 September and hand all property over to the Liberal Party.[118]

Before the UAP dissolution, Baker also denied that a split in non-Labor forces was planned and claimed that the 'old hands' welcomed 'many new and active members' who were creating 'a virile organisation'.[119] Baker was an ex officio member of the state council and as leader of the parliamentary party saw no need to hold an executive position, which would be 'contrary to practice elsewhere in Australia'. At its first meeting the Liberal Party state council had adopted a policy of co-operation between itself and the parliamentary party as a symbol of unity.

The crunch came when applications were called for candidates to contest the 1946 elections. President Wright dismissed the 'assertion' that the Liberal Party executive intended to endorse at most two or three members of the parliamentary Opposition, but did concede that the executive expected 'a large proportion of our candidates to be returned servicemen' and wanted to endorse 'the best team for Liberalism'.[120] Those who had called the Liberal Party 'the old crowd under a new name' must now realise that the party was 'a new party' containing 'no vested interests' or 'prejudices'. At a meeting between the members of the Opposition and the state executive on 10 November it was again agreed that both bodies would work together and that the Opposition would represent the Liberal Party in parliament until the next election, but the name Liberal Party would not be used in parliament until candidates were elected under that name.[121]

The conference of state council moved to the next step of preparing for the elections by adopting on 24 November a ten-point policy plan under the headings of parliamentary reform, taxation, housing, education, transport, industrial relationship, rehabilitation of service personnel, primary production, country facilities and social security.[122] *The Examiner* praised the plan for revealing 'a truly liberal and progressive outlook'.[123] It recognised 'private enterprise as the most fruitful and efficient productive system', but encouraged 'co-operative effort to ensure a just division of the rewards of work'. Other features were support for 'profits control', 'stabilised prices for primary products' and contributory social security provision. Even Labor's *Voice* found much to support in the ten-points as many policies were 'closely allied with Labor ideals, and if put into practice 100 per cent, would do an immense amount of good'.[124] That similarity and the Cosgrove Labor Government's consistently expressed disapproval of federal governments, both Labor and non-Labor, showed that there was 'not one good reason why Tasmania should become Liberal-minded'.

In January 1946 the Liberal Party decided openly to break with tradition by endorsing a candidate for the Legislative Council elections, which Wright claimed had been Labor Party practice for some time.[125] The Liberal Party wanted, said Wright, to counter Labor's 'very insidious and unjustified campaign' to undermine the Legislative Council, which Premier Robert Cosgrove had regularly criticised for blocking its legislation. Wright affirmed that the Legislative Council would remain a house of review and that Liberal Party candidates would not, as Labor candidates had been, be tied 'by any strict pledge which deprived them of independence of thought'. The Liberal Party endorsed Nationalist John Soundy, who had moved from the House of Assembly to contest the Legislative Council seat of Hobart.

Soundy narrowly won in May 1946 by forty votes from the young and relatively unknown ALP candidate Russell Lyons, who contested his first election and faced the obstacle of a restrictive franchise that favoured his opponent.[126] While Reg Wright attributed Soundy's victory to his long 'record in public life' and his adherence to 'the principles underlying Liberalism', Soundy affirmed that he would 'vote as he sees fit, and refuse to take any action that might halt progress'.[127] *The Mercury* claimed that Soundy was 'the first non-Labour official endorsement' for the Upper House, but the Bennetts's electoral handbook indicates that Arthur William Loone had won the Legislative Council seat of South Esk as a Liberal in May 1910.[128] Liberal indecision about endorsement to the Upper

House remained until 1954 when it became party policy to retain the Legislative Council as a non-party chamber.[129]

In March 1946 the Liberal Party began preparing itself for the federal and state elections to be held later in the year. After acting secretary Edwin Cottier had put the Liberal Party on a solid footing, he was replaced by Quentin McDougall as paid state secretary. McDougall was an accountant, who had recently been discharged from the Navy.[130] Other paid secretaries were appointed for the north, James Wilson Henty, and the north-west, Don Smith. In June the party appointed as its public relations officer Herbert John Turner, who served with the 40th Battalion and reached the rank of captain in World War II.[131] Various subsequent party officials are identified in Lucadou Wells, who also emphasises the importance to the party of publicity in newspapers and on radio, spreading its philosophy and gaining new members.[132]

For the elections, candidates of 'outstanding character and ability' would be selected and the names of all applicants would be kept secret by the selection committee.[133] Two continuing and three new candidates were selected for the House of Representative elections in September. The two continuing candidates were Enid Lyons in Darwin and one-time Labor member Allan Guy, who had represented the UAP in Wilmot since 1940.[134] The three new members were all returned servicemen. Dr John Bruce Hamilton was a specialist in eye surgery, who had served as a major and consulting oculist in the Middle East 1941-43 and on his return to Tasmania continued his military service at Campbell Town Military Hospital. Hamilton was the candidate for Denison. Twenty-five-year-old Flight-Lieutenant Charles William 'Bill' Falkinder had served overseas from 1941-45 and was 'the most decorated navigator' in the RAAF in Europe, being awarded a DSO and DFC and Bar. Falkinder was the candidate for Franklin and represented the archetype new Liberal candidate – a 'young and distinguished ex-serviceman with flair, presence and ability'.[135] Lieutenant-Colonel Harry Edward

Spotswood served in both the First and Second World Wars, had been council clerk of Derby and Scottsdale and was active in the RSL. He was the candidate for Bass.[136] For the Senate, two existing senators were selected. Herbert Hays had represented the north-west since 1922 and Burford Sampson had represented the north since 1925.[137] The new Senate candidate representing the south was Arthur Beck, a World War I veteran, who replaced retiring Senator John Blyth Hayes.

Menzies visited Tasmania in the week or so before the elections set for 26 September 1946. In Hobart his meeting was 'the best attended of any in Australia'.[138] Although not reported in Tasmanian newspapers, but widely so in mainland newspapers, Menzies allegedly made a 'sneering reference' to a rowdy section of his Launceston audience that he was 'not addressing … the descendants of convicts, but … free Australian citizens'.[139] Condemning this 'unseemly reference to our forebears', ALP secretary Ernest Newton West claimed electors will view this 'as a token of what is in store for them if brought under the feudalistic domination of a Menzies-led government'. *The Examiner*, which did not report Menzies's remarks, was confident that voters would give the Liberals 'a clear majority' because the Chifley Government had shown itself 'incapable of leading Australia to prosperity', an assessment which conveniently forgot the wartime prosperity enjoyed by many.[140]

Despite a swing towards it, the Liberal Party did not as it had hoped win office at the federal poll. Instead, it was the first time Labor had won two consecutive federal elections. In Tasmania the Liberals, perhaps due to Menzies's visit in the week before voting, had won 'the highest percentage in the Commonwealth', but the election results were on balance disappointing.[141] In the traditionally 'anti-Labor seat' of Wilmot a complacent Allan Guy was unexpectedly defeated by Labor newcomer Gil Duthie, whose tireless 'getting-to-know-you' doorknocking gave him a healthy victory.[142]

On the other hand, Bill Falkinder defeated Labor incumbent and Minister for Repatriation Charles Frost by a mere 73 votes. This left the status quo at three House of Representatives seats for Labor and two for Liberal, with Enid Lyons securing a convincing victory in Darwin. In the Senate, none of the three Liberals were elected.[143] President Reg Wright said the results emphasised 'the need for unity of the forces opposed to Socialism … it is a challenge to the Liberal Party to increase its strength'.[144]

In the referendum submitted at the 1946 elections, Tasmanians voted yes to giving the federal government power over a range of social services, but voted no to empowering it to legislate for the marketing of primary products and exempting it from the freedom of interstate trade requirement, and no again to giving the federal government power to make laws for regulating employment in industry.[145] For the social services power Tasmanians voted yes by the slimmest of margins (1.16 per cent). They voted no to the marketing power by the largest of margins (14.9 per cent) and voted no by even more to the industrial employment power (17.26 per cent). Moreover, in the 1948 Australian rents and prices referendum Tasmanians voted against by 64.55 per cent to 34.55 per cent, this time running second to Queensland. These results had more to do with the typical Tasmanian elector's reluctance to give a government of either side in Canberra more power than opposition campaigning from local Liberals or at best lukewarm support from the Labor Party.

Thirty candidates or six per electorate were chosen to contest the state elections.[146] In April 1946 a sub-committee of three women was charged with forming a Tasmanian Liberal women's group to mobilise the women's vote and party workers, but not, it seems, women candidates, perhaps due to what Lucadou Wells called 'a male supremacist attitude' that permeated the party.[147] Only one of the thirty candidates was a woman – Joyce Heathorn contesting Denison – probably because, despite Liberal rhetoric, women were expected to continue their traditional roles as wives and mothers.

Northern executive chairman Fotheringham said the party had responded to 'an outcry for new blood, young blood and returned servicemen' in its selections.[148]

Of the thirty candidates, only six had 'previous political experience' with five sitting members out of ten recontesting and one other, Allen Hollingsworth, mayor of Launceston, who had served as the member for Bass from 1934-41.[149] Of the other sitting members, one retired for health reasons; Henry Baker ostensibly for business reasons but in reality because his 'dour' personality was considered out of place in the new party; and Soundy because he was contesting the Legislative Council elections. Two sitting members were not endorsed – John Featherstone Ockerby aged 83 and former Premier Sir Walter Lee aged 72, perhaps casualties of the desire for younger members.

The Advocate thought the candidates were well chosen, with 'promise of much good material', a 'well diversified' area of selection from all over Tasmania, and candidates from primary industry were 'well represented'.[150] Indeed, as secretary of the northern area, James Henty, pointed out, of the Liberal Party's seventy branches only twenty-five were from the cities, which meant that ninety of the 140 delegates came from rural areas and accounted for the large number of rural candidates.[151] The dominance of rural interests in the Liberal Party removed the need for a Country Party in Tasmania as proposed by some.

The *Voice* dwelt on the selection of the 'old timers' from the remnants of the UAP, who were 'not remarkable, either for their progressive ideas or for their skill in propounding them'.[152] Walter Lee complained that the endorsed candidates were 'decided by fewer than half the number of delegates entitled to be present', but Wright countered that the selection committee was made up of two representatives from each branch in the electoral division.[153] Wright proudly proclaimed again that the party had shown it was 'a new party inheriting no allegiance to any past organisation or member'.

The Liberals felt confident in the state elections because they had selected so many ex-servicemen and had been buoyed by Falkinder's victory in Franklin.[154] They hoped, wrote *The Mercury*, that so many new candidates espousing 'a clear and progressive Liberal policy' would appeal to electors seeking a 'fresh approach' to Tasmania's problems.[155] *The Advocate* also felt the 'many new faces', including young men, were an advantage, that it had been many years since the non-Labor forces had been 'so well equipped' to fight an election and that the Liberal program was 'progressive' and appealed to different sections of the community.[156] But it highlighted 'a remarkable correspondence between the rival platforms so the question largely resolves itself into one of which is deserving the greater trust'.

The Cosgrove Labor Government had achieved its highest vote in 1941, felt it had a strong record, and was confronted with a new and experienced but uninspiring Liberal leader, Tamar orchardist Neil Campbell, so it decided to hold the state elections on 23 November 1946.[157] Labor received a shock when its vote dropped from the high of 62.59 per cent in 1941 to 50.97 per cent in 1946 with the Liberals 34.25 per cent (two per cent lower than the Nationalists in 1941) and independents 14.79 per cent. Ten of the nineteen sitting Labor members who recontested their seats were defeated, many by new faces on the Liberal team. Only one Labor minister topped his electorate and in Denison Premier Cosgrove dropped by 4,445 votes on his 1941 triumph. Labor had dropped from twenty seats to sixteen, the Liberals increased from ten to twelve seats, and two independents won seats. One of the independents, Rex Townley, had been a former ALP member.

Liberal Party secretary Quentin McDougall seemed upbeat about the entry of seven new members into the House of Assembly to present 'the ideas of a younger generation mixed with ideas gained in their travels as members of the fighting forces'.[158] McDougall was encouraged by the good performance of Joyce

Heathorn, 'the first woman to stand for the party in Tasmania' at state elections, who would give other Liberal women the 'incentive' to contest future elections. Two important steps were taken after the 1946 elections. In 1947 the Young Liberals were formed with the full support of the parliamentary party.[159] On 1 July 1948 Joy Piesse began work as woman organiser to capitalise on the growing interest of women in politics and maintain the involvement of women in Liberal branches in the run up to the state elections on 21 August.[160]

The 1948 elections were held under unusual circumstances that should have worked in the Liberal Party's favour. Facing bribery, corruption and conspiracy charges, Cosgrove as premier resigned in December 1947 and faced a Supreme Court trial in February 1948, which acquitted him of all charges.[161] But his trial had emboldened his enemies. The Liberal Party Young Turks became 'increasingly pugnacious' and urged the Legislative Council to throw Labor out.[162] On 8 July the recalcitrant Legislative Council voted to grant two months' supply only if Cosgrove called a general election.[163] The August election was fought over constitutional issues, but the Liberal Party team with more new faces ('too young, immature and of poor quality' as *The Mercury* and *The Examiner* later observed) could not dislodge Cosgrove's moderate and anti-strike Labor team, which secured fifteen seats to the Liberals' twelve with three independents.[164] This time the Labor vote fell to 49.38 per cent, but remained stable, the Liberals rose to 37.84 per cent, but with much ground to make up, and the independents dropped to 12.66 per cent. Two independents – Rex Townley and William George Wedd – said they would support Labor, but reliance on independents, dissident Labor members, and a hostile Legislative Council left the future uncertain for Labor, which somehow managed to cling to power for the next twenty years.[165] One Liberal parliamentarian, John Orchard, strongly criticised Liberal leaders for failing to take their opportunities to oust Labor.[166]

WRIGHT
FOR FRANKLIN
ENERGY AND ABILITY TO FIGHT.
For integrity in Government and Freedom from Canberra control and Development of Tasmania.
Vote [1]
WRIGHT, R. C.,
And for the Franklin Liberal Team in order of your preference:
STOP SOCIALISM—
VOTE LIBERAL.
(Authorised by A. W. Potter, 50 Elizabeth St., Hobart.)

R. C. WRIGHT.

Reg Wright's 1948 Tasmanian state election advertisement. From *The Mercury* (Hobart), 12 August 1948.

The state elections were not the triumph the Liberals had anticipated and must have been a blow to morale. The mood changed after the 1949 federal elections when Menzies defeated a besieged Chifley Government, gaining 74 Coalition seats (only 24 of which were old members) to 47, but in terms of overall votes the difference was only 202,417 votes.[167] The redistribution of seats increased the number of electorates and made the swing to the Liberals more effective. In Tasmania the Coalition polled 53.5 per cent, second only to Queensland at 56.3 per cent. Two Tasmanian House of Representative seats changed hands. Liberal Bruce Kekwick narrowly defeated sitting Minister for Repatriation Claude Barnard in Bass and independent turned Liberal Athol Townley (younger brother of Rex) easily defeated Henry Cosgrove (son of Robert) in Denison, leaving only Gil Duthie as the sole Labor member after his convincing victory in Wilmot.

Enid Lyons won Darwin easily. Despite the 'sourness' she showed Menzies and against his own preference, Lyons was appointed to the honorific position of vice-president of the executive council – what she called a 'toothless position' – the first woman to be appointed to federal cabinet.[168] The Liberal Party won four out of the seven Senate seats, with Reg Wright topping the votes and Labor won three Senate positions, but retained a majority in the Senate because most of its senators did not have to contest the election.[169] The total votes cast for the Liberals were 71,994 or 8,420 more than Labor. In the 1950s the Liberal Party more than held its own in winning Senate spots. This helped Menzies retain control of the Senate and indicated that electors were willing to support conservatives – Senator Wright being the supreme example – who protected their state's rights against central government intrusion, which aligned with the position of conservative state Labor governments.[170]

Epilogue

By September 1950 the Liberal Party had formed 100 branches in Tasmania with 6,717 members, had a new 'popular' leader in Rex Townley and, despite lacking adequate funds, had become well established as a political party.[171] Yet the Liberals could not dislodge Labor from government, even when it clung precariously to power with the support of independents, until 1969 because of their own failings: in appointing leaders who could not cut through and win public confidence or sell party policies or develop more imaginative policies that would appeal to a broad spectrum of electors; selecting politicians who did not always hold the party line; divisions between the parliamentary party and the state executive; and, to a lesser extent, in the early 1960s the emergence of a rival non-Labor party, the Country Party, which proved to be electorally ineffective and soon crumbled.[172] Outside the party, factors included the general prosperity of the community and a consistently moderate ALP, which did not have a strongly militant left wing and did not offend conservative voters.[173]

Yet, with time, the formation of a more modern, organised and proactive Liberal Party changed the political landscape in Tasmania and Labor could no longer claim to be the natural party of government. From 1969 to 2024, Labor held office for twenty-nine years and the Liberals for twenty-six years; the Liberal rise is more obvious when we note that from 1982 to 2024 the Liberals held office for 23 years and Labor 19 years.[174] Over this long period of 'post-modern flux', controversial neoliberal policies and globalisation, many economic, social, demographic and political factors accounted for the Liberals' greater electoral success.[175] One reason might be that under a new generation of leaders (from 1981 to 2016 Labor had ten leaders compared with five leaders from 1939-81) and university educated members Labor arguably became less conservative in an effort to counter the siphoning off of votes to Tasmania's most significant minority party the Greens, while the Liberals mostly retained a moderate conservatism based on assertive pro-growth policies with expedient concessions to environmental concerns, and kept a safe distance from the Greens.[176] The Tasmanian electorates' predilection to vote for the most conservative option offered by a strong leader might not explain the full story, but it can certainly not be discounted as a factor in the rise of the Liberal Party from the late twentieth century.

---

1 Hughes, *Case for Labor*, p. 118.

2 Petrow, 'The State', pp. 483-4.

3 Caldwell, 'Population, p. 26.

4 Denholm, 'The Lyons Tasmanian Labor Government', p. 45.

5 Townsley, *Government of Tasmania*, p. 41.

6 Ibid., p. 40.

7 Ibid., p. xi.

8 Davison, 'Urbanisation', pp. 491-96; Townsley, *Government of Tasmania*, p. 3.

9 Batt, 'Tasmania's Depression Elections', p. 111; Tasmanian economist HF Giblin declared in 1929 that Tasmania was 'a poor country, and will never be a very rich community compared with the rest of the world', *The Mercury*, 12 February 1929, p. 6.

[10] Reynolds, 'Regionalism in Nineteenth-Century Tasmania', pp. 14-28.

[11] Townsley, *Government of Tasmania*, p. 28.

[12] Tanner, 'Press, Tasmania', pp. 358-60.

[13] Davis, *History of the Tasmanian Labor Party*, pp. 60-61; Davis, '"A real and quiet affinity"', p. 73

[14] Townsley, *Government of Tasmania*, p. 11.

[15] Ibid., p. xi.

[16] Bennett, *Tasmanian Electoral Handbook*, pp. 10-15; Denholm, 'The Lyons Tasmanian Labor Government', p. 51.

[17] Bennett, *Tasmanian Electoral Handbook*, pp. 10-15.

[18] Townsley, *Government of Tasmania*, p. 88, 91.

[19] Ibid., p. 32.

[20] Bennett, *Tasmanian Electoral Handbook*, pp. 11-12. The details of the Hare-Clark system are too detailed to be discussed in this chapter.

[21] Weller, 'Tasmania', p. 371.

[22] Davis, *History of the Tasmanian Labor Party*, pp. 10-11; Townsley, *Government of Tasmania*, pp. 26-27.

[23] Townsley, *Government of Tasmania*, pp. 22-24.

[24] Rydon, 'The Conservative Electoral Ascendancy Between the Wars', pp. 65-7.

[25] Townsley, *Government of Tasmania*, pp. 24, 41.

[26] Ibid., p. 41.

[27] Scott, 'Parties and Parliament', p. 36.

[28] Davis, 'A real and unique affinity', p. 74.

[29] Scott, 'Parties and Parliament', pp. 36-7.

[30] His main publication is Davis, *History of the Tasmanian Labor Party.*

[31] Alexander, 'Communism in Tasmania', pp. 61, 63, 65, 71-5.

[32] Davis, *History of the Tasmanian Labor Party*, pp. 14, 31, 39-43, 46, 59, 79, 83, 121.

[33] Weller, 'Organisation of Early Non-Labor Parties', pp. 137-8.

[34] Weller, 'Tasmania', pp. 365-66.

[35] Weller, 'Tasmania', pp. 366-7; Weller, 'Organisation of Early Non-Labor Parties', pp. 137-8.

[36] Davis, *History of the Tasmanian Labor Party*, p. 9.

[37] Weller, 'Tasmania', p. 368; Weller, 'Organisation of Early Non-Labor Parties', pp. 139-41.

[38] Weller, 'Organisation of Early Non-Labor Parties', pp. 141-42; *The Examiner*, 21 July 1909, p. 6; *Daily Post*, 22 July 1909, p. 3; *The Mercury*, 5 August 1909, p. 2.

[39] Weller, 'Tasmania', pp. 374-5; Weller, 'Meetings of the Early Non-Labor Parties', p. 129.

[40] Reynolds, 'Premiers and Political Leaders', p. 209; Townsley, *Government of Tasmania*, p. 54.

[41] Weller, 'Tasmania', pp. 375-6, 378; Weller, 'Organisation of Early Non-Labor Parties', pp. 143-5.

[42] 1912 Tasmanian state election; Davis, *History of the Tasmanian Labor Party*, p. 15.

[43] Reynolds, 'Premiers and Political Leaders', pp. 209, 216.

[44] Bennett, 'Solomon, Albert Edgar (1876-1914)'.

[45] Denholm, 'Playing the Game', p. 150.

[46] Lake, *Divided Society*, pp. 93-6.

[47] Lloyd, 'Formation and Development of the United Australia Party', p. 24.

[48] Lake, *Divided Society*, pp. 104-5, 128.

[49] Bennett, *Tasmanian Electoral Handbook*, pp. 174-6.

[50] Lake, *Divided Society*, pp. 104, 128, 184; Results of the 1919 Tasmanian State Election.

[51] Denholm, 'The Lyons Tasmanian Labor Government', p. 45; Robson, *Short History of Tasmania*, p. 95.

[52] 1922 Tasmanian state election; McRae, *Tasmanian Farmers*, pp. 33-35; Costar and Woodward, *Country to National*, pp. 5-6.

[53] Denholm, 'The Lyons Tasmanian Labor Government', p. 46; Davis, *History of the Tasmanian Labor Party*, p. 48.

[54] Denholm, 'The Lyons Tasmanian Labor Government', p. 28.

[55] *The Mercury*, 5 July 1929, p. 6; Davis, *History of the Tasmanian Labor Party*, p. 51.

[56] Henderson, *Joseph Lyons*, p. 169.

[57] *The Mercury*, 19 May 1926, 6.

[58] Denholm, 'The Lyons Tasmanian Labor Government', 1977, p. 58; Robson, Short History of Tasmania, p. 97.

[59] Henderson, *Joseph Lyons*, pp. 250-6.

[60] Lonie, 'From Liberal to Liberal', p. 47.

[61] Lloyd, 'Formation and Development of the United Australia Party', pp. 148-50.

[62] *Daily Telegraph*, 7 March 1928, p. 4; *The Mercury*, 8 March 1929, p. 12; *The Advocate*, 25 February 1931, p. 9; Sawer and Simms, *A Woman's Place*, p. 193.

[63] Results of the 1931 Tasmanian state election; Davis, *History of the Tasmanian Labor Party*, p. 80.

[64] Lloyd, 'Formation and Development of the United Australia Party', pp. 148-50; *The Examiner*, 18 April 1931, p. 7, 20 August 1931, p. 9, 14 October 1931, p. 7; *The Advocate*, 6 May 1931, p. 2; *The Mercury*, 23 July 1931, p. 5.

[65] Lloyd, 'Formation and Development of the United Australia Party', pp. 151-5; *The Examiner*, 28 November 1931, p. 10: *The Mercury*, 7 December 1931, p. 7.

[66] Lloyd, 'Formation and Development of the United Australia Party', pp. 197-201, 244, 296; *The Examiner*, 22 October 1935, p. 12; *The Mercury*, 26 November 1935, p. 10, 24 July 1936, p. 9.

[67] *The Mercury*, 23 October 1935, p. 3, 7 October 1936, p. 7.

[68] *The Mercury*, 28 October 1937, p. 8; Roe, *Albert Ogilvie and Stymie Gaha.*

[69] *The Mercury*, 10 November 1943, p. 2; Martin, *Robert Menzies*, Vol. II, pp. 1-2.

[70] *The Advocate*, 10 November 1943, p. 2.

[71] *The Examiner*, 12 November 1943, p. 4.

[72] *The Examiner*, 31 August 1944, p. 4; Hancock, *National and Permanent*, pp. 32, 36; Menzies, *Afternoon Light*, p. 286; Henderson, *Menzies' Child*, p. 77; Williams, 'Emergence of the Liberal Party', p. 17.

[73] *The Examiner,* 14 October 1944, p. 5.

[74] *The Mercury*, 26 July 1933, p. 5; *The Examiner*, 6 October 1944, p. 4.

[75] Henderson, *Menzies' Child*, p. 76.

[76] Hazlehurst, *Menzies Observed*, p. 281.

[77] *The Mercury*, 21 July 1941, p. 1.

[78] *The Examiner*, 10 August 1943, p. 3, 19 August 1943, p. 6; *The Mercury*, 10 August 1943, p. 2, 18 August 1944, p. 9; *The Advocate*, 12 August 1943, p. 5.

[79] *The Advocate*, 17 October 1944, p. 5.

[80] Ibid.; Henderson, *Enid Lyons*, p. 294.

[81] *The Advocate*, 20 October 1944, p. 5.

[82] Hoddinott, '"Independent peasants"', p. 20.

[83] *The Examiner*, 30 October 1944, p. 4.

[84] *The Mercury*, 28 November 1944, p. 9; *The Advocate*, 29 November 1944, p. 2.

[85] *The Examiner*, 19 December 1944, p. 5.

[86] *The Mercury*, 16 January 1945, p. 5; Lucadou Wells, *50 Year History of the Liberal Party*, p. 2.

[87] *The Examiner*, 17 January 1945, p. 4.

[88] The *Advocate*, 18 January 1945, p. 2.

[89] *The Advocate*, 1 February 1945, p. 5.

[90] *The Examiner*, 5 February 1945, p. 4; Lucadou Wells, *50 Year History of the Liberal Party*, p. 1.

[91] Ibid.; Ibid., p. 3.

[92] *The Examiner*, 14 February 1945, p. 4.

[93] Ibid.

[94] Ibid.

[95] *The Mercury*, 16 March 1945, p. 7.

[96] *The Mercury*, 22 May 1945, p. 17.

[97] *The Advocate*, 7 April 1945, p. 7; *Voice*, 16 June 1945, p. 1.

[98] *The Mercury*, 23 May 1945, p. 11.

[99] *The Mercury*, 16 March 1945, p. 7; Lucadou Wells, *50 Year History of the Liberal Party*, p. 4.

[100] *The Advocate*, 28 May 1945, p. 2.

[101] *The Examiner*, 25 1945, p. 6.

[102] *The Mercury*, 8 June 1945, p. 7.

[103] *The Mercury*, 22 June 1945, p. 5.

[104] *The Examiner*, 26 June 1945, p. 5.

[105] Lucadou Wells, *50 Year History of the Liberal Party*, p. 42.

[106] *Saturday Evening Express*, 21 July 1945, p. 12; *The Examiner*, 23 July 1945, p. 4.

[107] *The Examiner*, 23 July 1945, p. 4.

[108] Ibid.

[109] West, *Power in the Liberal Party*, p. 194.

[110] *The Examiner*, 23 July 1945, p. 4.

[111] Ibid.

[112] *The Examiner*, 23 July 1945, p. 4, 7 September 1945, p. 4.

[113] *The Examiner*, 23 July 1945, p. 4.

[114] *The Examiner*, 16 August 1945, p. 4.

[115] *The Mercury*, 16 August 1945, p. 3.

[116] *The Examiner*, 1 September 1945, p. 6.

[117] *The Examiner*, 3 September 1945, p. 4.

[118] *The Examiner*, 17 September 1945, p. 4.

[119] *The Examiner*, 4 September 1945, p. 4.

[120] *The Mercury*, 27 October 1945, p. 5.

[121] *The Examiner*, 13 November 1945, p. 5.

[122] *The Examiner*, 26 November 1945, p. 4.

[123] *The Examiner*, 27 November 1945, p. 4.

[124] *Voice*, 1 December 1945, p. 1.

[125] *The Examiner*, 14 January 1946, p. 4, 15 January 1946, p. 4.

[126] *The Mercury*, 4 February 1946, p. 8; *Voice*, 11 May 1946, pp. 1, 4.

[127] *The Mercury*, 8 May 1946, p. 2.

[128] *The Mercury*, 4 February 1946, p. 8; Bennett, *Tasmanian Electoral Handbook*, p. 51

[129] West, *Power in the Liberal Party*, p. 193; Lucadou Wells, *50 Year History of the Liberal Party*, pp. 33-5.

130 *The Examiner*, 22 March 1946, p. 4; Lucadou Wells, *50 Year History of the Liberal Party*, p. 6.

131 *The Mercury*, 10 June 1946, p. 2.

132 Lucadou Wells, *50 Year History of the Liberal Party*, pp. 8-11, 14 -20.

133 Ibid., p. 29.

134 *The Mercury*, 4 March 1946, p. 8.

135 Hancock, *National and Permanent*, p. 69.

136 *The Examiner*, 1 April 1946, p. 1; *North-Eastern Advertiser*, 2 April 1946, p. 1.

137 *The Examiner*, 11 March 1946, p. 4.

138 *The Mercury*, 24 September 1946, p. 1, 25 September 1946, p. 20, letter by Leicester Warburton.

139 See, for example, *The Age*, 25 September 1946, p. 3; *The Mercury*, 27 September 1946, p. 3.

140 *The Examiner*, 28 September 1946, p. 6.

141 *The Mercury*, 27 September 1946, p. 3, 28 October 1946, p. 10.

142 *Voice*, 21 September 1946, p. 1; Duthie, *I Had 50,000 Bosses*, pp. 24-30.

143 Bennett, 'Hays, Herbert Ephraim Digby (1869-1960)'.

144 *The Mercury*, 30 September 1946, p. 11.

145 *Handbook of the 44th Parliament* (2014); *Voice*, 5 August 1944, p. 1, 12 October 1946, p. 1.

146 *The Mercury*, 29 March 1946, p. 2, 1 April 1946, p. 8; *Examiner*, 30 March 1945, p. 6.

147 Lucadou Wells, 'Women in the Liberal Party', pp. 1, 13.

148 *The Examiner*, 1 April 1946, p. 1.

149 *The Advocate*, 2 April 1946, p. 2; West, *Power in the Liberal Party*, p. 195.

150 *The Advocate*, 2 April 1946, p. 2.

151 *The Examiner*, 10 June 1946, p. 4.

152 *Voice*, 6 April 1946, p. 4.

153 *The Mercury*, 11 April 1946, p. 2.

154 *The Mercury*, 26 October 1946, p. 2.

155 *The Mercury*, 28 October 1946, p. 10.

156 *The Advocate*, 30 October 1946, p. 2.

157 Davis, *History of the Tasmanian Labor Party*, pp. 124-5; Bennett, 'Tasmanian Labor Under Attack', p. 67; *The Mercury*, 30 November 1946, p. 1; West, *Power in the Liberal Party*, p. 195

158 *The Mercury*, 30 November 1946, p. 1, 5 December 1946, p. 12.

159 *The Mercury*, 25 June 1947, p. 10.

160 *The* Advocate, 22 May 1948, p. 7.

[161] Townsley, 'Cosgrove, Robert (1884-1969)'.

[162] Bennett, 'Tasmanian Labor Under Attack', pp. 69, 76.

[163] Townsley, 'Cosgrove, Robert (1884-1969)'.

[164] *The Examiner*, 28 August 1948, p. 2; Davis, *History of the Tasmanian Labor Party*, p. 133; Bennett, 'Tasmanian Labor Under Attack', p. 79.

[165] Bennett, 'Tasmanian Labor Under Attack', pp. 67-9.

[166] Orchard, *Not To Yield*, pp. 125-37.

[167] Duthie, *I Had 50,000 Bosses*, pp. 90-3; Martin, *Robert Menzies*, Vol. II, pp. 125-6.

[168] Henderson, *Enid Lyons*, pp. 299-302.

[169] *The Mercury*, 30 December 1949, p. 2; Henderson, *Menzies' Child*, p. 109.

[170] Bennett, 'Wright, Reginald Charles (1905-1990)'.

[171] Hancock, *National and Permanent*, p. 121; West, *Power in the Liberal Party*, p. 197; Lucadou Wells, *50 Year History of the Liberal Party*, pp. 21-25.

[172] West, *Power in the Liberal Party*, pp. 200-9; Lucadou Wells, *50 Year History of the Liberal Party*, pp. 47-52.

[173] Lucadou Wells, *50 Year History of the Liberal Party*, p. 39; Townsley, *Government of Tasmania*, p. 59.

[174] The later, more successful, history of the Liberal Party is partly related in two autobiographies, see Gray and Tilt, *Proud to be Tasmanian*; Cheek, *Cheeky*.

[175] Robson, *Short History of Tasmania*, chapter 9; Reynolds, *History of Tasmania*, chapters 12 and 13; Davis, *History of the Tasmanian Labor Party*, *passim*; Lucadou Wells, *50 Year History of the Liberal Party*, pp. 52-62.

[176] One exception was the Rundle Liberal government (1996-1998), which depended on Green support but without signing any formal compact, Davis, *History of the Tasmanian Labor Party*, p. 332. One way or another from 1982 the Greens had a notable impact on the success and length of Tasmanian governments, but never came close to holding office on its own.

10

The Australian Capital Territory: Liberalism's furthest frontier

Gary Humphries[1]

The Liberal Party, as befits the most federally-conceived of Australia's political parties, was born in the national capital, Canberra, in October 1944. Though state-based divisions of the new party were quickly established, it would be a further five years before the party would have an organisational presence in the federal city itself, and even then, only as an outpost of the NSW Division. At this time, the citizens of the Australian Capital Territory elected none of those who made decisions on their behalf and, as democratic structures were slowly erected to address this omission, the Liberal Party competed for representation as a counterweight to the Labor Party.[2] Nonetheless, despite some electoral successes and even, after the arrival of self-government, tasting power locally on two occasions, Canberra's Liberals have long battled a sense of being outsiders – alien to the Territory mainstream, a right-of-centre party in a community that leans left. The party has accordingly experienced extended periods of electoral failure, but not complete failure. Adversity fostered innovative approaches to coalition-building, to capitalise on those (rare) opportunities to take government as have arisen under the Territory's unusual electoral system. The party's operations, both parliamentary and extra-parliamentary, represent a significant departure from the practice of Liberalism elsewhere.

The difficulty of winning legislative majorities is attributable in part to the strong identification by Canberrans of the local Liberals with their federal counterparts. In a city where many eyes are trained on the federal parliament, national perceptions easily overwhelm local ones. Thus, when the stocks of the federal parliamentary Liberal

Party are high (in Canberra), the Canberra Liberals have tended to do well. The converse is also true – an inconvenience for the local Liberals because the federal party's stocks are not infrequently buoyant elsewhere but low in Canberra, particularly when Coalition governments have cut the size of the Australian Public Service (APS). Whereas state Liberal governments have often achieved a measure of separation by attacking 'those idiots in Canberra' (albeit Liberal idiots), physical proximity has made insulating the ACT Liberals from decisions of 'the Feds' a higher order of difficulty.

Establishing a foothold

The sense of the ACT party as the handmaiden of its federal parent was underlined by the manner of its establishment. There was no impetus to replicate the party apparatus in Canberra until 1948, four years after the party's birth, when the Chifley Government announced its intention to give the ACT a seat for the first time in the House of Representatives, albeit one carrying voting rights limited to ACT matters – an arrangement similar to one already in place for the Northern Territory. The perceived need of the Opposition led by Robert Menzies to bid for this seat led to a public meeting being organised in Canberra on 3 June 1948, at the Albert Hall. Attended by about 25 residents, it was addressed by the member for Fawkner, Harold Holt, who advised that the 'task confronting the party was to break up the atmosphere of class bitterness and class warfare which exists today'. A branch in Canberra would have the advantage, he said, that 'a higher proportion of the people are more politically knowledgeable than elsewhere in Australia'. The meeting resolved that it was 'desirable that a branch of the Liberal Party of Australia be formed in Canberra … as soon as practicable'.[3] The NSW general secretary, John Carrick (later Senator Sir John Carrick), was tasked by the federal executive to satisfy this call, one which necessitated amendments to both the federal and NSW party constitutions (the former had not contemplated branches existing in the territories).[4] Meanwhile, local Labor representatives chided the Liberals for their 'sudden concern' with the Territory, in contrast to an ALP presence of more than 20 years' standing.[5]

The Albert Hall again did service on 27 January 1949, as host to the Canberra branch's inaugural meeting (suitable meeting venues in the small city being limited). 54 citizens attended, of whom 42 signed up as party members. They were addressed by the chief organiser of the NSW Division, Major RT Tarrant, who intoned that the Liberal Party 'was not governed by any financial cliques', but rather followed 'a policy of financial freedom'. He added that the party 'will not become the wind in a concertina for anybody to play a tune on'. Tarrant's comments made allusion to the debate playing out across the nation about the identity and character of the new party, in particular its relationship with big business.[6] There was a desire to avoid the perception that had clung to the Liberals' predecessor, the United Australia Party, that it was the creature of business cliques. So encouraged, the new members duly elected prominent local architect Malcolm Moir as their first president.[7] The newly-minted branch was set apart from other NSW state branches by having the authority to choose Liberal parliamentary candidates.[8] By May 1949, the branch had 127 members (who were 'keen but need some direction', Carrick opined), a healthy membership considering that there were then just 9,400 electors in the Territory.[9] On 29 June 1949, at the Gloucester Hotel in Civic, the inaugural meeting of the ACT Liberal women's branch was held, attended by 24 women. The creation of the branch reflected the preoccupation of the party's founders that it should provide a voice for the concerns of women.[10] Its first president was Mrs G Thomas.[11]

Notwithstanding its optimistic beginnings, the branch's original raison d'être was frustrated when Moir, its candidate at the December 1949 election, missed the Menzies landslide and achieved just 22.5 per cent of the formal vote despite a spirited and well-funded campaign. The successful independent candidate, Lewis Nott, was in turn beaten in 1951 by Labor's Jim Fraser, inaugurating the long-term, iron-like grip by the ALP on the Capital Territory's Lower

House seats. On only three occasions in the ensuing 70-odd years would the Liberal Party succeed, however briefly, in loosening that grip. Fraser himself held the ACT seat for almost 20 years, leading to laments by ACT Liberals that his position as the Territory's sole elected representative gave him 'too many opportunities with regard to public functions', opportunities which occasional Liberal challengers could not hope to match.[12]

A succession of challengers nonetheless attempted to defy the advantages of incumbency. Mary Stevenson was chosen to stand at the 1954 poll; Scottish born, she was a leader or committee member of countless community organisations that held together the social fabric of the young city.[13] She linked Fraser to allegations that Communists had defaced the Australian War Memorial in 1951: 'LABOUR [sic] AND RED POLICIES ARE IDENTICAL', her newspaper ads declared.[14] In 1955 Robert Greenish urged voters to back him to 'PUT THE ACT IN THE GOVERNMENT TEAM!'. He was an accountant who had served as a naval commando during the war. Ann Dalgarno, a nurse and 'matron-secretary' of the Nurses Club, warned in 1958 that voting Labor meant 'higher taxes' and 'high prices'.[15] Canberrans were unmoved by these entreaties.

The nascent branch attracted an eclectic membership, albeit one dominated by men with ex-service and business backgrounds. The ACT electorate conference chair in 1950, John Gannon, admitted to his members that he was a past president of the Port Moresby branch of the ALP ('there being no other political parties in existence in New Guinea in 1940'). On the branch executive in 1953 was one JR Willoughby – presumably the same JR Willoughby who served then as federal director of the party.[16] Eager to fly the Liberal flag, the branch turned its attention to contests other than the sole federal seat. The Scullin Labor Government had established an 'Advisory Council for the Territory' in 1930, notionally as a halfway house toward greater self-determination 'within a few years'.[17] This ambition was overstated; the Advisory Council was to subsist for the next 44 years, argumentative but impotent, the democratic fig leaf on the Commonwealth's unbridled overlordship of the Territory. Journalist Warren Denning was able to speak of the ACT, with a measure of exaggeration, as 'virtually a Fascist State'.[18] The Advisory Council consisted of a majority of government-appointed members, but the proportion of elected members steadily grew until they made up a majority from 1953 onwards. There were periodic pushes for real self-determination, including – at times – by the Liberal Party branch, but these efforts evoked mixed feelings among Canberra residents. Many public servants saw their role in Canberra through the prism of their employment rather than their place of residence.[19] Some regarded the push for greater local control with disdain, identifying in the Commonwealth stewardship an expression of a broader national interest that they, as public servants, were in Canberra to serve, albeit often temporarily. 'Canberra is not 18th-century Paris', the *Canberra Times* observed: 'The paving stones look pretty secure'.[20]

The ACT branch was conflicted on whether to support self-government, and stood no candidates for the 1949 Advisory Council elections (party politics should not intrude into 'domestic spheres', said Moir), but by 1951 attitudes had shifted and the party decided to enter the fray.[21] Its boldness was rewarded. Mary Stevenson became both the first successful Liberal candidate and the first woman elected to public office in the ACT when she won one of five contested positions on the Council.[22] She would be re-elected three times.

This initial breakthrough did not herald a pattern for future elections, however. Over the next 20 years, endorsed Liberals received only modest preferment from the electorate; while Liberals won two of the six seats in 1957, they picked up just one out of nine in 1959. With the party in the doldrums federally and the branch short of funds, it decided not to field candidates for the 1961 Council election.[23] Funding was but one factor in such decisions. ACT voters, with their jaundiced view of 'local' government, showed a persistent preference for independents. These succeeded at every election and dominated the elected contingent of councils as late as 1967, often outnumbering the members chosen by parties.[24] It reflected a common Australian attitude at municipal elections – that government at this level ought to be non-political, by which they meant parties should stay out of it.[25] The Liberal Party, at that time reluctant anywhere in Australia to anoint candidates for local government, oscillated in Canberra between endorsing Liberal candidates and giving tacit support to certain 'independents'.[26] Thus, Dalgarno and Greenish were elected under that banner in both 1961 and 1964 despite having previously been federal Liberal candidates in the ACT.[27] It was decided not to expel party members who stood against endorsed Liberal candidates because a Council election 'was not an election under [a] State or Federal body'.[28] The branch agonised over whether to contest elections for the Canberra Community Hospital board, but decided that it would 'in view of the fact that these elections are held on party lines'.[29] These campaign endeavours, both official and unofficial, together with federal elections and crossing the border to assist their NSW brethren at state elections, sharpened the political skills of the members of the capital's branch.

On the issue of the development of party policy, however, it seems that little skill-sharpening among Canberra members was necessary. Within months of its establishment branch representatives were in Sydney arguing, at the NSW party convention, that the term 'White Australia Policy' should be eschewed because of the offence it caused other (non-white) nations.[30] Perhaps they had taken to heart Holt's prediction at the branch's birth in 1948 that it would become 'one of the most influential, intelligent and powerful branches in the Commonwealth'.[31] Spirited debate about party policy and contemporary political issues were regular features at branch meetings, and occasionally at levels of candour and intensity which alarmed the party hierarchy in Sydney. Motions ranging from state aid to Catholic schools, to the release of Japanese war criminals, and the opening hours of the Canberra Tourist Bureau were carried.[32] Carrick, evidently tiring of the stream of policy ideas from the ACT Liberals, resorted to lecturing them in April 1958:

> … we do not attempt to formulate policies on public issues as a body distinct from the Federal Government. The whole concept of the Liberal Party Constitution is one of freedom to our Parliamentary members to devise policies in accordance with their own conscience.[33]

This Burkean admonishment from Sydney would have rankled some Canberra members; the constraint on policy contributions did not sit well with some of the best educated and most policy-literate party members in the country. Indeed, some years later the branch – by now an independent division of the Liberal Party – would adopt a constitution giving party members the power to lay down binding policy on Liberal members of the ACT legislature, setting the division apart from state counterparts and taking a leaf from the ALP's playbook. The political culture of the ACT, for so long a distinctive subset of the Australian political tradition, influenced in turn the character and behaviour of the local Liberal apparatus which sat in its midst.

The branch continued to be a burr under Carrick's saddle during the 1950s. It sought a dedicated seat on the NSW state executive, a proposition that was rebuffed. It entertained at least one motion of 'no confidence in Ash Street' (the Sydney headquarters of the NSW Division).[34] In 1956 a motion was debated (but defeated) that the branch 'take steps to dis-affiliate from the NSW Division of the Party, and sets itself up as an independent Branch' – a notion Carrick considered 'entirely off the rails'.[35] He wrote testily to Stevenson in February 1958 that:

> … some of the correspondence which stems from the ACT branch is remarkably belligerent in tone. It seems to me that, in the enthusiasm for pursuing certain issues, the promotion of the Liberal cause is not always foremost.

(He added in a postscript that she was 'quite a "hit" on TV', then a very new medium for political debate, perhaps indicating that the branch's views were not being aired exclusively behind closed party doors.)[36] On another occasion he confessed to being 'frankly amazed' that the 'troublesome' ACT branch had challenged a report given to the state executive, and on yet another complained of the 'consistently critical nature of your branch's correspondence. Out of some 450 branches within our administration they are unique in this regard.'[37] (Equating the Capital Territory with a local suburban branch would not have calmed frayed tempers in Canberra.) He would later attribute this 'turbulence' to 'the presence of Public Servants who desire to seek an outside Forum'.[38]

The Canberra Liberals themselves took a somewhat different perspective on the problem of being a private-sector party in a public-sector town. Small business supporters, particularly as donors, were hard to engage. Problems existed for members who were public servants; Carrick's habit of referring branch motions to the relevant federal minister caused consternation, since 'no one will stand up and be counted at our meetings or even join the Liberal Party here if his views are to be channelled back to his department'.[39] There was an underlying instability in the membership base as public servants were posted into and out of the Territory.[40] The ACT electorate conference president, John Murray, wrote plaintively to Carrick in 1961 about the state of the ACT party. Explaining that the conference was more than £100 in debt, he proposed that it not contest the federal election due that year. The party had fewer than 150 ACT members, partly because, he said, bureaucrats 'of the Liberal viewpoint generally follow the principle that public servants should not disclose their political views', a principle 'not so slavishly followed' by ALP-inclined bureaucrats. In addition:

> Many Liberal Members of Parliament appear to be contemptuous of the citizens of Canberra and give the impression that they are determined to withhold from them any opportunity to manage, even in a small way,

> the equivalent of municipal affairs. The repeated assurances of the Labour [sic] Member for the ACT, who is a most astute politician, that this injustice will be remedied with a change of government has a decided appeal ... Many Canberra citizens feel that it is desirable, in our present disenfranchised circumstances, to have, as the local member, someone who can dig the needle into the Ministers concerned with ACT control and administration.[41]

He ended with an appeal for financial support to the branch from Sydney. The records do not disclose whether that financial support was forthcoming, but the conference did field a federal candidate in 1961. Whether ACT voters at that time felt 'disenfranchised' by the absence of local government is open to debate; what is less doubtful is that Murray accurately identified a long-term impediment facing the local party, namely the feeling by Liberal-voting public servants that party membership was improper, or at least unwise. Historically those public servants who have joined have tended to be from the more junior ranks of the public service.

The 1960s: growth and opportunity

While the Canberra branch struggled for relevance and confronted existential challenges in the 1950s, the rapid growth of the city in the 1960s transformed the environment in which it operated. Menzies as a young parliamentarian had regarded Canberra as a place of exile. With a population of just 30,000 in 1955, it was still a far cry from cosmopolitan Melbourne. The prime minister's conscience was pricked, however, by the complaints of his wife and daughter, who struggled to push his grandchild's pram over bad or non-existent footpaths around the Lodge; in time he became 'the high priest' of 'the Canberra idea', the creation of 'a worthy capital ... that would be a focal point for national pride and sentiment'.[42] In pursuit of that goal, in April 1956 he asked the interior minister, Allen Fairhall, to 'straighten out' the city's development. This prime ministerial nudge set balls rolling. The transfer to Canberra of 1,100 defence services employees was announced the following year, the beginning of a sustained program to drag the central offices of Commonwealth departments from Melbourne, sometimes 'by the hair on their heads'. Major housing projects were announced to support those transfers. It was 'a time of expanding horizons supported by postwar prosperity'.[43] Most significantly, in 1957 Fairhall introduced the National Capital Development Commission Bill, under which the new super authority would be given 'the broadest possible powers' to 'undertake and carry out the planning, development and construction of the City of Canberra as the National Capital of the Commonwealth'.[44]

As the population burgeoned during the decade, participation in the local Liberal Party also grew. To bolster the still-small party infrastructure the branch had been incorporated into the NSW Division's country southern regional conference in May 1958.[45] As the branch struggled with internal divisions and a lack of money in 1960, Carrick had encouraged it to invest in membership growth, reasoning that 'current difficulties appear to be clashes of personalities due to the relative smallness of the organisation. These would disappear if we had the numbers'.[46] He supported a membership drive, with 'Visitors' trained to visit selected households and encourage the inhabitants to sign up, applying a model that had been used successfully in Sydney. The initiative succeeded; a second geographical branch, in north Canberra, was established in 1960, followed by a branch in a new 'town centre' in the south, Woden, in 1966. A 'special branch' existed by 1965 at the Australian National University, which had by this time taken on undergraduates.[47] With multiple branches the organisational peak of the party in the Territory was now the ACT federal electorate conference.

Members debated at length their attitude to the Advisory Council, and to the ACT self-government of which it was a harbinger. Some noted that the Council was powerless, and self-government 'contentious' among Canberra voters. Others regarded it as a breeding ground for future federal candidates, and as a forum where the party could attract media attention which was then monopolised by Fraser.[48] After sitting out the 1961 and 1964 elections, the party decided to contest the 1967 poll, a decision which disappointed Carrick, who considered that the ACT party gave the Council 'more prominence than I think it merits'.[49] The decision yielded modest gains, with the party winning two seats out of nine, to Labor's four.

Party divisions over whether to contest Advisory Council elections were unsurprising; they reflected sharp divisions within the broader community. Elected members now made up the majority of the Council, and among the councillors – including Liberal ones – there was a profound conviction that the Territory deserved and needed at least some limited form of self-rule. They were incensed when their repeated appeals for this to the minister were rebuffed. Lawyer and businessman Jim Leedman, the sometime Council Liberal leader, decried a 'profound arrogance' affecting Liberal and Country Party ministers and their senior departmental staff, bordering, in the case of some ministers, on a 'colonial mental attitude'.[50] Anger spilled over in March 1969 when the elected Council members resigned *en masse* in response to the proposed closure of the Canberra abattoir and the imposition of new municipal taxes. A stand-off with the interior minister, the Country Party's Peter Nixon, continued until December when the rebels backed down and returned to their seats, having won some small, face-saving concessions.[51] The minister's sang-froid to the Council's demands was probably educated by an awareness that many citizens regarded it as something of a joke. This had been illustrated by the election in 1967 of journalist Alan Fitzgerald to the Council. He nominated, half in jest, as the representative of the True Whig Party, on a platform of building six service stations on posh Mugga Way. He polled the third highest number of votes and served two terms. Fitzgerald's election suggests an underlying community belief that the Territory's administration was better left with federal autocrats than handed over to the likes of the councillors. This left the Council in the bind that it 'was taken seriously neither by the electors it was supposed to represent nor the Minister it was supposed to advise'.[52]

The largesse lavished on the national capital by Menzies in the 1960s did not immediately translate into electoral gratitude to the Liberal Party. Liberal hopefuls took on Jim Fraser at each poll, but he continued to retain the ACT seat comfortably (the prize made more glittering when its member achieved full voting rights in the federal parliament in 1966). Though the Liberal Party did succeed in dislodging his brother, Allan Fraser, from the neighbouring NSW seat of Eden-Monaro in the landslide of that year. Menzies held no illusions about the political loyalties of the capital; he scotched a proposal in 1965 to give each territory a senator on the basis that this would give the 'Government city' of Canberra 'a militant voice in Parliament'.[53] After his departure from the Lodge, however, an optimism grew, both in Sydney and in some corners of the federal parliamentary party, that the higher educational attainments and disposable incomes of ACT residents would eventually deliver ACT seats. Such hopes were fuelled in 1968 when left-wingers in the ACT branch deposed Fraser as the Labor candidate; Carrick thought the seat winnable with 'a First Class Candidate', and tried to enlist a popular former federal MP, Jo Gullett, to nominate.[54] The president of the Canberra Young Liberals sent Carrick a detailed analysis of the Liberal prospects of winning the seat; Carrick humoured him with a compliment, unaware that the young man, Malcolm Mackerras, would one day be Australia's pre-eminent psephologist.[55] Sensing danger, the ALP hierarchy reinstated Fraser and saved the seat, but Liberal appetites were again whetted in 1970 when Fraser died, necessitating a by-election.

Prime Minister John Gorton, himself a long-term Canberra resident, thought this was the breakthrough the party needed. No stone was left unturned; Nixon was given the job of identifying 'possible issues' for the by-election and Defence Minister Malcolm Fraser was enjoined to facilitate postal voting by Australian service personnel based overseas.[56] Gorton personally attended the preselection of local magistrate Clarrie Hermes as the Liberal candidate and, in turn, Hermes's campaign launch in May 1970 at the Hughes Community Hall.[57] There, the prime minister announced the effective abolition of land rents in Canberra's leasehold system, making it probably the most expensive electoral inducement ever offered in an Australian by-election (on one estimate Gorton gave away lease revenue worth $230 million that night). It was certainly the most futile inducement, dollar for vote, for the Liberal tally barely improved.[58] The city's loyalty to Labor seemed unshakeable.

Whitlam's gift

The election of a federal Labor government in 1972 transformed ACT politics as much as it did the politics of the nation. Gough Whitlam's legacy to the ACT Liberals was a very positive one; he created two new electoral forums in which the party thrived, and his government's performance fostered the conditions both for the first break in the ACT party's long winter of electoral discontent and, in turn, for the long-sought separation from NSW and the creation of an independent ACT Division.

Whitlam paid lip service to the idea of ACT self-rule, but in practice preferred to retain Commonwealth control to showcase Canberra as a social laboratory for Labor's various urban renewal schemes.[59] He replaced the Advisory Council with a Legislative Assembly, but its title was a misnomer – it had no more powers than its predecessor. By the time of the first election for this body in September 1974, disenchantment with government policies retarded Labor's performance.[60] The Liberals won seven seats to Labor's four; it was the first time in 25 years that the party had eclipsed its rival. Other opportunities emerged: population growth gave the ACT a second House of Representatives seat, and Whitlam legislated for the territories to have two senators each, though persistent Coalition resistance meant that the measure had to await the joint sitting of August 1974. The government's tendency to cut administrative corners (the Khemlani loans affair being but the most conspicuous example) had particular resonance in the city dominated by public servants, to the extent that the Liberal Party was able to grab some of the new electoral spoils. At the 1975 dismissal election, the Liberals' John Knight won a seat in the Senate (he became the first-elected of the Territory's two senators by pipping Labor's Susan Ryan in the count) and John Haslem the seat of Canberra, putting its representation in the Territory on a par with the ALP's.[61]

This new flowering of Canberra Liberalism meant that its status as an adjunct to the NSW Division had to be reassessed. With the creation of a second federal electorate conference in 1974, the party was now constituted as the 'ACT Council' of the NSW Division, but a limited apportionment of autonomy did not satisfy the yearning of many members for a separate identity. The ACT Council president was Margaret Reid, a family lawyer originally from South Australia (like almost all senior ACT Liberal Party figures, born outside the ACT). She argued for a separate ACT structure: 'In a sense we have nothing more in common with NSW than we do with Victoria … On national issues our members' voices ought to be as significant as theirs'.[62] Her members continued to rock the Liberal boat, pressing the case for separate representation on the federal council and federal executive, for example, and supported the ACT acquiring Senate seats while the federal parliamentary party was opposed.[63] This restlessness was fuelled by a rapidly expanding party membership, courtesy of Whitlam's missteps. There were three local branches in 1970, but by 1977 there were 18. A membership of 303 in 1973 had burgeoned to 1,124 by 1977.[64] The writing was on the wall. A 'divisional sub-committee' was set up in 1973 to negotiate Canberra's independence from the NSW Division. By October 1975 an ACT constitution was in its seventh draft. The local party opened its first office in January 1976.[65] In September 1976 federal council approved the establishment of an ACT Division of the party, with an entitlement to four federal council delegates.[66] Reid joshed at the September council meeting that this was not 'the beginning of a campaign for Statehood', but also observed more seriously to

The Australian Liberal that the new structure was a chance to show ACT voters 'that we are not conservative'.[67]

The inauguration of the new division on 25 November 1976 at the art deco Institute of Anatomy in Acton was a brief but buoyant affair. Goodwill telegrams from Prime Minister Fraser and federal party President John Atwill were read out. Carrick, by now a senator and Fraser's education minister, was an apology but no doubt breathed a sigh of relief to see his former cantankerous chook fly the NSW coop. Capital Territory Minister Tony Staley addressed the meeting, predicting that the party could outpoll Labor in the next ACT Senate election, as it had done in the last.[68] Reid was elected as inaugural divisional president, only the third woman to head a major party organisation in Australia.[69] The meeting adjourned to a champagne supper.[70]

The heyday was not destined to last. With Whitlam's political demise and the installation of the Fraser Government, complete with a 'razor gang' charged with the job of cutting public spending, the Canberra Liberal bloom began to wilt. At the 1979 House of Assembly (as the Legislative Assembly was necessarily renamed following the failure of a 1978 plebiscite on self-government) election, disenchantment with Fraser handed the ALP eight seats out of 18, while the Liberals attracted just 20 per cent of the vote.[71] A year later Labor recaptured the federal seat of Canberra from Haslem. Senator Knight died suddenly in 1981, with Reid chosen to replace him as the Territory's, by now, sole federal Liberal representative. The party again won fewer seats than Labor at the 1982 Assembly election but the Liberal MHAs under Jim Leedman, now inured to the persistence of Labor's plurality, began to devise new strategies to outflank their old enemy. In a portent of the political plasticity which would be deployed in the later era of self-government, the Liberals were able to string together a coalition with two independents, two Family Team members and an Australian Democrat to snatch the privileges of the controlling majority, such as they were in the 'pretend parliament'.[72] The pretence was further enhanced by the minister bestowing parliamentary titles, so that Leedman now became leader of the House and independent Harold Hird rejoiced in the title of speaker.[73] For the Liberal Party, long actuated by its relationship with power rather than with ideology, a valuable lesson had been learned.

Despite the absence of opportunities to hold public office, Canberra's Liberals were careful to nurture new talent, particularly among their younger members. Young Liberal branches were in existence from the 1960s, and possibly earlier; the senior party seemed to rely on their energy and enthusiasm from an early stage. Over the years that enthusiasm helped several Young Liberals to hold public office while in their 30's; examples include Greg Cornwell (later speaker of the Legislative Assembly), Tim McGhie, Alistair Coe and Candice Burch (all elected MLAs while still Young Liberals). The Liberal Club at the ANU was also the incubator of future parliamentarians, particularly in the wake of campus radicalism in the 1960s and 1970s; its alumni included Michael Yabsley (later a minister in the NSW Greiner Liberal Government) and me (later ACT chief minister and senator).

The 1980s were a lean period for the Liberals in Canberra. The House of Representatives seats remained stubbornly out of reach, and even the Liberal-led local coalition came to an end when the House of Assembly lapsed in 1986, leaving the party with just one elected representative at any level, Senator Reid. The Hawke Labor Government applied more conservative fiscal settings than the Whitlam Government, calming public servants and depriving ACT Liberals of the leverage they had enjoyed courtesy of Whitlam's mistakes. The division remained a powerhouse for policy development, including doubling down on its advocacy for self-government, and acquired its own building, part of which it leased out for revenue and part of which became its headquarters. Nonetheless, it was hampered by the absence of a forum in which it could be competitive – a greyhound without a racecourse to run on.

A new arena: self-government

This changed in 1988. From Canberra's inception, the indifference of its residents to the idea of self-rule had dovetailed neatly with the attitude of successive federal governments. Most administrations saw Canberra as a national responsibility, an idea inconsistent with its own residents having a significant say in its planning and direction. A one-time interior minister, Gorton, considered that Commonwealth autocracy 'worked beautifully'. He thought it 'absurd' that 'a little packet of land like this' should be given equality of status with the states.[74] The plebiscite of Canberra residents engineered by the Fraser Government in 1978 rejected self-government – an outcome many suspected satisfied the minister, Bob Ellicott, who wanted an unfettered hand in shaping the national capital.[75] At each of these junctures Liberal governments danced around a philosophical contradiction; as the champions of decentralisation and subsidiarity, they granted self-government to the Northern Territory in 1978 and even tiny Norfolk Island in 1979, but seemed to have no difficulty denying the Canberra community the same measure of autonomy. Perhaps Canberra was too much the symbol of centralised power for it to be considered a candidate for decentralisation itself.

What finally triggered the countdown to ACT self-government was the preoccupation of the Hawke Labor administration, in common with governments everywhere at that time, with economic rationalism and managerialism, including 'user pays' principles. These called for reducing the role of government to core activities and transferring non-core ones elsewhere. Running Canberra's schools and hospitals, at a cost heavily subsidised by other Australians, offended the rising 'economic rationalism' of the era. An initial Self-Government Bill in 1986 foundered in the Senate over disagreement on an appropriate electoral system, but a second attempt – employing the European d'Hondt electoral system of proportional representation – succeeded in late 1988.

The first election for the 17-member Legislative Assembly was set down for 4 March 1989. What suited the major parties, however, did not suit the Canberra electorate. Supposedly outraged that the emphatic rejection of self-government at the 1978 plebiscite had been disregarded, and fearful that Commonwealth subsidies would soon wither, voters turned away from the major parties. At the election, Labor and Liberal sank to their lowest share of the vote anywhere since 1910 (23 per cent and 15 per cent respectively).[76] With the newborn legislature at the mercy of recently-emerged minor parties, even the prospect of a Labor-Liberal coalition government was publicly canvassed before Howard, the then federal Opposition leader, intervened to quash the idea.[77] Labor under Rosemary Follett formed a minority government of five members, facing four other parties including two committed to the abolition of self-government. Instability was all but guaranteed, and seven months later the Liberal-led Alliance Government was installed under Trevor Kaine, in a coalition of three parties. Though this coalition commanded a majority in the Assembly, it became increasingly divided over cost-cutting measures made necessary by the withdrawal of Commonwealth subsidies – particularly the closure of schools and the Royal Canberra Hospital. It collapsed in June 1991 and Follett returned, securing another term at the second election in 1992.

The Liberal Party's brief taste of power in the first Assembly had taught it valuable lessons. It had built alliances with left-of-centre MLAs, accommodating a variety of their social policy agendas, while pursuing central tenets of Liberal belief – in particular, balancing budgets, a conspicuously-difficult task as federal generosity rapidly ebbed away. This ideological flexibility was deployed again when Kate Carnell, a Queensland-born pharmacist, replaced Kaine as leader in 1993. She advanced policy positions which confounded traditional perceptions of Liberalism, an important device in a community which had rarely embraced a conservative philosophy. For example, she advocated liberalised drug policies, including the trialled supply of heroin to registered addicts, producing both a bemused doubletake by voters and a warmer relationship with a left-wing independent, Michael Moore. Underpinning this approach was an appreciation that the Hare-Clark electoral system, adopted at a referendum in 1992, would virtually mandate minority or coalition governments into the future.

The Carnell strategy paid dividends at the 1995 election. An 11 per cent swing delivered a minority Liberal government with the support of Moore and another independent. It was arguably the zenith of the Liberal Party's performance in its 75-year history in the Capital Territory: for the first time, a Liberal administration had been installed by popular choice, and Carnell became the first woman to head a Liberal government anywhere in the nation.[78] This momentum propelled the party still further; with the Keating Labor Government now nationally unpopular, Liberal Brendan Smyth won a by-election for the federal seat of Canberra the following month, only the third time that the seat has been wrenched from Labor's grasp.[79]

With the ACT health system in crisis and the budget in deficit, Carnell took on the roles of both health minister and treasurer. She was also careful to maintain an (ideological) distance from John Howard, who led the federal party to victory in 1996 and who set about cutting the size of the public service, a move which took a heavy toll on the party's stocks in the national capital. Once again, the carving out of a philosophical niche distinctive from Liberalism elsewhere aided the ACT party; in February 1998 Carnell's Liberals comfortably defeated the Labor Party at the Assembly election, but at the federal election eight months later the Liberal vote in Canberra plunged, almost costing Senator Reid her seat.

Carnell broke new political ground following the 1998 election by inviting Moore to take a seat in the Liberal cabinet, as health minister, while remaining an independent. Moore generally supported the government but preserved the right to step outside cabinet and vote against it on occasions. The arrangement proved to be remarkably resilient. Meanwhile, the ACT Labor Party regrouped after its loss under a new leader, the factionally-unaligned Jon Stanhope. Carnell had aggressively pursued business and investment opportunities in Canberra to offset stalled Commonwealth spending, and the Opposition focused on what it alleged were administrative recklessness and procedural failures in these ventures. Eventually Carnell was forced to resign in 2000 in the wake of a damning auditor-general's report on irregularities in the redevelopment of the Bruce Stadium, and I became chief minister. The Liberal tide, both in the states and in Canberra, was ebbing however, and Stanhope led Labor back into government at the 2001 election. Whereas in Opposition it had been antagonistic to the Assembly crossbench, in government Labor replicated – and perhaps eclipsed – the Liberal Party's ken for dealmaking and coalition building. Over the next 23 years it succeeded in governing through such arrangements, mainly in alliance with the ACT Greens, now a fixture of ACT politics.[80] Stanhope was succeeded in turn by Katy Gallagher and Andrew Barr. A succession of Liberal leaders has, to date, enjoyed little success in displacing the ALP's hegemony.

Conclusion: the furthest frontier of Liberalism

Nowhere has the battlefield terrain faced by the warriors of the Liberal Party been harsher, more unforgiving than in the Australian Capital Territory. This is partly because it has always fought with one hand tied behind its back, philosophically-speaking. As the party of small government and minimal bureaucratic intervention in the lives of citizens, it has generally struggled to win hearts and minds in a city which naturally prospers when government is expansive and its agenda ambitious. Its occasional triumphs over the Labor Party have tended to occur when the latter has fallen into administrative or fiscal malfeasance, rather than when the Liberal credo has had greater resonance than Labor's. This ideological disparity has not been helped in recent years by the ACT party adopting a more conservative profile, echoing its federal arm; this has been a factor in six successive Legislative Assembly defeats and the loss of the Liberal Senate seat to an independent in 2022. The party has also struggled to rekindle the pragmatism that had presented it with its main successes. Significant challenges remain. As ever, the sensitivity of the ACT economy and workforce to policy affecting the APS plays a significant role in shaping public attitudes, attitudes which disfavour the party which is perceived to advocate a smaller, less influential APS. There is now also the structural problem that high rates of tertiary education nationally correlate with ALP and Greens voting, a problem for the Liberals in the ACT with its well-educated population.

The patchy record of electoral success by Canberra's Liberals ought not to obscure their achievements. Political adversity has fostered resilience and adaptability at Liberalism's furthest frontier. Significantly, these Liberals blazed trails in two important areas – pathways that may be useful as the modern Liberal Party addresses present challenges.

The first, reflecting the progressive veins in ACT politics, was the party's success in promoting women as political leaders. From the ranks of the Canberra Liberals came the first woman elected to public office in the Territory, the first woman to head a Liberal government anywhere and the first female president of the Senate.[81] Moreover, they produced the first female-majority Liberal party room and the first all-female Liberal leadership line-up.[82] Notably, these milestones were achieved without quotas or other rules preferring women. They occurred rather quietly.

The second achievement was its success in forming government by working with left-of-centre parties and independents. The Alliance Government of 1989-91 was the only governing coalition (other than with the Country/National Party) ever entered into by the Liberal Party.[83] Similarly, the Carnell and Humphries governments of 1998-2001 were the first to share executive power with an independent, an example which has since been applied elsewhere.[84]

Both these innovations facilitated Liberal-led ACT administrations. The compromises necessary to make these arrangements work did not come at the cost of core Liberal objectives, particularly responsible fiscal management. In an age when support for the major political parties has been eroding and majority governments have become more elusive, the ability to negotiate and compromise needs to be in the toolkit of every party leader.[85] Conspicuously, an inability to negotiate and compromise with crossbenchers has cost the Liberal Party the privilege of power in other contexts.[86]

No appraisal of the Liberal Party's relationship with Canberra would be complete without reference to its role in building the national capital. Modern Canberra is the creation of successive Liberal governments. Decisions of the Menzies Government in particular transformed Canberra from a country town into a true national capital. Almost all of the great national institutions and structures in Canberra, which define that role and which give expression to the Australian identity, were the product of Liberal governments' decisions: they include the National Library, the National Museum, the National Gallery, the National Portrait Gallery, Lake Burley Griffin, the Australian Institute of Sport, and Parliament House. There is no small irony in the fact that the party which has been Canberra's chief benefactor, at least in a physical sense, has been generally passed over when its citizens have gone to the ballot box.

---

1 Gary Humphries is a former ACT Liberal chief minister and senator. He is currently undertaking a PhD thesis at the Australian National University on the history of ACT self-government.

2 See Monnox, *ACT Labor 1929-2009.*

3 *The Canberra Times*, 4 June 1948, p. 4.

4 Minutes of NSW State Council, 29 June 1948, *Records of the New South Wales division of the Liberal Party of Australia, 1949-1970, State Library of New South Wales*, Box Y4625,2.

5 *The Canberra Times*, 13 July 1949, p 5; *Liberal Opinion* newsletter, July 1949, p. 3, ACT Liberal Party archives.

[6] See for example McLennan, 'Menzies and the Movement: Two Pillars of Australian Anti-Communism', pp. 24-6.

[7] *The Canberra Times*, 28 January 1949, p. 4; *Liberal Opinion* newsletter, February 1949, p. 13, ACT Liberal Party archives.

[8] Letter, JR Willoughby to John Carrick, 23 April 1948, *Records of the NSW Liberal Party*, Box Y4629,4.

[9] Memorandum, John Carrick to WH Spooner, 20 May 1949, *Records of the NSW Liberal Party*.

[10] Hancock, *National and Permanent?*, pp. 83-5.

[11] *The Canberra Times*, 30 June 1949, p 5; 'Mary Stevenson (1896-1985)', *The Australian Women's Register*, https://www.womenaustralia.info/entries/stevenson-mary/.

[12] Fraser's own diligence as a local member was a factor in his success. Carrick would concede in 1968 that Fraser 'does his Electorate work very well indeed and he avoids all major National Issues': Letter John Carrick to Senator RC Cotton, 29 May 1968, *Records of the NSW Liberal Party*, Box Y4616,3. See also Sparke, *Canberra 1954-1980*, pp. 198-9.

[13] 'Mary Stevenson (1896-1985)', *The Australian Women's Register*, https://www.womenaustralia.info/entries/stevenson-mary/.

[14] *The Canberra Times*, 28 May 1954, p. 6.

[15] *The Canberra Times*, 5 November 1955, p. 2; 10 December 1955, p. 4; 18 September 1958, p. 2; 20 November 1958, p. 20.

[16] Federal selection nomination form, John Gannon, 26 March 1951, *Records of the NSW Liberal Party*, Box Y4686,1; State Branch membership records, *Records of the NSW Liberal Party*, Box YV1173.

[17] Gibbney, *Canberra 1913-1953*, p 161; *House of Representatives Hansard*, 12 March 1930, p. 39.

[18] Denning, *Capital City*, p. 82.

[19] Atkins, *The Government of the Australian Capital Territory*, p. 10.

[20] Quoted in Sparke, *Canberra*, p. 271.

[21] *The Canberra Times*, 27 July 1949, p. 5.

[22] Though one could argue that she owes this distinction to being the first woman elected to the board of the Canberra Community Hospital in 1947, without Liberal endorsement.

[23] Letter Robert Greenish to John Carrick, 17 June 1961, *Records of the NSW Liberal Party*, Box Y4646,2.

[24] *ACT Advisory Council Elected Members, 1930-1974* (compiled by Chris Monnox), Libraries ACT https://www.library.act.gov.au/find/history/frequentlyaskedquestions/personal_stories/act_advisory_council,_1930-1974/elected_members,_act_advisory_council,_1930-1974. Although Jim Pead sat in its successor bodies as an independent, in the Advisory Council he represented the ACT Progress and Welfare Association.

[25] Monnox, 'Canberra's Local Council? The ACT Advisory Council', p. 24.

[26] See, for example, Report of the Local Government Sub-committee of [NSW] State Council, 11 September 1958, *Records of the NSW Liberal Party*, Box Y4710,1.

[27] *The Canberra Times*, 18 September 1958, p. 2. Mrs Dalgarno may have been a 'real' independent in 1961 as there was some disputation between her and the ACT conference in 1960; see Letter NC Hyett to John Carrick, 31 October 1960, *Records of the NSW Liberal Party*, Box Y4646,2.

[28] Minutes of ACT Federal Electorate Conference, 17 May 1967, ACT Liberal Party archives.

[29] 'Recommendations from the Policy Sub-Committee, Canberra General Branch', 28 May 1957, *Records of the NSW Liberal Party*, Box Y4646,2.

[30] *Liberal Opinion*, July 1949, p 7, ACT Liberal Party archives.

[31] *The Canberra Times*, 4 June 1948, p. 4.

[32] Letter John Carrick to Mary Stevenson, 25 July 1956, *Records of the NSW Liberal Party*, Box Y4606,4; Letter John Carrick to Robert Greenish, 26 July 1957, *Records of the NSW Liberal Party*, Box Y4607,1; Letter Robert Greenish to John Carrick, 18 June 1961, *Records of the NSW Liberal Party*, Box Y4646,2.

[33] Letter John Carrick to Colin Watson, 1 April 1958, *Records of the NSW Liberal Party*, Box Y4607,8. Some irritation at Sydney headquarters was understandable, such as when the ACT branch raised for its attention the issue of divorce proceedings by a certain vice-president of the United Nations Association!

[34] Letter John Carrick to Colin Watson, 26 February 1958, *Records of the NSW Liberal Party*, Box Y4607,5; Letter Colin Watson to John Carrick, 26 March 1958, *Records of the NSW Liberal Party*, Box Y4646,2; Letter John Carrick to Colin Watson, 23 April 1958, *Records of the NSW Liberal Party*, Box Y4607,9.

[35] Letter John Carrick to JR Willoughby, 13 August 1956, *Records of the NSW Liberal Party*, Box Y4606,4.

[36] Letter John Carrick to Mary Stevenson, 19 February 1958, *Records of the NSW Liberal Party*, Box Y4607,5. For an example of the kind of correspondence Carrick was referring to, see Letter Robert Greenish to John Carrick, 12 July 1957, *Records of the NSW Liberal Party*, Box Y4646,2.

[37] Letter John Carrick to Robert Greenish, 19 July 1957; Letter John Carrick to Mary Stevenson, 18 July 1957, *Records of the NSW Liberal Party*, Box Y4607,1, Letter John Carrick to Colin Watson, 23 April 1958, *Records of the NSW Liberal Party*, Box Y4607,9.

[38] Memorandum, General Secretary to State President, 17 May 1968, *Records of the NSW Liberal Party*, Box Y4616,3.

[39] Letter Robert Greenish to John Carrick, 28 June 1958, *Records of the NSW Liberal Party*, Box Y4646,2.

[40] Correspondence Book 1966-73, ACT Liberal Party archives.

[41] Letter John Murray to John Carrick, 27 May 1961, *Records of the NSW Liberal Party*, Box Y4646,2.

[42] Menzies, *The Measure of the Years*, p. 143; Sparke, *Canberra,* p 31; *Interview, Heather Henderson with Gary Humphries*, 15 November 2018, author's archive.

[43] Davies, Hoffman and Price, *A history of Australia's capital,* p. 94; Evans, 'The intertwined history of Canberra and the Parliament', p. 18.

[44] Brown, *A History of Canberra*, pp. 144-6.

[45] Letter John Carrick to PJ Osborne, 23 May 1958, *Records of the NSW Liberal Party*, Box Y4607,9.

[46] Letter John Carrick to Mary Stevenson, 25 July 1960, *Records of the NSW Liberal Party*, Box Y4609,3.

[47] Letter John Carrick to E Rowe, 15 February 1965, *Records of the NSW Liberal Party*, Box Y4612,8.

[48] Minutes, ACT Federal Electorate Conference, 9 March 1967; Minutes of meeting of Combined Branches of ACT Liberal Party, 6 April 1967, ACT Liberal Party archives.

[49] Memorandum, General Secretary to State President, 17 May 1968, *Records of the NSW Liberal Party*, Box Y4616,3.

[50] *Oral history interview with Jim Leedman*, conducted by Bill Oakes & Lynne Reeder, 4 April 1990 (ACT Heritage Library); *Interview, Gary Humphries with Jim Leedman*, 28 April 2018, author's archive.

[51] Sparke, *Canberra,* pp. 269-71.

[52] Brown, *A History of Canberra,* p 171; Sparke, *Canberra,* pp 269-70; Grundy, Oakes, Reeder and Wettenhall, *Reluctant Democrats,* pp. 58-9.

[53] Hancock, *National and Permanent?* p. 227.

[54] Letter John Carrick to Senator RC Cotton, 29 May 1968, *Records of the NSW Liberal Party*, Box Y4616,3; Memorandum, John Carrick to State President, 27 November 1968, *Records of the NSW Liberal Party*, Box Y4616,7.

[55] Letter Malcolm Mackerras to John Carrick, 20 November 1968, *Records of the NSW Liberal Party*, Box Y4619,2.

[56] Letter John Carrick to Peter Nixon, 22 April 1970; Letter John Carrick to Malcolm Fraser, 6 May 1970, *Records of the NSW Liberal Party*, Box Y4618,1.

[57] Minutes of the ACT Preselection Committee, 30 April 1970, ACT Liberal Party archives.

[58] Gorton had also neglected to inform Nixon of his intention to make this announcement: Sparke, *Canberra*, pp. 199-201.

[59] Sparke, *Canberra*, pp. 203-6; Brown, *A History of Canberra,* pp. 179, 185.

[60] Chris Monnox, *ACT Labor*, p. 28.

[61] Knight's win in 1975 was the only time that the Liberal Party has gained a plurality over Labor in this contest.

[62] *The Australian Liberal*, June 1976, p. 12, ACT Liberal Party archives.

[63] Minutes, ACT Federal Electorate Conference, 19 March 1973, 18 April 1973, ACT Liberal Party archives.

[64] Minutes, ACT Federal Electorate Conference, 20 June 1973; Minutes of ACT Council, 15 June 1976; Minutes, ACT Division Executive, 2 June 1977, ACT Liberal Party archives.

[65] Minutes, ACT Council Executive, 22 January 1974; 27 October 1975; 22 January 1976, ACT Liberal Party archives.

[66] Minutes, ACT Council Executive, 16 August 1976, ACT Liberal Party archives.

[67] *The Australian Liberal*, June 1976, p. 12; September 1976, p. 3, ACT Liberal Party archives.

[68] (It didn't.) *The Canberra Times*, 26 November 1976, p. 1.

[69] https://www.aph.gov.au/About_Parliament/Parliamentary_Departments/Parliamentary_Library/pubs/rp/rp1314/QG/FemalePolLeaders#_ftn13

[70] Minutes, ACT Divisional Council of the Liberal Party, 25 November 1976, ACT Liberal Party archives.

[71] Monnox, *ACT Labor*, pp. 31-2.

[72] *The Canberra Times*, 17 July 1982, p. 1.

[73] Sparke, *Canberra*, p. 334.

[74] *Oral history interview with Sir John Gorton*, conducted by Bill Oakes & Lynne Reeder, 14 February 1990 (ACT Heritage Library).

[75] *Oral history interview with Bob Ellicott*, conducted by Bill Oakes & Lynne Reeder, 22 February 1991 (ACT Heritage Library).

[76] https://www.elections.act.gov.au/elections_and_voting/past_act_legislative_assembly_elections/1989_election/first_preference_results_1989_election

[77] *The Canberra Times*, 3 May 1989, p. 1; 4 May 1989, p. 1. Howard's opinion may not have mattered; he was deposed as leader by Andrew Peacock six days later.

[78] It would take a further 22 years for another woman, Gladys Berejiklian in NSW, to replicate this achievement.

[79] Like so many ACT Liberal victories, it was short lived; Labor regained the seat at the following year's general election.

[80] Only once has any ACT single-party government been able to govern in majority, the Stanhope Labor government of 2004-08.

[81] These distinctions belong to Mary Stevenson, Kate Carnell and Margaret Reid respectively.

[82] The ACT legislative Assembly Liberal Party room consisted of six women and five men from 2017 to 2020. In March 2021 Elizabeth Lee became leader and Giulia Jones deputy leader of the parliamentary Liberals. The present leadership team is also all-female: Elizabeth Lee and Leanne Castley.

[83] The Rundle Tasmanian Government 1996-98 entered into an agreement with the Tasmanian Greens without including them in the ranks of the government.

[84] Examples include the Rann and Weatherill South Australian Governments of 2004-10 and 2014-18 respectively.

[85] In the Australian context, see, for example, the Australian Election Study: chrome-extension://efaidnbmnnnibpcajpcglclefindmkaj/https://australianelectionstudy.org/wp-content/uploads/Trends-in-Australian-Political-Opinion-Results-from-the-Australian-Election-Study-1987-2022.pdf.

[86] Examples include the failures of the Kennett Victorian Government in 1999 and the Abbott federal Opposition in 2010. The re-election of the Rockliff Tasmanian Government in 2024 is a (rare) example of where this trend has been reversed.

11

The Liberals Up North

Shane Stone[1]

An account of the Liberal Party up north is a challenging task given the party did not long endure as a separate entity. A Liberal Party associated with the Victorian Division emerged in 1966. It would last less than eight years before exiting NT politics, but not before overseeing with the then Country Party (NSW Division), the birth of the merged and enduring entity, the Northern Territory Country Liberal Party, in 1974.

In 1995 the CLP invited the late Associate Professor Alistair Heatley of NTU to research the CLP's history. The CLP did not commission the study and it was never intended as an official history; archives were made available; and party officials and elected members were encouraged to cooperate with Heatley in the preparation of his publication. Some financial assistance was forthcoming to assist with research. The result, *The Territory Party: The Northern Territory Country Liberal Party 1974-1998* published by Northern Territory University Press, was launched by Chief Minister Shane Stone MLA on 20 November 1998 at Parliament House Darwin.[2] Many of those participating in the launch are now deceased. Copyright of the Heatley publication is acknowledged and relied on extensively in what follows.

Writing in his introduction, Heatley observed 'In the scholarly literature on Territory politics, treatment of parties has largely been located within analyses of elections and institutions or within general works on the Territory polity. Although the development of parties before 1974 has been traced in works on the Legislative Council (Walker 1986 and Jaensch 1990) and in an early account of the Territory's political system (Heatley 1979), the coverage was cursory and partial. There have been few substantial publications about the Territory's political parties post-1974 save for the early publications by Dean Jaensch, 1988 and 1985, and the publication by Jolly 1991 who examined the history of Territory Labor between 1974 and 1990'.[3] Additionally, former Deputy Chief Minister Barry Coulter AO wrote and delivered a paper at an Alice Springs branch meeting detailing the history of the Country Party in the years leading up to the formation of the CLP in 1974.

With such paucity of publications and primary material I apologise in advance for any inaccuracies and misdescriptions and most importantly the omission of names of those associated with the Liberal Party pre-CLP. Records have been misplaced and lost over the years.

The Liberal Party in the Northern Territory was a short-lived yet important chapter in our political development and history. There is no Liberal Party in the Northern Territory. The Country Liberal Party was created when both the Liberal and Country (now National) parties withdrew from the Territory and the Country Liberal Party was born in 1974. The CLP is not a division of the Liberals and Nationals; we attend annual conferences, council, management and executive committees as observers. When elected in federal elections, the House of Representatives members sit with the Liberals and the senators with the Nationals, although this is not mandated. The CLP is the fourth member of the Coalition, a fact often overlooked by commentators.

Notwithstanding CLP members have played key roles in our sister Coalition parties – members and senators (Calder, Tambling, Kilgariff, Dondas, Tollner, Griggs, Scullion and Price), ministers (Tambling and Scullion, the latter also held leadership roles in the Nationals Senate team), whip (Kilgariff), shadow minister (Jacinta Price, shadow minister for Indigenous affairs), party leadership (Stone, Liberal federal president during the six latter years of the Howard Government 1999-2004 and one of the few federal life members as well as accorded same by LNP QLD and Victoria). Most importantly the CLP over successive federal elections has facilitated key campaign operatives (not members of the CLP), at various times dominating key roles in CHQ – Textor (of Crosby Textor fame), Conran, Murphy, Cowdy, Swinstead and Stone. The CLP has punched well above its weight and has been associated with several of the Coalition's greatest successes. Conran served on the personal staff of Howard and Morrison. He was later appointed as the federal cabinet secretary in the Morrison Government. The CLP Perron Government through expert treasury advice sought to assist Dr John Hewson on various matters associated with the 'Fight Back' package in 1993. At state level, the CLP Hatton Government assisted the incoming Greiner Government's 'transition to Government' in 1988. The Perron CLP Government assisted the incoming Kennett Government in formulating education and schools' policy in 1992. In 1996, the Stone CLP Government assisted the Tasmanian Rundle Government on various policy issues, albeit unsuccessful.

The merged Coalition entity styled the Northern Territory Country Liberal Party owes a great deal to the contemporary Liberal Party for its survival and ultimate revival. True to the saying 'success has many parents and failure is an orphan' it is worth reflecting on what was achieved by the new entity, the CLP, following the withdrawal of the Liberal and Country parties from the Territory. Dating from the first fully elected Legislative Assembly in 1974 the CLP won every Territory election for the rest of the century, ultimately defeated in 2001 with the fall of the Burke Government. In terms of highlights on 30 August 1997 the CLP were returned to office for the sixth time since self-government on a record vote and the eighth time since 1974 (the 1997 general election represented a high-water mark for the CLP receiving 54.7 per cent of the first preference vote, an increase of 2.8 per cent from the 1994 election result. Territory Labor's vote was down by 2.9 per cent to 38.5 per cent. In two-party preferred terms support for the CLP increased

1.6 per cent to 57.9 per cent). Post our defeat in 2002 we returned for a single term in 2012 to ultimately suffer a humiliating defeat in 2016 where the CLP were reduced to two members of the Assembly after a single term including the Chief Minister Adam Giles losing the seat of Braitling in Alice Springs. Our result in federal elections has been less spectacular as we are on an equal footing with Labor. At the time of writing Labor hold both Territory federal seats Solomon and Lingiari. The CLP and Labor have a senator each.

At a Territory level the NT Labor Party has dominated the last 20 years (save 2012-16), to a point where we who had invested in the CLP over decades pondered whether it was possible to retake the government benches ever again. In party forums, discussions turned on formally merging with either the Liberals or the Nationals. The Nationals' forerunner the Country Party (NSW Division) had played a pivotal role in conservative politics in the NT and can claim to have fostered and supported the CLP in the party's formation and early success.

In January 1941 Prime Minister Robert Menzies flew by Qantas Empire flying boat to Brisbane, Gladstone, Townsville and Darwin before heading to the Dutch East Indies. Given the isolation and remoteness of the NT, he would have found a mostly itinerate northern outpost of circa 5000 people, soon to be recoiling from the Japanese bombing of Darwin commenced in 1942 and continued until 1943 with an estimated 260 casualties. Darwin was a city with limited resources; a poorly equipped and demoralised military outpost. Whether the prime minister met with any like-minded political supporters during the visit I have not been able to ascertain. His main address was to an AIF unit, to whom he said specifically 'I am not here to talk politics', although he did touch on his upcoming meetings with Churchill.[4] He noted in his diary that he was 'assured on every side that if not for unions Darwin would progress',[5] suggesting he received at least some local political intel. In any event, the Liberal Party had not yet emerged on the national scene and the Menzies UAP Government was a minority destined for defeat.

The first Territory conservatives with a UAP/ Liberal disposition came from 'down south' and resided primarily in Darwin. The Country Party's strength was to be found in Central Australia. There was also the North Australia Party (NAP) established in the 1960s by the formerly independent member for Alice Springs Colonel Lionel Rose, 'to promote the economic, social and political development of northern Australia.'[6] This enjoyed some initial success with the assistance of a campaign organiser from the NSW Division. But the simple reality of Territory politics was that whilst the states and the Commonwealth provided ample opportunities for passionate electoral contests, this was not the case in the Territory. Until the creation of the Legislative Council in 1947 the only contests going were for a single seat in the Commonwealth parliament (with no voting rights save on matters affecting the NT), Darwin municipality until 1930, and Advisory Councils between 1926 and 1931.

The Labor Party got an early foothold in the Territory stemming from trade unions around Darwin, and was contesting Town Council elections from 1915. It was not until 1922 that an NT Reform League emerged as an alternative to Labor who were riven by internal dissent and competing factions. The inauguration of a Legislative Council in 1957 and a municipal council in Darwin did not prompt the formation of a permanent conservative party. Labor continued to field candidates with moderate success while others preferred to be independents. The reality was that Darwin had a small and churning population, and due to poor communications, the locals were somewhat removed from national news and events notwithstanding a few local papers.

Heatley documents the brief history of the NAP as follows:

> Jaensch has described the October 1965 Council general election as 'the genesis of a Northern Territory party system'. It was the first 'where a majority of candidates were party nominees, and the first election where Labor faced a party team'. The NAP fielded five contestants, three in

central Australia, one in the seat around Katherine and one in Darwin. Labor ran seven. After a fiery campaign on the hustings and in the media, where *The Northern Territory News* (NTN) in Darwin and the CA in Alice Springs vigorously opposed the NAP … the new party gained but one seat; Greatorex was elected in Stuart, the largely pastoral constituency in the south of the Territory. Rose lost his place narrowly to Labor. In Darwin, the NAP hopeful polled poorly. An interesting, albeit arguable, comment on the NAP was made by the NTN; it saw the party as a 'Liberal Party – front organisation'. As evidence, it pointed out that the organiser of the campaign had been provided by the NSW Liberals, that the NAP's top official in Alice Springs had attempted to form a local Liberal branch, that the resources expended on the election were large (and therefore by implication received from outside the Territory) and that the NAP had concentrated on attacking the ALP. It concluded that 'if the Liberal party wants to move in then this should be done openly. The party would receive, as such, considerable support from many sections of the community' (NTN, 21 October 1965). The NAP survived into early-1966 to contest two further elections. In a byelection for the seat based on Tennant Creek in February, it was unsuccessful but, in the same month, it achieved its best results in the election for the five community representatives on the Alice Springs Town Management Board. In a small turn-out (17 per cent), it won all positions, swamping the Labor team. One commentary referred to the NAP success as 'the greatest political reversal ever seen in The Centre' (*The Inland Review*, 2:5, December 1967, 18). Nonetheless, it soon faded away with its place as opposition to Labor being soon taken by the Country Party and the Liberals. Several of those who had been

> connected to the NAP were later to become involved with the Country Party, particularly in Alice Springs.[7]

The death of the NAP left a political vacuum which would give birth to the NT Liberals:

> Several earlier invitations had been made to the Liberal Party to establish a presence in the Territory and one candidate in a 1963 Darwin by-election had styled himself a 'Liberal' but the party only became active in 1966, and for similar reasons which had spurred the interest of the CP. A Darwin branch, which later became associated with the Victorian Division, was founded in late September (NTN, 28 September and oral history transcript of Harold Cooper, NT Archives). Like the CP, the Liberal Party had a small membership, largely drawn from the commercial and professional community. It did not stand a candidate in the 1966 federal poll, preferring instead to support Calder (Country Party). Until the lead-up to the 1968 Council election, there was little public political activity from the party.[8]

The leading figure of the Darwin branch was Norman Harold Cooper OBE, mayor of the city from 1959-66, a former soldier who had entered the stevedoring business and become an active member of the Chamber of Commerce.[9] A humanitarian, Cooper had received interstate press attention for threatening to resign in opposition to a proposal to bar Indigenous Australians from using the municipal swimming pool,[10] and backing two Malayan residents in a fight against their deportation.[11] He also led a successful campaign to stop the wreckage of the first Japanese aircraft shot down over Australia from being relocated from Darwin to Canberra.[12] The timing suggests that the first Liberal branch may have been founded partly in response to Cooper's defeat as mayor at the 1966 council elections.

Heatley concludes:

> In August 1968 a second branch was created in Darwin and an executive structure established (NTN, 20 August and oral history transcripts of Tom Lawler and Ella Stack, NT Archives). The Liberal Party stood six candidates in the October 1968 election – five in Darwin-based seats and the other in Arnhem. Although it conducted a strong campaign and won nearly 30 per cent of the primary vote, none of its candidates was elected. Nor were endorsed Liberal candidates successful in two by-elections in Darwin in late 1969 and early-1970; they were won by former Liberal members running as independents. Rivalry over preselection was one factor in weakening the party. After the run of electoral disappointments, it ceased to operate as an organised body; in the 1971 Council elections, several erstwhile party officials, candidates and members again participated under an independent label. When it became clear in 1973 that the next election would be for a fully elected legislature, there were discussions among Liberal supporters about party revitalisation. But they were overtaken by the events which surrounded the formation of the CLP in mid-1974.[13]

The rest is now history. The minutes of the Liberal Party in Darwin 1966-74 have been lost but some names are remembered by family members and friends. They include Cooper, Alf Hooper (first president CLP 1974), Paul Everingham (subsequently first chief minister), Neville Skews, Albert Albany, Maizie Rainer, Rex Jettner, Tom Lawler, Ella Stack, (subsequently lord mayor of Darwin 1975-79), Ron Dickson, and Tony Watson-Brown. Other leading identities at the time were Calder, Letts, Vale, Kilgariff and Rex Jettner associated with the Country Party. This is not an exclusive list of Liberal and Country Party identities.

Menzies is not forgotten in the north. The Menzies School of Health Research, named for Sir Robert Menzies was established in

1985 by a CLP Government as a body corporate of the Northern Territory Government under the *Menzies Act 1985*. This Act was amended in 2004 to formalise the relationship with Charles Darwin University (CDU). Menzies is now a major partner of CDU and constitutes a school within the University's Institute of Advanced Studies. The school is one of Australia's leading medical research institutes dedicated to improving the health and well-being of Aboriginal and Torres Strait Islander peoples. They are also a leader in global and tropical health research into life-threatening diseases.

---

[1] The Honourable Shane L Stone AC KC is the current president of the Country Liberal Party. He was formerly chief minister of the Northern Territory (1995-9) and federal president of the Liberal Party (1999-2004).

[2] To see a photographic record of the launch see www.stonefamilyinaustralia.com.au search Shane Stone's archive for Alistair Heatley.

[3] Heatley, *The Territory Party*, p. xi.

[4] 'Prime Minister at Darwin', *The Age*, 4 February 1941, p. 6.

[5] Menzies, *Dark and Hurrying Days*, p. 20.

[6] 'New political party to develop north', *Canberra Times*, 12 August 1965, p. 9.

[7] Heatley, *The Territory Party*, p. 3.

[8] Ibid., p. 4.

[9] Heatley, *A City Grows*, p. 129. There is photographic evidence suggesting that Cooper may have met and even sailed with Menzies during the latter's 1954 trip to Darwin.

[10] 'Would resign if natives banned from pool', *Canberra Times*, 28 June 1960, p. 6.

[11] 'Malays', *The Bulletin*, 7 October 1961, p. 8.

[12] 'Save Our Zero', *The Bulletin*, 28 July 1962, p. 9.

[13] Heatley, *The Territory Party*, p. 7.

12

The Country Party, the foundation of the Liberal Party, and the birth of the modern Liberal-Nationals Coalition

John Anderson and Terry Barnes

Introduction

On its birth in 1944, the Liberal Party joined the centre-right of Australian politics, taking a place beside its rural and regional cousin, the Country Party.

Sometimes, it is opponents who define a rival political party or movement. It was the Labor-aligned senior public servant and political scientist, 'Fin' Crisp, who framed the Liberal and Country parties as the 'parties of town and country capital':[1] a lazy definition, yet in many ways not a wholly inappropriate one.[2]

But as the shattered and loose alliances of the United Australia Party coalesced into Menzies's child, the opportunity to weld all centre-right forces into a single national party, including the Country Party, was passed over. Was this by accident, design, or simply inertia?

This chapter considers the Country Party's relationship with the Liberal Party's formation. It looks at the relationship between the parties and their leading personalities in the mid-1940s, the state of the Country Party itself, and asks whether overtures of amalgamation and unity on either side after the Coalition parties lost office to John Curtin's Labor in 1941 were anything more than lip service and being seen to be going through the motions.

It also looks briefly at the impact the Country Party had on Australian federal and state politics once its Liberal Coalition partner had established itself and, in a postscript, suggests what the Country Party's greatest gift to the Liberal Party in 1944 may well have been.

Background

To understand why the Liberal and Country parties ended up as separate entities, and Menzies's attitude towards keeping them so, some basic points of historical context are important.[3]

The main one is that the Country Party had emerged in the wake of the 1919 federal election in direct protest against the then mainstream centre-right party, the Nationalists.[4] The notion that a single centre-right party, whose main electoral and donor base was overwhelmingly urban, would not understand and advocate the interests of rural and regional people and communities, became the Country Party's raison d'etre. This was, of course at a time when the Australian economy was heavily agrarian and dependent on primary industry, famously riding 'on the sheep's back'.

Also relevant was that, at that time, the Nationalists were headed by an ex-Labor leader in Billy Hughes – hence the Country Party's emergence may be partly attributed to the manner in which Hughes failed in government to practise liberal values like subsidiarity and decentralisation, values he had never claimed to believe in. Indeed, when the major centre-right party did embody those values, such as the original Commonwealth Liberal Party headed by Prime Minister Sir Joseph Cook (who made a deliberate pitch to rural voters in 1914),[5] no such split occurred.

Although there were other factors at play, most notably the introduction of preferential voting which made separate centre-right parties less of an automatic electoral gift to Labor, and Australian liberalism's longstanding opposition to the representation of so-called 'sectional interests' in politics. As the 1920s dawned therefore, the stars aligned for the forming of a Country Party and its immediate electoral success, which in 1922 forced the Nationalists to depose Hughes for Stanley Bruce, in return for their parliamentary support.

For this, there is another curious Menzies connection. The new but unaligned Liberal member for Kooyong, and future (after he eventually joined them in 1925) Nationalist and UAP leader, John Latham KC, was elected on a 'Hughes must go' platform. Country Party Leader Earle Page invited Latham to sit in the Country Party room as an observer, given their common interest in removing Hughes. Here, Latham assisted Page unofficially but was instrumental in what led to the Stanley Bruce-Earle Page Government, Page writing of this informal alliance that '(Latham) was more than an honoured guest for over a year, giving us the benefit of his practical wisdom and his sage legal advice' in dealing with Hughes and the Nationalists.[6]

There was also significant political blood spilt in fights between Nationalists and Country Party candidates when the latter emerged, directly affecting Menzies and his family. Robert Menzies of Jeparit's outlook on the relationship inevitably was influenced by the fact that the previous politicians in his family, who all represented rural seats, were toppled by Country Party opponents. These included his father James Menzies (Victorian MLA for Lowan until 1920); his father-in-law John Leckie (federal member for Indi until 1919); and his uncle and political mentor Sydney Sampson (federal member for Wimmera until 1919). Sampson was not even a dyed-in-the-wool Nationalist; he had openly advocated rural interests, supported most of the Country Party platform, and was actively recruited to become a Country Party candidate. But Sampson steadfastly refused to sign up to the party's Labor-resembling pledge, hence the party felt the need to make an example of Sampson.[7]

Menzies's family experiences, and his succeeding Page's 1922 collaborator Latham in Kooyong, also must have given him cause to think about the relationship and personalities of the two Coalition parties. Perhaps these background factors influenced his decision not to try to entice the Country Party into his 1939 ministry after Page refused to serve with the UAP.[8] But, as Arthur Calwell of all people later pointed out somewhat admiringly, 'I thought his attitude to the Country Party was more than generous because he must have always felt chagrined when he remembered that the Country Party, figuratively speaking, held three scalps of the Menzies clan on their belt'.[9]

A final point to note is how generally fractious was the relationship between Coalition partners before the birth of the Liberal Party. As noted earlier, in the wake of the 1922 election, the Country Party insisted on the removal of Hughes if they were to form a government with the Nationalists. While the resulting Bruce-Page ministry was generally a productive partnership, subsequently the United Australia Party under Joe Lyons would jettison the Country Party to rule by itself from 1931-34. Then, after less than five years of co-governance, Menzies himself would form an all-UAP ministry in April 1939, only reverting to a Coalition arrangement because of the circumstances of the war.

The Country Party in 1944

Essential to the Liberal Party's actual foundation story is that the UAP, and the assortment of MPs, individuals and organisations allied with it, were in a state of utter disarray and incapable of offering a coherent alternative to John Curtin and his then-predominant Labor Party.

But any assumption that, while the UAP was collapsing, the Country Party was blissfully happy and unified, with its parliamentary representatives, federal and state organisations, and affiliated supporters working together in serene harmony, is wrong.

In the mid-1940s, the Country Party had more than a few problems of its own that permeated the war years, and contributed to the conservative parties' heavy defeat by Curtin in 1943.

Federally, the Country Party room was riven by its own divisions and personality conflicts. In 1939, Page resigned as leader after his vicious personal attack, under parliamentary privilege, on Menzies. Unfortunately for party unity, he was replaced by Archie Cameron, a curmudgeonly South Australian who failed to understand being a parliamentary leader meant being civil to his colleagues. When, in petulant frustration, Cameron quit after failing to find support for his renomination as leader after a poor 1940 federal election result, the leadership was contested by Page and John McEwen, who tied in the voting.[10] Only then did Arthur Fadden become acting leader of the party,[11] as a compromise candidate well-liked by his colleagues,[12] but who also had quit the party room for a time in protest over Page's denunciation of Menzies.

Fadden, an accountant by profession whose affability and 'hail fellow, well met' personality, combined with ministerial acumen, earned the respect of his colleagues, did much to unite and soothe the bruised egos of his parliamentary party. He even successfully buried the hatchet with Page after the party room split of 1939.[13] Menzies appointed him treasurer; he was acting prime minister during Menzies's mission to Britain and the Middle East in 1941; and, after the UAP toppled Menzies later that year, Fadden was prime minister for, famously, 'forty days and forty nights' until he and his government were, in turn, toppled by two independents, Arthur Coles and Alex Wilson.

It is generally forgotten today that it was Country Party internal divisions that finally brought down the Menzies-Fadden Government in October 1941. One of those two independents who switched their support to Curtin, member for Wimmera and wheat-grower advocate Wilson, was a disaffected Country Party member who had won his seat in 1937 against the party's endorsed candidate. In crossing the floor on 3 October, Wilson declared 'he had always had some sympathy for the ALP and that the platform of his party in Victoria (the United Country Party) was similar to that of Labor.'[14]

At state level, the shape of the Country Party was not wildly different from the UAP, in terms of being an unstable conglomerate of notionally allied interests. State party organisations were laws unto themselves, each with their own structures and policy priorities reflecting the interests of the farmers' and rural groups affiliated with them, rather than coordinating and cooperating with each other on issues of common concern. Indeed, they rarely talked with each other, let alone worked together, even for federal election campaigns: their priorities were their own states. In a time where mass communication on a nationwide basis was still limited, even federal election campaign planning and execution mostly were parochial at state and electorate level, rather than national.

As far as the UAP went, state Country Party organisations had ambivalent relationships with their UAP 'colleagues', even when in Coalition. In the one state where the parties were fused, South Australia, the Liberal and Country League still had its share of cross-party tensions.[15] The most egregious example, however, was Victoria. There in the late 1930s and 1940s the Country Party (calling itself the United Country Party), led by rural populist Premier Albert Dunstan, formed a minority government supported by Labor, with the UAP as its Opposition.[16] Moreover, Dunstan was hostile even to his federal party, a reality highlighted by the defection of Dunstan-supporting Alex Wilson to back Curtin and Labor in late 1941.[17] Even after the non-Labor parties notionally reconciled in Victoria years later, Victorian Liberal figures, including Henry Bolte, maintained their personal hostility to the Country Party, and even for a time the state Liberal Party was renamed the Liberal and Country Party to undercut its rival in regional Victoria.[18]

With an anaemic federal organisation, fiercely independent state parties, a wide range of affiliated interests, and ambivalent relations with the UAP and the likes of Menzies and the UAP's interregnum leader and Page's bête noir, Billy Hughes,[19] in 1944 Fadden had more than enough Country Party cats of his own to herd. His concern, and that of his federal MPs, was first and foremost to give the

Curtin Government vigorous and effective Opposition. However fragile was their own unity, after the 1943 defeat they welcomed the Country Party's UAP partners, under Menzies's leadership, demolishing and rebuilding their own house to get it in order.

Amalgamation of the non-Labor parties?

The Country Party and UAP working together in Coalition was one thing; amalgamation was another altogether. Nevertheless, the challenges of the non-Labor parties staying effective and united in wartime caused some consideration of the possibility, even before 1944. Interestingly, it was the Country Party that first flirted with the idea.

As the late Country Party historian Paul Davey has related, Fadden broached the possibility as early as April 1941, while he was acting for the absent Menzies. Fadden convened a unity meeting of Queensland Country Party and UAP MPs, under the banner of the Country National Organisation (CNO) – not dissimilar to South Australia's Liberal and Country League, but with MPs remaining 'true to their own organisations, but co-operating for electoral contests'.[20] The CNO arrangement lasted until the 1943 federal election but, as Gerard Henderson notes, not all Country Party MPs accepted it.[21] Some organisational elements of the Queensland CNO would survive to attend Menzies's 1944 Unity Conferences.

Fadden raised the question again just weeks later, telling a meeting in Wagga Wagga that he would welcome an amalgamation with the UAP, at least for the duration of the war. In doing so he antagonised members of his own parliamentary party, including his close friend and member for Richmond, Larry Anthony.[22] In assessing Fadden's motives, Davey suggests that the acting prime minister was primarily concerned about fostering stability and giving direction to the teetering Menzies Government, as UAP dissatisfaction with Menzies's leadership swirled and undermined the Coalition's fragile unity.[23] Subsequent events, however, killed off amalgamation talk, while Fadden continued, once becoming PM and Coalition leader, to keep the parliamentary Country Party's relations with the UAP and its new leader and Coalition deputy Billy Hughes, as close as possible.

Nonetheless, at federal level at least, before Menzies's return to the UAP leadership in late 1943 the preconditions for a potential merger were there. Unable to find a dynamic leader of their own, until Menzies and his National Service Group (NSG) became open dissidents and a policy ginger group on the Opposition benches, UAP MPs bumped along under the leadership of Hughes, but were comfortable working with the Country Party under the overall leadership of the affable but competent Fadden. Indeed, the fact that the UAP under Hughes never held its own party room meetings and relied exclusively on joint Coalition meetings was one of the NSG's main complaints.[24] However, on the whole Opposition MPs were keen not to rock the boat too much when it came to the conduct of the war.

The question also came up on the UAP side. In February 1943, the UAP Opposition leader in New South Wales, former Premier Alexander Mair, denied there was any suggestion of a merger between the UAP and the Country Party, adding 'there was always ground for co-operation between the two parties, which have a great deal in common.'[25] But despite official denials like Mair's, the question was in play. As the movement to forming the Liberal Party progressed in 1944 and 1945, and no doubt recalling Fadden's floating amalgamation in 1941, some UAP figures and affiliated groups called for bringing the Country Party in.

There was, however, one leading UAP figure who had no interest whatsoever in merging with the Country Party, and was determined that it would not happen: Robert Menzies.

The Country Party and the formation of the Liberal Party

Menzies's return to the leadership after the 1943 election, and his insistence that he, as leader of the largest Coalition party, should be

Opposition leader, sent a clear message to both Coalition parties about who was boss. Whether it was with a clear sense of direction for the future, or simply a show of bravado while he contemplated his own future,[26] Menzies ended the comfortable co-existence with the Fadden Country Party for a relationship that was edgier, more aloof, and very definitely separate.

No doubt this was partly because the 'CP' had been less than kind to Menzies himself, over and above his family's political history. In his home state of Victoria, he was at odds with the Country Party Premier Albert Dunstan, and their detestation was mutual. His personal dislike and distrust of Page was deep, and not only because of Page's bitter 1939 attack on his character. As for Fadden, there was lingering resentment about Fadden's role in replacing him as prime minister, despite Fadden not being one of the Country Party ministers calling for a new leader when the issue came to a head.[27]

Regardless of why, from the outset of his project to form the Liberal Party out of the ashes of the moribund UAP, Menzies did not see the Country Party's involvement as necessary, let alone essential. The late 1943 undated memorandum written by Menzies and unearthed by journalist and political historian, Troy Bramston, demonstrates that conclusively.

Headed 'Some Lessons from the 1943 Election' it is, if not a hard blueprint for what followed over the following year, certainly a general road map to the establishment of what Menzies tentatively called the Australian Liberal Democratic Party. In relation to the Country Party, Menzies wrote:

> Nothing will destroy us more completely than our continued subservience to the Country Party – which is of necessity sectional … it is one thing to have an alliance with the C.P.; it is another to be annexed by it. The U.A.P. signed its own death warrant when it agreed to serve under a C.P. leader. Under these circumstances, for the

> U.A.P. to abandon the leadership was to acknowledge its own bankruptcy, and it can scarcely be wondered that the electors took it at its own valuation.[28]

Given sentiments like that, and Menzies regarding the Country Party as 'of necessity sectional', it is clear that Menzies had no intention of welcoming the Country Party to shelter under his new Liberal umbrella. That did not mean, however, that he rejected the Country Party as an ally and partner to his new party: on returning to the leadership he valued the relationship, re-established the Coalition and working positively with Fadden.

For his part, Fadden kept his counsel ever after about the Country Party's role in the immediate Liberal formation story. Of relinquishing the Opposition leadership to Menzies, Fadden wrote that he had 'no regrets'.[29] Of the moves to form and launch the Liberal Party initiated and spearheaded by Menzies, Fadden simply chose to say the Country Party stood aside and let the 'urban' conservatives and liberals sort themselves out.

That is not to say that Menzies and others did not put out feelers in 1944 to gauge the Country Party's interest in joining the Liberal project. Twenty-five years later, Fadden wrote, laconically but tantalisingly, for historians:

> (Menzies) even tried to lure the Country Party into participation but, adhering to our traditional principle of separate entity, we declined to attend the conference of October 1944 at which the other groups emerged.[30]

That any such feelers were more than just good form on both sides, being seen to explore the possibility if only to dismiss it, is however moot. Both Menzies and Fadden could then say to supporters that the possibility had at least been raised. In September 1944, just prior to the Canberra Unity Conference, Menzies wrote to his son Ken:

> Two things are at any rate established. One is that my

> own position has been very much strengthened, as 'nothing succeeds like success'; the other is that I am now able to get out invitations to all non-Labour bodies (*other than the Country Party, with which we can always negotiate later on*) to attend a conference in Canberra in about a month's time to have a shot at setting up an Australia-wide organization.[31]

Indeed, Menzies told the Canberra conference that the Country Party sent neither delegates or observers because it 'already had an interstate conference at which a high degree of unity was achieved', and it had an expectation that 'those of us who espouse the general liberal cause should become equally united so that we may be in a position to discuss co-operation or alliance, or even fully organic unity.'[32]

As Gerard Henderson has pointed out, the creation of the Liberal Party 'at least settled the relationship between the major non-Labor party and the Country Party'.[33] As subsequent history has shown, it was settled as a relationship based on partnership, and the Coalition has equally suited the Country Party, now the Nationals.

The Country and National parties since 1944: a story of (mostly) partnership and cooperation

They may not have amalgamated in 1944, but in the decades since – with a few rough moments such as 1987's Joh for Canberra push and regular clashes over three-cornered electorate contests – the federal Liberal and Country (now National) parties have generally worked constructively and cooperatively together. This has, of course, been mostly in Coalition, but even in the periods where there was no formal coalition arrangement, notably after the 1972 election loss, and even during the bitter acrimony of Joh for Canberra, the Country/National Party has been key to the centre-right's overall dominance of Australian electoral politics since 1949.

So crucial has the Country Party been seen by Menzies and other Liberal leaders, especially Harold Holt in 1966, Malcolm Fraser in 1975 and 1977, and John Howard in 1996, that when the Liberals won enough House of Representatives seats to govern in their own right, there was no thought of doing so. This contrasted sharply with the approach of the Liberals' pre-1944 predecessors, as outlined earlier.

In 1968, John McEwen characterised the place of the Country Party in the Australian political scene thus:

> The most important thing is that we have a total national concept of the Australian need. ... So, we conceive our role as a dual one of being at all times the specialist party with a sharp fighting edge, the specialists for rural industries and rural communities. At the same time, we are the party which has the total co-ordinated concept of what is necessary for the growth and safety of the whole Australian nation.[34]

There are three key factors that have meant the Country Party has remained vital to the Coalition, and therefore influential, so enduringly.

Firstly, the Country Party principally has concentrated and husbanded its resources and its vote in its regional electorate catchments, maximising the clout of its support base and seat numbers by understanding its rural and regional constituency, and regional voters' specific needs and aspirations. The result has been a disproportionate Country Party parliamentary presence relative to its national and state vote shares. In 1946, the first federal election contested by the Liberal Party, the Liberals won 15 seats with 28.6 per cent of the total Lower House primary vote; the Country Party 12 seats with 10.7 per cent; and the LCL won two seats with 4.4 per cent.[35] Such numerically disproportionate results have continued to the present day, despite a relative decline in Country Party vote shares: in the most recent federal election, in 2022, the Liberals won 40 seats with almost 30 per cent share of the nationwide primary vote for the House of Representatives, and the Nationals won 18 seats with a six per cent vote share, with much of that concentrated in Queensland.[36]

The adoption of joint Senate tickets in Queensland (prior to the 2008 Liberal National Party amalgamation), New South Wales and Victoria, with guaranteed Country/National winnable positions, has both minimised friction with the Liberals and boosted the numerically-smaller party's presence and joint party room influence.

The second key factor is the party's concentrating on its strengths, and keeping itself close and responsive to its natural regional constituency. The Country Party, and now the Nationals, have been strongest and most influential when they speak for their regional and rural constituents and communities in national and state politics. In a lesson to some in the contemporary Liberal Party who have lost their way as to who they are and what they stand for, the Country Party has only faltered when it has strayed too far from its rural and regional roots, as it did briefly and damagingly in 1987. Consequently, it has succeeded in holding seats even when the electoral tide is strongly against the Coalition as a whole.

That the Country/National Party has a tradition of seeking strong parliamentary candidates drawn from the communities they represent, who are able to understand and empathise with their constituents in good times and bad, has also served the party well in its relations with the Liberals, and in the Canberra joint party room. The overall small-c social and economic conservatism, balanced by adroit political pragmatism,[37] of Country/National Party leaders and MPs over the years has also been a major factor that has kept the Coalition in the electoral mainstream, tempering the temptations of their Liberal partners to veer too far to either the left or the right, and ensuring that Liberal leaders and MPs remember that Australia is more than just its capital cities, and Sydney and Melbourne in particular.

The intangible power and influence of personal relationships

The third and most crucial factor, however, is not institutional or electoral, but *personal.*

The Country/National Party has punched above its weight with the Liberals because of the strength and quality of personal relationships, especially between their leading figures. This intangible but very personal element has given the so-called 'junior' Coalition partner considerably more influence on the direction of the Coalition, and through it the nation, than even its strength in parliamentary numbers relative to the Liberals.

From the beginning in 1944, personal relations between Country/Nationals and Liberal leaders have been crucial to the Coalition's long-term success. Menzies maintained warm if not intimate relations with Fadden, overcame (if not wholly set aside) his animosity and personal differences with Page for the good of his team,[38] and highly respected and valued the advice of McEwen, whose record as a minister and leader – especially his championing the reopening of Australia's formal economic relations with a former bitter enemy through the Australia-Japan Commerce Agreement in 1957 – must have helped prove to Menzies that the Country Party was truly a party serving the whole Australian nation, and not just a party for 'sectional interests' as he characterised it in the 1930s and 1940s.

Such personal friendships and positive working relationships have smoothed over many a policy or political difficulty between the parties, their MPs, and their organisations. Indeed, Menzies and Fadden showed how opposites can complement each other in politics. Fadden's defence of Menzies against Page's unjustified and unfairly bitter and personal 1939 attack on him would have been appreciated by Menzies (and Pattie), but the two were not natural intimates by personality and background. When Fadden came to nominate the greatest figure in Australian public life in his lifetime ('and I don't care who knows it'), he pointedly named not Menzies, but John Curtin.[39] Perhaps reading 'Artie's' 1969 memoir coloured

Menzies's comments on Fadden in 1970, where he described his former leadership counterpart as 'a genial and popular soul...a good politician and a good political companion, but as a political general he never seemed to me ... to develop a coherent grand strategy or penetrative tactics'.[40]

Being, perhaps, more easy-going and approachable than Menzies, Fadden was also, for Menzies, a reliable sounding board for what his MPs – Liberal as well as Country Party – were thinking. Fadden may not have been the grandest of strategists, but he was an excellent treasurer for his times, a sound parliamentary and political tactician, and a source of wise counsel, in Opposition and then in government. In each leader's character sketch of the other, therefore, is not only a reminder that no political leader is perfect, but also a fascinating joint insight as to how the different personalities and talents of Fadden and Menzies, when combined together in Coalition, made them such a formidable political and leadership team.

That sort of personal leadership rapport, that Menzies and Fadden established, was a beneficial legacy to the Coalition. In later years, Malcolm Fraser – himself a grazier and country member for Wannon in Victoria – was similarly considerably closer to deputy prime minister, Doug Anthony, and National Country Party cabinet ministers Peter Nixon, Ralph Hunt and Ian Sinclair, than to many of his own Liberal colleagues. Later still, John Howard had excellent rapport with Sinclair, Tim Fischer, John Anderson and Mark Vaile, and Tony Abbott got on very well with Barnaby Joyce.

Looking at cabinet representation over the decades, having Country/National Party ministers around the table tended to provide the 'go to' voice of regional Australia in decision making. Their presence, and being called on in this way, may well have blocked the progression to the ministry and cabinet of otherwise qualified and talented regional Liberals.[41]

When these relationships were poor, the Coalition as a whole suffered. Most notorious was the 'Bill, I don't trust you' relationship between McEwen and William McMahon that blocked McMahon from the prime ministership on Harold Holt's death in 1967 (but effectively opened the door to the chaotic and flawed prime ministership of John Gorton), Howard and Joh Bjelke-Petersen in 1987 and, most recently, Malcolm Turnbull and Joyce.

But as with Menzies and Page, poor relationships can be, and have been, overcome and rebuilt for the common good of the shared cause. Most notably, the Joh-for-Canberra fiasco ultimately strengthened the Coalition, made Howard a better and more resilient leader, and encouraged him to work with the Nationals as full and highly valued partners, and embrace successive Nationals leaders as close confidants,[42] even when as in 1996 the Liberals could govern alone on the parliamentary numbers.

Arguably too, those personal relationships have helped to manage and massage ideological and policy differences between the parties, of which there have been many over the years, some quite deep and bitter. Indeed, an advantage of Coalition for the leaders of both parties is that one could confide in, and advise the other on matters which were difficult to share with their own party colleagues.[43]

Amalgamation talk since 1944

While amalgamation at federal level never eventuated, at state level there have been two notable amalgamations: South Australia's Liberal and Country League from 1932-74, and the current Liberal National Party of Queensland from 2008. At the time of writing the latter boasts, remarkably, the two current federal Coalition leaders: Peter Dutton for the Liberal Party and David Littleproud for the Nationals.

At the federal level, the possibility of amalgamating the two Coalition parties has been canvassed by figures in both parties, particularly following election defeats. In 1973 former prime minister, William McMahon, proposed a merger, suggesting it would improve the quality of the Opposition,[44] and then Liberal leader, Bill Snedden, said similarly immediately after the Coalition's close 1974 double dissolution defeat by Gough Whitlam's Labor.[45] The 1983 Valder report, commissioned by the Liberal federal executive following that year's election loss, canvassed ways of improving the party's performance and quality of representation in regional Australia, but did not consider amalgamation with, by then, the National Party.[46]

On the Country/National Party side, after the 1990 election defeat, former Fraser-Anthony minister Peter Nixon – the principal author of 1988's major review of the National Party structure and performance – publicly concluded that amalgamation should be considered, setting off a bitter and public internal debate. Former leader Doug Anthony agreed with Nixon, while his successor Ian Sinclair rejected the idea flatly and the new incumbent leader, Tim Fischer, represented the status quo. Sinclair believed, like McEwen before him, that the differences between the characters and constituencies of the two parties were too fundamental for amalgamation to work, and that it was better for two Coalition parties to work cooperatively and in partnership as they traditionally had: his view prevailed, and amalgamation talk petered out.

Similar questions were raised after the Howard Government's defeat in 2007, but this time they were considered very seriously by the Nationals' federal executive. A committee of senior party figures, led by former Deputy Prime Minister John Anderson, was tasked with advising the party on its future in a world where it is competing with the Liberals for funding and support, as well as for electorates and political influence; when contemporary election campaigns are presidential and focus on the major party leaders is paramount – effectively meaning the Liberal leader gets the media attention while the Nationals and its leaders largely are bypassed on the so-called 'wombat trail'; the reality that what constitutes 'regional' in twenty-first century Australia is increasingly blurred, meaning Liberals and Nationals are increasingly competing for the same turf; and the demographics of some regional seats – particularly in north coast New South Wales and coastal Queensland – are evolving in favour of not just the Liberals, but also Labor and the Greens.[47]

The Anderson committee's frank report canvassed three options: keep the status quo in terms of party structure, organisation and reach; 'lifting our game' in terms of making the party more fit for purpose in the contemporary political and fundraising climate; and amalgamation with the Liberals. While it was agreed the status quo was untenable, the debate between reform and amalgamation was intense, and the management committee was divided. In the end, reform was narrowly preferred over amalgamation at the federal level. Subsequently the Nationals indeed lifted their game and succeeded in achieving relative stability in their parliamentary numbers over the decade, compared to the Liberals: notably, in 2016 and 2022 the Nationals (including Nationals-affiliated MPs of the Queensland LNP) held their seats, whereas the Liberals lost heavily.[48] In 2016, therefore, the Nationals saved the Coalition from defeat by Labor, and in 2022 they helped save sufficient seats to keep the Coalition as a viable fighting force in Opposition.

At the state level, since South Australia's Liberal and Country League shed itself of its explicitly rural element to become simply a 'Liberal Party' in the mid-1970s, state party amalgamation has occurred only in Queensland, where the current Liberal National Party was established in 2008.[49] It has to be said that, even after 15 years, the verdict on the success of the Queensland LNP venture, especially in balancing Nationals and Liberal representation and interests, and minimising tensions and personality clashes between the two wings, is still out.

After the 2022 election loss, amalgamation was not at all raised at federal level. This is unsurprising: despite the occasional tensions between the parties, not least over 'demarcation disputes' over three-cornered electorate contests,[50] as well as policy and party room disagreements, the Coalition on the whole has held firm, and proven as a source of mutual support and strength in Opposition as well as in government.

Effectively, the Coalition as re-established by Menzies and Fadden lives on in John Howard's 'broad church', but as a church with two denominations. In that form, it has served the Australian nation, and Australians who want a strong and effective centre-right alternative to the Labor Party, and now the Greens, extraordinarily well.

The Country Party's greatest gift to the Liberal Party: Menzies himself?

There would never have been a Liberal Party without the driving motivational force of Robert Menzies. It thus follows that ensuring that Menzies was on the scene after the great disappointments of the 1943 federal election was essential to the party's creation.

After that election drubbing for the UAP, Menzies was, understandably, despondent and personally demoralised. So much so was he that, as Anne Henderson writes elsewhere in this book,[51] it is believed that Menzies allowed his name to go forward to be appointed as chief justice and lieutenant-governor of Victoria to replace the retiring Sir Frederick Mann, who resigned in late 1943.

Certainly, such a vacancy would have appealed to Menzies, allowing him to pursue his love of the law and apply his forensic legal mind, and judicial temperament, while also allowing him to return home permanently to Melbourne to be with Pattie and his family. The Victorian Supreme Court and the Victorian Bar also meant a great deal to Menzies personally,[52] and it would be consistent with his life and career history if he did allow himself to be considered for the chief justice appointment.

Unfortunately, there are no hard records or surviving correspondence that prove with certainty that Menzies did declare his interest formally, to be considered by the Victorian government of the day.[53] Nevertheless, at the time there was some press speculation that Menzies's hat was in the ring.[54]

If indeed it was, however, the appointment was not to be. The Victorian cabinet recommended to the governor that a serving lieutenant-general and Rhodes Scholar, Sir Edmund Herring, be appointed chief justice: Herring went on to hold the office with distinction from February 1944 to September 1964 and remained as lieutenant-governor until 1972.

As good of an appointment as Herring was, politically it was no wonder that Menzies was passed over if he was in contention. As noted earlier, the Victorian government of the day was a minority United Country Party government, headed by radical rural populist Albert Dunstan. Not only was Dunstan at constant odds with Fadden and his federal party; the Dunstan Government had for years been propped up by support from Labor on the crossbench, with the UAP under 'Tuke' Hollway in Opposition. Furthermore, Dunstan had no love for Menzies himself, and the dislike was mutual.

Therefore, if Menzies was ever recommended for the judicial appointment, Dunstan most certainly rejected the recommendation, effectively leaving Menzies where he was, as leader of the federal UAP Opposition recovering from its heavy 1943 defeat. It also, of course, left Menzies free in 1944 to pursue his vision and determination to unite anti-Labor forces in a new, effective political grouping – the Liberal Party.

It may well be that, as well as leaving the field open for Menzies to work his magic in 1944, the Country Party thus gave, thanks to the personal dislikes and parochialism of its Victorian premier, the greatest possible gift to the Liberal Party, and Australian centre-right politics ever since: Sir Robert Menzies himself.

Conclusion

Looking back on the formation of the Liberal Party eighty years ago, and the motivating force in its creation that was Sir Robert Menzies, Sir Arthur Fadden wrote:

> By determined effort and persuasion Menzies picked up the unpromising bits and wove them into a united party fabric, the Liberal Party. In doing so he achieved one of his greatest political triumphs.[55]

Fadden understood then, as in 1944, that Menzies's mission to 'unite the right', while leaving the Country Party as an independent force with its own constituency, was in the best interests of each party and, far more importantly, of Australia. Ever since, the Coalition between the two parties has been a huge positive for the nation, and has helped make the Liberal and Country/National parties the dominant federal governing force since the end of World War II.

In *Afternoon Light*, Menzies wrote:

> (Through) my long membership of the Commonwealth Parliament, my party heavily outnumbered the Country Party. We were and are separate entities. In substance, we have the same political philosophy; over the years, we have, with a little give and take, succeeded in presenting common policies to the electors. The Country Party has, as the name indicates, a particular association with rural interests; though this is not exclusive, as many of my own party members represent country seats. Under these circumstances, there can be local contests, and occasionally some friction. But in effect the association between the two parties has been sustained and fruitful.[56]

To Menzies, the Country Party was an indispensable asset to the success of the Liberal Party. In his retirement press conference in January 1966, Menzies nominated successful relations with the Country Party as one of the two political achievements that gave him greatest pride: the other was the formation of the Liberal Party itself. When asked whether he could ever envisage the Liberals governing without the Country Party, Menzies said:

> I don't. If you are asking me, at any time over these years if I had come back with an absolute majority for the Liberal Party on the floor of the House, I still would have said to the Country Party, 'I want you to be in' because I believe it is in this alliance, this conjunction of affairs, that a great deal of strength has existed.[57]

Menzies's commitment to the Coalition, and maintaining strong relations with his Country Party allies and partners, has been a major part of his legacy to all the Liberal leaders who followed him. It is an essential and integral part of his, and Fadden's as his Country Party counterpart in 1944 and deputy prime minister from 1949-58, political legacy.

---

[1] Crisp, *Australian National Government*, Chapter 9.

[2] In his partisan way, Crisp also characterised the Coalition parties as 'anti-Labor' although, as the Country Party itself demonstrated in the 1930s and 1940s, especially in Victoria, this was not always so.

[3] The authors are very grateful for the advice of Robert Menzies Institute historian, Dr Zachary Gorman, on this section.

[4] The 1919 election saw the Australian Farmers' Federal Organisation endorse candidates, although they would not formally become the Country Party until the following year.

[5] Gorman, *Joseph Cook*, p. 90.

[6] Page, *Truant Surgeon*, p. 114, quoted in Davey, *Ninety Not Out*, p. 24.

[7] Gorman, 'Sampson, Sydney (1863-1948)'.

[8] Although Page's personal attack on Menzies in 1939 must have made his acceptance of Page's breaking the Coalition easy. Nevertheless, in the exigencies of war the Coalition was re-formed in 1940, not long after Page stepped down as Country Party leader.

[9] Calwell, *Be Just and Fear Not*, pp. 74-5. Calwell also noted that 'Menzies of course was happy' when a Liberal, William Dowling Bostock, eventually won back Leckie's former seat of Indi in 1949. The seat remained Liberal-held until 2013, before going to independents.

[10] Davey, *Ninety Not Out*, pp. 71-2.

[11] In his laconic way, Fadden wrote in 1969, 'I continued as Acting Leader until, at a meeting on 12 March 1941, a united party unanimously decided I had made the grade and gave the full title and honour of Leader of the

Country Party. This I retained until I retired in 1958'. Fadden, *They Called Me Artie*, p. 45.

[12] Interestingly, the longest-serving Victorian premier, Sir Henry Bolte, became leader of Victoria's then-named Liberal and Country Party in similar circumstances.

[13] Ibid, pp. 81-2

[14] Jones and Lamb, 'Wilson, Alexander (1889–1954)'. Wilson returned 'home' to the Country Party room after the 1943 election, but jumped ship again in 1945 to become Ben Chifley's appointment as Administrator of Norfolk Island.

[15] Which went federal in 1940, when spurned Country Party leader, Archie Cameron, defected from the Country Party to the UAP, yet still remained a Liberal and Country League MP. Cameron later speaker of the House of Representatives after the Coalition's election in 1949.

[16] The rollicking story of the Country Party in Victoria from its foundation to 1945 is covered in an excellent doctoral thesis by former Labor federal MP, the late Tony Lamb. See Lamb, *Of Measures and Men*.

[17] Lamb, *Of Measures and Men*, chapter 9.

[18] Abjorensen, 'Keeping the Country in the Coalition', *Inside Story*, 23 February 2018.

[19] Hughes was a slippery, wilful and devious political partner, but Fadden liked him immensely as a person. Indeed, Fadden devoted a whole chapter of his memoir to Billy Hughes anecdotes.

[20] Davey, *Ninety Not Out*, pp. 73-4.

[21] Henderson, *Menzies' Child*, p. 62.

[22] Father of future party leader Doug, and grandfather of Howard-Fischer government minister, Larry junior.

[23] Davey, *Ninety Not Out*, p. 74.

[24] Menzies, 'Why We Did It' radio broadcast, 9 April 1943.

[25] *The Canberra Times*, 27 February 1943.

[26] See below.

[27] The four Country Party ministers were Page, McEwen, Collins and Anthony: Martin, *Robert Menzies*, Vol. I, p. 381. Interestingly, Menzies's eventual Liberal successor, Harold Holt, wanted Fadden as Opposition leader after the 1943 election, rather than Menzies.

[28] The memorandum is reproduced in facsimile in Bramston's recent biography of Menzies: Bramston, *Robert Menzies*, pp. 322-4.

[29] Fadden, *They Called Me Artie*, p. 88. It is worth noting, however, that elsewhere in his memoir Fadden implicitly criticises Menzies's shortcomings as a leader, especially in his lifelong difficulty in tolerating fools gladly.

[30] Ibid.

[31] Menzies to Ken Menzies, 5 September 1944, quoted in Martin, *Robert Menzies*, Vol. II, pp. 7-8. The italics are the author's.

[32] Menzies, address to the Canberra conference in October 1944, quoted in Henderson, *Menzies' Child*, p. 90.

[33] Ibid.

[34] McEwen, 1968, quoted in the National Museum of Australia's web page on the Country Party. McEwen said similar, but less pithily, in his speech opening the Country Party secretariat's John McEwen House on 4 November 1968.

[35] Stephen Barber, 'Federal election results 1901-2016', Parliamentary Library Research Paper, 31 March 2017.

[36] Calculated with Queensland seats won by the amalgamated Liberal National Party (LNP) of Queensland distributed by which party held or received the two-party preferred vote in each seat immediately prior to amalgamation.

[37] These policy debates and differences such as, for example, the central importance of Protection for Australian primary and secondary industry to the McEwen-era Country Party, are important but beyond the scope of this chapter.

[38] Although Dame Pattie Menzies did not. Near the end of her life, Dame Pattie told Gerard Henderson that she never forgave Page for his 1939 parliamentary slurring of Menzies's character, and Page's name was mud in the Menzies household ever after: Gerard Henderson, in conversation with Terry Barnes, July 2024.

[39] Fadden, *They Called Me Artie*, pp. 80-1.

[40] Menzies, *The Measure of the Years*, pp. 13-14.

[41] John Anderson AC, in conversation with Terry Barnes, July 2024.

[42] Ibid.

[43] Ibid.

[44] *The Canberra Times*, 13 March 1973.

[45] Ibid., 23 May 1974.

[46] Valder et al, *Report of the Committee of Review: Facing the Facts*, especially pp. 80-1.

[47] Examples are the northern NSW federal seats of Page and the former Anthony family stronghold of Richmond, which are now firmly Labor seats underpinned by Greens preferences.

[48] For 2016: Parliament of Australia, 2017, *Federal Election Results 1901-16.* For 2022: www.aec.gov.au.

[49] Judging the success of the LNP merger is beyond the scope of this chapter.

[50] The convention being that a seat vacated by a Liberal or National Party MP may be contested in the following general or by-election by either or both parties, enabling a three-cornered contest with Labor and (in theory at least) the preferences of one Coalition party flowing to the other.

[51] See Chapter 3.

[52] Anne and Gerard Henderson, in conversation with Terry Barnes, July 2024.

[53] There are no formal or archived records of Victorian cabinet decisions before 1982, and any correspondence between Menzies and the Victorian government on the chief justice appointment – if such correspondence ever occurred – has been lost.

[54] For example, the Adelaide *News*, 4 January 1944.

[55] Fadden, *They Called Me Artie*, p. 88.

[56] Menzies, *Afternoon Light*, p. 55.

[57] Menzies, 'Press, radio and television conference given at Parliament House, Canberra, 20 January 1966', Department of the Prime Minister and Cabinet.

Bibliography

Archives

ACT Liberal Party Archives

Records of the ACT Liberal Party.

Australian National University Archives

Records of the Institute of Public Affairs, AU NBAC N136.

John Oxley Library, State Library of Queensland:

'Queensland People's Party: Our Objective', Queensland People's Party pamphlet dated 25 November 1943, held at John Oxley Library, State Library of Queensland.

TA Hiley, Sir Thomas Hiley Transcript, Box 5321, OM Acc 974, 1974 [recording of an interview 21 March 1974 between Suzanne Walker and TA Hiley for the National Library of Australia's oral history program], John Oxley Library, State Library of Queensland.

Mitchell Library, Sydney

Liberal Party of Australia (NSW Division) Records, MSS 2385.

National Library of Australia

Dame Enid Lyons interviewed by Mel Pratt, ORAL TRC 121/30.

Henry Bolte interviewed by Mel Pratt, 1976.

Papers of Donald Cleland, MS 9600.

Papers of Ernest K White, MS 6455.

Records of the Liberal Party of Australia, MS 5000.

Papers of Sir Robert Menzies, MS 4936.

Privately Held

Institute of Public Affairs (Victoria) papers.

University of Melbourne Archives

Records of the Liberal Party of Australia (Victorian Division).

Newspapers/Magazines

The Advertiser (Adelaide).

The Advocate (Tasmania).

The Age

The Argus (Melbourne).

The Bulletin.

Burnie Advocate (Tasmania).

The Canberra Times.

The Camperdown Chronicle (Victoria).

Courier Mail (Brisbane).

The Daily News (Perth).

Daily Telegraph (Sydney).

Daily Post (Tasmania).

The Dowerin Guardian and Amery Line Advocate (WA).

The Examiner (Tasmania).

Geraldton Guardian and Express (WA).

The Herald (Melbourne).

The Kalgoorlie Miner (WA).

Labor Call.

The Mercury (Tasmania).

North-Eastern Advertiser (Tasmania).

Pix. (Sydney).

Saturday Evening Express (Tasmania).

Sun News Pictorial (Melbourne).

Sunday Times (Perth).

Sydney Morning Herald.

The Victorian Liberal.

Voice (Tasmania).

The Weekend Australian.

The West Australian.

Books and Theses

Aimer, EP 'Liberal Organisation in Victoria 1945 – 68', PhD Thesis, Australian National University, 1970.

-- *Politics, Power and Persuasion: The Liberals in Victoria*, James Bennett, Melbourne, 1974.

Anderson, WH. *The Liberal Party of Australia: Its Origin, Organisation and Purpose*, Liberal Party of Australia (Victorian Division), Melbourne, 1948.

Atkins, Ruth. *The Government of the Australian Capital Territory*, UQ Press, St Lucia, 1978.

Bennett, Scott and Barbara. *Tasmanian Electoral Handbook 1851-1982*, History Project Incorporated, Kensington, 1986?

Berzins, Baiba. 'The Nationalist Party, 1919-1930: organisation and ideology', PhD Thesis, 1972.

Black, David. *The House on the Hill: A History of the Parliament of Western Australia 1832-1990*, Parliament of Western Australia, Perth, 1991.

Blazey, Peter. *Bolte: A Political Biography*, Jacaranda Press, Brisbane, 1972.

Bollen, JD. *Protestantism and Social Reform in New South Wales 1890-1910*, Melbourne University Press, Melbourne, 1972.

Bolton, Geoffrey. *A Thousand Miles Away: A History of North Queensland to 1920* (1963), Australian National University Press, Canberra 1972.

—— *The Oxford History of Australia Volume 5: 1942–1995: The Middle Way* (1990), Oxford University Press, South Melbourne, 1996.

Bongiorno, Frank. *Dreamers and Schemers: A Political History of Australia*, La Trobe University Press, Collingwood, 2022.

Bramston, Troy. *Robert Menzies: The Art of Politics*, Scribe Publications, Brunswick, 2019.

Brown, Nicholas. *A History of Canberra*, CUP, Port Melbourne, 2014.

Buxton, Jeremy. *Commemorating 70 Years: Electoral History - Liberal Party of Western Australia*, Liberal Party of Australia (WA Division), Perth, 2015.

Calwell, Arthur. *Be Just and Fear Not*, Lloyd O'Neill, Hawthorn, Vic., 1972.

Carrick, John. *The Liberal Way of Progress*, Liberal Party of Australia (N.S.W. Division), Sydney, c.1948-9.

Cheek, B *Cheeky: Confessions of a Ferret Salesman*, Pipeclay Publishing, Sandy Bay, 2005.

Clune, David. *Jack Lang*, Australian Biographical Monograph 15, Connor Court, Brisbane, 2022.

-- 'Labor government in New South Wales, 1941 to 1965 : a study in longevity in government', PhD Thesis, University of Sydney, 1990.

Colebatch, Hal. *Dick Hamer: The liberal Liberal*, Scribe, Brunswick, 2014.

Costar, B and D Woodward (eds). *Country to National: Australian Rural Politics and Beyond*, George Allen and Unwin, Sydney, 1985.

Cramer, John. *Pioneers, politics and people: a political memoir*, Allen & Unwin, Sydney, 1989.

Crisp, LF *Australian National Government*, Longman Cheshire, Melbourne, 1965

Cunningham, Matthew. *Mobilising the Masses – Popular Conservative Movements in Australia and New Zealand During the Great Depression,* ANU Press, Canberra, 2022.

Davey, Paul. *Ninety not out: the Nationals 1920-2010*, UNSW Press, Sydney, 2010.

Davidson, Dianne. *Women on the Warpath*, University of Western Australia Press, Perth 1997.

Davies, EV, JE Hoffman, and BJ Price. *A history of Australia's capital, Canberra*, Ministry of Health, Education and the Arts, Canberra, 1990.

Davis, RP. *A History of the Tasmanian Labor Party 1902-2017*, Sassafras Books, Hobart, 2017.

Denning, Warren. *Capital City: Canberra Today and Tomorrow*, The Publicist, Sydney, 1938.

Duthie, G. *I Had 50,000 Bosses: Memoirs of a Labor Backbencher 1946-1975*, Angus and Robertson, Sydney, 1984.

Earnshaw, Beverley. *One Flag, One Hope, One Destiny: Sir Joseph Carruthers and Australian Federation*, The Kogarah Historical Society Inc., Sydney, 2000.

Eggleston, FW. *Reflections of an Australian Liberal,* F. W. Cheshire, Melbourne, 1953.

Evatt, HV. *Australian Labour Leader: The story of W. A. Holman and the Labour movement*, Angus & Robertson, Sydney, 1940.

Fadden, Arthur. *They called me Artie: the memoirs of Sir Arthur Fadden*, Jacaranda, Milton (Qld.), 1969.

Fairfax, Warwick. *Men, Parties and Politics*, John Fairfax & Sons, Sydney, 1943.

Fitzgerald, Ross, Lyndon Megarrity, and David Symons. *Made in Queensland: A New History*, University of Queensland Press, St Lucia, 2009.

Fitzhardinge, LF. *William Morris Hughes: A Political Biography, vol 2, The Little Digger 1914-1952*, Angus & Robertson, Sydney, 1979.

Fitzherbert, Margaret. *Liberal Women: Federation – 1949,* The Federation Press, Annandale, 2004.

Forming the Liberal Party of Australia: Record of the Conference of Representatives of non-Labour Organisations, convened by the Leader of the Federal Opposition, Rt. Hon., R. G. Menzies, K.C., M.P., and held in Canberra, A.C.T., on 13th, 14th and 16th October 1944.

Gibbney, Jim. *Canberra 1913-1953*, Australian Government Publishing Service, Canberra, 1988.

Gorman, Zachary. *Joseph Cook*, Australian Biographical Monograph 19, Connor Court, Redland, 2023.

-- *Sir Joseph Carruthers: Founder of the New South Wales Liberal Party*, Connor Court, Brisbane, 2018.

Gray, R and A Tilt. *Proud to be Tasmanian: Robin Gray & The Liberal Led Recovery*, Proud Tasmanian Pty Ltd, Launceston, 2020.

Green, Antony. *New South Wales Election Results 1856-2007*, Parliament of New South Wales, Sydney, 2007.

Gregory, Alan (ed). *The Menzies Lectures*, Sir Robert Menzies Lecture Trust, Melbourne, 1999.

Grundy, Philip, Bill Oakes, Lyne Reeder, and Roger Wettenhall. *Reluctant Democrats: The Transition to Self-Government in the Australian Capital Territory*, Federal Capital Press, Canberra, 1996.

Hancock, Ian. *National and Permanent?: The Federal Organisation of the Liberal Party of Australia 1944-1965*, Melbourne University Press, Carlton South, 2000.

-- *The Liberals: A History of the NSW Division of the Liberal Party of Australia, 1945-2000*, Annandale NSW, Federation Press, 2007.

Hayek, FA. *The Road to Serfdom*, Routledge, London, 1944.

Hazlehurst, C. *Menzies Observed*, George Allen and Unwin, Sydney, 1979.

Head, Brian and James Walter (eds). *Intellectual Movements and Australian Society*, Oxford University Press, Melbourne, 1988.

Heatley, Alistair. *A City Grows: A History of the Darwin City Council 1957-1984*, ANU North Australia Research Unit, Brinkin (NT), 1986.

-- *The Territory Party: The Northern Territory Country Liberal Party 1974-1998*, Northern Territory University Press, Darwin, 1998.

Henderson, Anne. *Enid Lyons Leading Lady To A Nation,* Pluto Press Australia, North Melbourne, 2008.

-- *Joseph Lyons: The People's Prime Minister*, NewSouth Publishing, Sydney, 2011.

-- *Menzies at War,* NewSouth, Sydney, 2014.

Henderson, Gerard. *Menzies' Child*, HarperCollins Publishers, 1994.

Hogan, Michael. *The Sectarian Strand*, Penguin Ringwood, 1987.

Holt, Edgar. *Politics is People: The Men of the Menzies Era*, Angus & Robertson, Sydney, 1969.

Hughes, Colin A and BD Graham. *A Handbook of Australian Government and Politics 1890 to 1964*, Australian National University Press, Canberra, 1968

-- *Voting for the Queensland Legislative Assembly 1890–1964*, Australian National University, Canberra, 1974.

Hughes, WM. *The Case for Labor*, with an introduction by Sir Robert Menzies, first published in 1910, Sydney University Press, Sydney, 1970.

Jamieson, Ronda. *Charles Court: I Love This Place*, St George Books, Perth, 2011.

Kemp, David. *A Liberal State: How Australia chose liberalism over socialism, 1926-1966,* Melbourne University Press, Carlton, 2021.

-- *Consent of the People*, Miegunyah press, Melbourne University Publishing, Melbourne, 2022.

-- 'The Institute of Public Affairs, 1942–1947', Honours thesis, University of Melbourne, 1963.

-- *The Land of Dreams*, Miegunyah Press, Melbourne University Publishing, Melbourne, 2018.

Kerr, Colin. *Archie: the Biography of Sir Archibald Grenfell Price*, MacMillan, 1983.

Keynes, JM. *The General Theory of Employment, Interest and Money*, Easton Press, Norwalk, CT, (1936), 2004.

Lack, Clem et al. *Three Decades of Queensland Political History 1929–1960*, Government Printer, Brisbane, 1962.

Lake, M. *A Divided Society: Tasmania During World War I*, Melbourne University Press, Carlton, 1975.

Lamb, Tony. *Of Measures and Men: The Victorian Country Party, 1917 to 1945*, PhD Thesis, Swinburne University of Technology, 2009.

Laski, HJ. *Democracy in Crisis*, Chapel Hill, 1935.

Looking Forward: A Post War Policy for Australian Industry, Institute of Public Affairs, Melbourne 1944.

Loughnan, Paul E. 'A History of the Askin Government 1965-1975', PhD Thesis, University of New England, 2013.

Loveday, P and AW Martin. *Parliament, Factions and Parties: The First Thirty Years of Responsible Government in New South Wales 1856-1889*, Melbourne University Press, Melbourne, 1966.

Lloyd, CJ. 'The Formation and Development of the United Australia Party, 1929-1937', PhD Thesis, Australian National University, 1984.

Lucadou Wells, R. *50 Year History of the Liberal Party (Tasmanian Division)*, Liberal Party (Tasmanian Division), Hobart, 1994.

Lyons, Enid. *Among the Carrion Crows*, Rigby, Adelaide, 1972.

-- *So We Take Comfort*, Heinemann, London, 1965.

Lutton, Nancy. (ed.). *My Dearest Brown Eyes, Letters between Sir Donald Cleland and Dame Rachel Cleland during World War II*, Nancy Pandanus Books, Canberra, 2006.

Macintyre, Stuart. *The Oxford History of Australia Vol 4, 1901-1942*, Oxford University Press 1990.

Martin, AW. *Robert Menzies: A Life*, Volume I 1894-1943, Melbourne, Melbourne University Press, 1993.

-- *Robert Menzies: A Life*, Volume II 1944–1978, Melbourne, Melbourne University Press, 1999.

McMullin, Ross. *The Light On The Hill: The Australian Labor Party 1891-1991*, Oxford University Press, Melbourne, 1991.

McRae, J. *The Tasmanian Farmers, Stockowners & Orchardists Association, 1906-1958*, Hobart, 1961.

Megarrity, Lyndon. *Northern Dreams: The Politics of Northern Development*, Australian Scholarly Publishing, North Melbourne, 2018.

-- *Robert Philp and the Politics of Development*, Australian Scholarly Publishing, North Melbourne, 2022.

Menzies, Robert. *Afternoon Light: Some Memories of Men and Events*, Cassell, Melbourne, 1967.

-- *Dark and Hurrying Days: Menzies' 1941 Diary*, ed AW Martin and Patsy Hardy. National Library of Australia, Canberra, 1993.

-- *Speech is of Time*, London, Cassell,1958.

-- *The Forgotten People and other Studies in Democracy*, Angus and Robertson, Sydney, 1943.

-- *The Measure of the Years*, Cassell, Melbourne, 1970.

Monnox, Chris. *ACT Labor 1929-2009: A Short History*, Ginninderra Press, Port Adelaide, 2013.

Orchard, JR. *Not To Yield: The John Orchard Story, 1906-1982*, J.R. Orchard, Launceston, 1982.

Popper, Karl. *The Open Society and Its Enemies*, Routledge, London 1945.

Puplick, CJ and RJ Southey. *Liberal Thinking*, Macmillan, Melbourne, 1980.

Robson, LL. *A Short History of Tasmania*, updated by Michael Roe, 2nd ed, Oxford University Press, 1997.

Roe, M. *Albert Ogilvie and Stymie Gaha: World-Wise Tasmanians*, The Parliament of Tasmania, Hobart, 2008.

Sawer, M and M Simms. *A Woman's Place: Women and Politics in Australia*, Allen and Unwin, St Leonards, 1993.

Schumpeter, JA. *Capitalism, Socialism and Democracy*, Harper & Brothers, New York, 1942.

Smith, Babette. *Australia's Birthstain: The Startling Legacy of the Convict Era*, Canada, 2011.

Sparke, Eric. *Canberra 1954-1980*, Australian Government Publishing Service, Canberra, 1988.

Starr, Graeme. *Carrick: Principles, Politics and Policy,* Connor Court, Ballan, 2012.

-- *The Liberal Party of Australia: A Documentary History*, Heinemann Educational Australia Pty., Ltd., Richmond, Victoria, 1980.

Sydenham, Diane. *Women of Influence,* Women's Section Liberal Party of Australia Victorian Division, Adelaide, 1996.

Teague, Baden. *A history of the Liberal Party in South Australia, 1910-2022*, Wakefield Press, Adelaide, 2023.

Tiver, PG. *The Liberal Party: Principles and Performance,* Jacaranda Press, Brisbane, 1978.

Townsley, WA. *The Government of Tasmania,* University of Queensland Press, 1976.

Webb, S & B. *Soviet Communism: A New Civilisation*, Scribner, New York, 1938.

West, Katherine. *Power in the Liberal Party: A Study in Australian Politics*, F. W. Cheshire, Melbourne, 1965.

White, Denis. *The Philosophy of the Liberal Party of Australia*, Hutchinson, Melbourne, 1978.

White, Kathleen. 'A Political Biography of Thomas Tuke Hollway', Masters thesis, La Trobe University, 1975.

Wright, Clare. *You Daughters of Freedom – the Australian who won the vote and inspired the world,* Text Publishing, Melbourne, 2018.

Wright, Raymond. *A People's Counsel: A History of the Parliament of Victoria, 1856-1990*, Oxford University Press, South Melbourne, 1990.

Journal articles and chapters in edited collections

Alexander, A. 'Communism in Tasmania', *Tasmanian Historical Research Association Papers and Proceedings*, Vol. 65, No. 3, 2018, pp. 61-81.

Batt, N. 'Tasmania's Depression Elections', *Labour History*, No. 17, 1970, pp. 111-20.

Bennett, S. 'Hays, Herbert Ephraim Digby (1869-1960)', *The Biographical Dictionary of the Australian Senate*, vol. 2 '1929-1962', 2004.

-- 'Solomon, Albert Edgar (1876-1914)', *Australian Dictionary of Biography*, Volume 12, 1990.

-- 'Tasmanian Labor Under Attack 1947-8', *Tasmanian Historical Research Association Papers and Proceedings*, Vol. 33, No. 2, 1986, pp. 67-81.

-- 'Wright, Reginald Charles (1905-1990)', *The Biographical Dictionary of the Australian Senate*, vol. 3 '1962-1983', 2010.

Berzins, Baiba. 'Ley, Thomas John (Tom) (1880–1947)', *Australian Dictionary of Biography*, Volume 10, 1986.

Birman, Wendy. 'Robertson, Agnes Robertson (1882–1968)', *Australian Dictionary of Biography*, Volume 16, 2002.

Black, David. 'Brand, Sir David (1912–1979)', *Australian Dictionary of Biography*, volume 13, 1993.

Bourke, Helen. 'Weaver, Reginald Walter (1876–1945)', *Australian Dictionary of Biography*, Volume 12, 1990.

Boxall, Helen. 'Spooner, Sir William Henry (1897-1966)', *The Biographical Dictionary of the Australian Senate*, vol. 3 '1962-1983', 2010.

Caldwell, J. 'Population', in W. Vamplew (ed), *Australians: Historical Statistics*, Fairfax, Syme, Weldon Associates, Sydney, 1987, pp. 23-41.

Clune, David. '1947', in Michael Hogan and David Clune, *The people's choice: electoral politics in twentieth century New South Wales*, Volume Two 1930 to 1965, Parliament of NSW, Sydney, 2001.

-- '1950' in Michael Hogan and David Clune, *The people's choice: electoral politics in twentieth century New South Wales*, Volume Two 1930 to 1965, Parliament of NSW, Sydney, 2001.

-- 'Why Labor Lost', in David Clune and Rodney Smith, *From Carr to Keneally: Labor in office in NSW 1995-2011*, Allen & Unwin, 2012.

Coltheart, Lenore. 'Rankin, Dame Annabelle Jane (1908–1986)', *Australian Dictionary of Biography*, Volume 18, 2012.

Costar, Brian. 'Arthur Moore: Odd Man In', in Denis Murphy, Roger Joyce, Margaret Cribb and Rae Wear (eds), *The Premiers of Queensland*, University of Queensland Press, St Lucia, 2003, pp. 184–206.

-- 'National-Liberal Party Relations in Victoria', in PR Hay, J Halligan, J Warhurst and B Costar (eds.), *Essays on Victorian Politics*, Warrnambool Institute Press, Warrnambool, 1985.

Cunneen, Christopher. '1944' in Michael Hogan and David Clune, *The people's choice: electoral politics in twentieth century New South Wales*, Volume Two 1930 to 1965, Parliament of NSW, Sydney, 2001.

-- 'White, Sir Ernest Keith (1892–1983)', *Australian Dictionary of Biography*, Volume 18, 2012.

Davis, RP. '"A real and quite unique affinity": New Zealand and Tasmanian Labor 1934-1949', *Labour History*, No. 40, 1981, pp. 68-76.

Davison, G. 'Urbanisation', in A Alexander (ed), *The Companion to Tasmanian History*, University of Tasmania, Hobart, 2005, pp. 491-6.

de Garis, Brian. 'Western Australia', in Helen Irving (ed), *The Centenary Companion to Australian Federation*, Cambridge University Press, Cambridge, 1999.

-- 'Western Australia', in P Loveday, AW Martin and RS Parker (eds), *The Emergence of the Australian Party System*, Hale and Iremonger, Sydney, 1977,

Denholm, M. 'The Lyons Tasmanian Labor Government 1923-1928', *Tasmanian Historical Research Association Papers and Proceedings*, Vol. 24, No. 2, 1977, pp. 45-65.

-- 'Playing the Game: Some Notes on the Second Earle Government, 1914-16', *Tasmanian Historical Research Association Papers and Proceedings*, Vol. 23, No. 4, 1976, pp. 149-51.

Evans, Harry. 'The intertwined history of Canberra and the Parliament' in *Canberra Historical Journal*, 62, October 2009.

Golding, P. 'They called him Old Smoothie: John Joseph Cahill', *Journal of the Australian Catholic Historical Society* 31/2 (2010/11), pp. 75-82.

Goot, Murray. 'Askin, Sir Robert William (Bob) (1907–1981)', *Australian Dictionary of Biography*, Volume 17, 2007.

Gorman, Zachary. 'A Flawed Saint: The Popular Image of William Gladstone in the Australian Colonies', *The Journal of Imperial and Commonwealth History*, Volume 47, Issue 4, pp. 697-717.

-- 'George Reid's anti-socialist campaign in the evolution of Australian liberalism', in Greg Melleuish (ed), *Liberalism and Conservatism*, Connor Court, Ballarat, 2015, pp.17-38.

-- 'Sampson, Sydney (1863–1948)', *People Australia*, National Centre of Biography, Australian National University.

Hancock, Ian. 'Liberal Party of Australia', in Graeme Davison, John Hirst & Stuart Macintyre (eds) *The Oxford Companion to Australian History*, revised edition, Oxford University Press, Melbourne, 2001.

-- 'The Liberal Party Organisation, 1944-1966', in Scott Prasser, JR Nethercote & John Warhurst (eds.), *The Menzies Era. A Reappraisal of Government, Politics and Policy*, Hale & Iremonger, Sydney, 1995.

Harrop, Daniel. 'The Republic of Western Australia: The Legal Possibility of Western Australia's Secession from the Australian Federation', *The Western Australian Jurist 2*, 2011.

Hoddinott, A. '"Independent peasants": A Memoir of the Tasmanian Wright Brothers', *Tasmanian Historical Research Association Papers and Proceedings*, Vol. 57, No. 1, 2010, pp. 17-27.

Hogan, Michael. '1904', in Michael Hogan and David Clune, *The people's choice: electoral politics in twentieth century New South Wales*, Volume one 1901 to 1927, Parliament of NSW, Sydney, 2001.

Jones, Barry and Tony Lamb. 'Wilson, Alexander (1889-1954)', *Australian Dictionary of Biography*, Volume 16, 2002.

Kemp, David. 'A Leader and a Philosophy', in H. Mayer (ed), *Labor to Power*, Angus & Robertson, on behalf of the Australasian Political Studies Association, Sydney, 1973, pp. 48-59.

-- 'The Political Philosophy of Robert Menzies', in J Nethercote, *Menzies: The Shaping of Modern Australia*, Connor Court, Redland Bay, Queensland, 2016, pp. 1-26.

Laverty, John. 'Chandler, Sir John Beals (1887-1962)', *Australian Dictionary of Biography*, Volume 13, 1993.

Lonie, J. 'From Liberal to Liberal: The Emergence of the Liberal Party and Australian Capitalism, 1900-45', in G. Duncan (ed), *Critical Essays in Australian Politics*, Edward Arnold, Melbourne, 1978, pp. 47-76.

Loveday, P, AW Martin & P Weller. 'New South Wales', in *The Emergence of the Australian Party System*, Hale & Iremonger, Sydney, 1977.

Lucadou Wells, R. 'Women in the Liberal Party: Tasmanian Division from the 1940s Onwards 1948-1955', in R Lucadou Wells, *50 Year History of the Liberal Party (Tasmanian Division)*, Liberal Party (Tasmanian Division), Hobart, 1994, pp. 1-18.

Maddox, Graham. 'The Australian Labor Party', in Graeme Starr, Keith Richmond, Graham Maddox (eds.), *Political Parties in Australia,* Heinemann Educational Australia, Victoria, 1978.

McCarthy, John. 'Bertram (later Sir Bertram) Sydney Barnsdale Stevens' in David Clune and Ken Turner, *The Premiers of New South Wales: Volume 2 1856-2005*, The Federation Press, Sydney, 2006.

McCulloch, John. '100 Years of Women's Suffrage in Queensland 1905–2005', *Queensland Review*, vol. 12, no. 2, 2005, pp. 63–72.

McLennan, Lucas. 'Menzies and the Movement: Two Pillars of Australian Anti-Communism', in Zachary Gorman (ed), *The Menzies Watershed: Liberalism, Anti-Communism, Continuities 1943-1954*, Melbourne University Press, 2023.

Monnox, Chris. 'Canberra's Local Council? The ACT Advisory Council,' in *Canberra Historical Journal* 71, September 2013.

Moon, Jeremy and Campbell Sharman, 'Western Australia', in Jeremy Moon and Campbell Sharman (eds) *Australian Politics and Government: The Commonwealth, the States, and the Territories*, ed., Cambridge University Press, Cambridge, 2003.

Moore, Brigid. 'Sectarianism in NSW: the Ne Temere legislation 1924-1925', *Journal of the Australian Catholic Historical Society*, Volume 9, Issue 1, Jan 1987.

Nairn, Bede. 'Holman, William Arthur (1871–1934)', *Australian Dictionary of Biography,* Volume 9, 1983.

-- 'McGowen, James Sinclair (Jim) (1855–1922)', *Australian Dictionary of Biography*, Volume 10, 1986.

Paul, JB. 'Dunstan, Sir Albert Arthur (1882–1950)', *Australian Dictionary of Biography*, Volume 8, 1981.

Petrow, S. 'The State', in A Alexander (ed), *The Companion to Tasmanian History*, University of Tasmania, Hobart, 2005, pp. 483-90.

Radi, Heather. 'Preston Stanley, Millicent Fanny (1883–1955)', *Australian Dictionary of Biography*, Volume 11, 1988.

Reynolds, H. 'Regionalism in Nineteenth-Century Tasmania', *Tasmanian Historical Research Association papers and Proceedings*, Vol. 17, No. 1, 1969, pp. 14-28.

Reynolds, J. 'Premiers & Political Leaders', in F. C. Green (ed), *Tasmania:*

A Century of Responsible Government 1856-1956, Government Printer, Hobart, 1956, pp. 115-238.

Rydon, J. 'The Conservative Electoral Ascendancy Between the Wars', in C Hazlehurst (ed), *Australian Conservatism: Essays in Twentieth Century Political History*, Australian National University Press, Canberra, 1979, pp. 51-70.

Saunders, Cheryl. 'The Uniform Income Tax Cases', in HP Lee & George Winterton (eds.), *Australian Constitutional Landmarks,* Cambridge University Press, Cambridge, 2003.

Scott, R. 'Parties and Parliament: The Tasmanian House of Assembly 1909-1959', *Politics*, Vol. 1, No. 1, 1966, pp. 32-42.

Smart, Judith. 'Couchman, Dame Elizabeth May (1876-1982)', *Australian Dictionary of Biography*, Volume 17, 2007.

Smith, Rodney. 'The Opposition in New South Wales' in Scott Prasser and David Clune, *The Art of Opposition*, Connor Court, Brisbane, 2024.

Starr, Graeme. 'The Liberal Party of Australia', in Graeme Starr, Keith Richmond, Graham Maddox (eds.), *Political Parties in Australia,* Heinemann Educational Australia, Victoria, 1978.

Stevenson, Brian F. 'Morris, Sir Kenneth James (1903-1978)', *Australian Dictionary of Biography*, Volume 15, 2000.

Tanner, S. 'Press, Tasmania', in B Griffen-Foley (ed), *A Companion to the Australian Media*, Australian Scholarly Publishing, North Melbourne, 2014, pp. 358-60.

Townsley, WA. 'Cosgrove, Robert (1884-1969)', *Australian Dictionary of Biography*, Vol. 13, 1993.

Turner, Ken. 'A Labor State?' in Ernest Chaples, Helen Nelson & Ken Turner, *The Wran Model: Electoral Politics in New South Wales, 1981 and 1984,* Oxford University Press, Melbourne, 1985.

Ward, John M. 'Stevens, Sir Bertram Sydney (1889-1973)', *Australian Dictionary of Biography*, Volume 12, 1990.

Weller, P. 'Tasmania', in P Loveday, AW Martin and RS Parker (eds), *The Emergence of the Australian Party System*, Hale and Iremonger, Sydney, 1977, pp. 355-82.

-- 'The Organisation of Early Non-Labor Parties in Tasmania',

Tasmanian Historical Research Association Papers and Proceedings, Vol. 18, No. 4, 1971, pp. 137-48.

-- 'Meetings of the Early Australian Non-Labor Parliamentary Parties', *Political Science*, Vol. 25, No. 2, 1973, pp. 121-30.

Whitington, Don, 'Directors of the Liberals', *Nation*, 7 October 1961, pp. 7-8.

Williams, John R. 'The Emergence of the Liberal Party of Australia', *The Australian Quarterly*, Vol. 39, No. 1, March 1967.

Williams, Paul D. 'Pie, Arthur Bruce (1902–1962)', *Australian Dictionary of Biography*, Volume 15, 2000.

van der Jadt, Gilbert. 'Mair, Alexander' in David Clune and Ken Turner, *The Premiers of New South Wales 1856-2005, Volume 2 1901-2005,* The Federation Press, Sydney, 2006.

Index

Milton Keynes UK
Ingram Content Group UK Ltd.
UKHW021146271024
450226UK00008B/115